Lauer Series in Rhetoric and Composition

Series Editors, Catherine Hobbs and Patricia Sullivan

Lauer Series in Rhetoric and Composition
Series Editors, Catherine Hobbs and Patricia Sullivan

The Lauer Series in Rhetoric and Composition honors the contributions Janice Lauer Hutton has made to the emergence of Rhetoric and Composition as a disciplinary study. It publishes scholarship that carries on Professor Lauer's varied work in the history of written rhetoric, disciplinarity in composition studies, contemporary pedagogical theory, and written literacy theory and research.

Other Books in the Series

1977: A Cultural Moment in Composition by Brent Henze, Jack Selzer, and Wendy Sharer (2007)

Networked Process: Dissolving Boundaries of Process and Post-Process, by Helen Foster (2007)

Composing a Community: A History of Writing Across the Curriculum, edited by Susan H. McLeod and Margot Soven (2006)

Historical Studies of Writing Program Administration: Individuals, Communities, and the Formation of a Discipline, edited by Barbara L'Eplattenier and Lisa Mastrangelo (2004).

Rhetorics, Poetics, and Cultures: Refiguring College English Studies (Expanded Edition) by James A. Berlin (2003)

Untenured Faculty as Writing Program Administrators

Institutional Practices and Politics

Editors
Debra Frank Dew
Alice Horning

Parlor Press
West Lafayette, Indiana
www.parlorpress.com

Parlor Press LLC, West Lafayette, Indiana 47906

SAN: 254-8879

Library of Congress Cataloging-in-Publication Data

Untenured faculty as writing program administrators : institutional practices and politics / editors : Debra Frank Dew ; Alice Horning.

p. cm. -- (Lauer series in rhetoric and composition)

Includes bibliographical references and index.

ISBN 978-1-60235-016-8 (pbk. : alk. paper) -- ISBN 978-1-60235-017-5 (alk. paper) -- ISBN 978-1-60235-018-2 (adobe ebook)

1. English language--Rhetoric--Study and teaching--United States. 2. Report writing--Study and teaching (Higher)--United States. 3. Academic writing--Study and teaching--United States. 4. Universities and colleges--United States--Administration. 5. Writing centers--Administration. I. Dew, Debra Frank, 1955- II. Horning, Alice S.

PE1405.U6U58 2007

808'.0420711--dc22

2007026762

Cover design by David Blakesley.
Printed on acid-free paper.

Parlor Press, LLC is an independent publisher of scholarly and trade titles in print and multimedia formats. This book is available in paper, cloth and Adobe eBook formats from Parlor Press on the World Wide Web at http://www.parlorpress.com or through online and brick-and mortar bookstores. For submission information or to find out about Parlor Press publications, write to Parlor Press, 816 Robinson St., West Lafayette, Indiana, 47906, or e-mail editor@parlorpress.com.

Contents

Preface   *vii*
    Edward M. White
Acknowledgments   *xi*
Introduction: What is Wrong with THIS Picture?   *3*
    Alice Horning

1 The Importance of Untenured Writing Administrators
   to Composition and to English Studies   *15*
   Richard C. Gebhardt

2 Ethics and the jWPA   *40*
   Alice Horning

3 Defining Junior   *58*
   Suellynn Duffey

4 Negotiating the Risks and Reaping the Rewards:
   Reflections and Advice from a Former jWPA   *72*
   Martha A. Townsend

5 jWPAs and the Call to Serve   *97*
   Ruth Mirtz and Roxanne Cullen

6 Labor Relations: Collaring jWPA Desire   *110*
   Debra Frank Dew

7 The Center Will Not Hold: Redefining
   Professionalism in the Academy   *137*
   Martha D. Patton and Jo Ann Vogt

8 Demystifying the Asian-American WPA: Locations in
   Writing, Teaching, and Program Administration   153
   Joseph Eng

9 Graduate Students Hearing Voices: (Mis)Recognition
   and (Re)Definition of the jWPA Identity   172
   Brenda M. Helmbrecht with Connie Kendall

10 Redefining Our Rhetorical Situations:
   jWPAs in the Small College Context   191
   Rebecca Taylor Fremo

11 Administering Writing Programs in the "Betweens":
   A jWPA Narrative   219
   Sandee K. McGlaun

12 Fitness for the Occasion:
   How Context Matters for jWPAs   249
   Paul Ranieri and Jackie Grutsch McKinney

Conclusion: Ethical Options for Disciplinary Progress
   on the Issue of jWPA Appointments   279
   Debra Frank Dew

Contributors   293
Index   297

Preface

Edward M. White

The most interesting professional books are those that take a fresh look at what "everyone" knows to be true. I have frequently spoken for "everyone" on the subject of who should and should not become a writing program administrator; as a number of the contributors to this book point out, I have argued for many years that nobody should take on the job of WPA until achieving tenure. The argument is simple: the job is so sensitive and so demanding that, as one English department chair put it in a 1989 interview, it will ruin the career of any young faculty member.

Ah, but times have changed and old truths may not hold under new conditions. With 65 PhD programs in rhetoric and composition, some of them (like my own) offering courses in writing program administration (which I sometimes teach), our field has matured and gained respect. The thriving job market for faculty with the doctorate in various areas of rhetoric and composition testifies to the value even traditional English departments now place on scholarly leadership in a field long the domain of amateurs. Some of these attractive jobs are for new PhDs interested in becoming WPAs. On a few campuses, writing programs have left indifferent or hostile English departments and established new homes in more friendly territory for teachers and administrators. Are the old truth and the advice it contains simply out of date?

Not entirely. A number of the contributors to this volume reiterate the dangers for untenured faculty in becoming administrators too early in their careers. I know one potential contributor to this book who withdrew his chapter because his situation as an untenured WPA at a small private college was just too dire to describe without, he felt, jeopardizing his career. But enough other voices here suggest that some

newer faculty might well find the WPA post just what they are looking for, in the right institution. Is it reasonable and sensible to tell a
new PhD with a special interest in administration and wide experience
to wait six years or more before taking the job he or she really wants?
Maybe not.

For the first time now we have a book with a variety of perspectives on the subject, enriched by much experience at different kinds
of institutions. It introduces a new set of initials for junior faculty,
who have become writing program administrators (jWPAs) and makes
special claims for the position. While it remains a risky one—an administrative job with much more responsibility than authority—it offers young faculty unusual opportunities for wide influence, creative
pedagogies, applied research, and even higher salaries.

Even more important, this book offers new ways of thinking about
the job itself, its place within institutions, and the traits needed to
be effective on the job. The WPA is traditionally a mature manager,
keeping things on track, speaking judicially for all writing activities on
campus, solving problems with TAs, adjuncts, students, and parents,
and protecting the finances that allow the writing program in all of
its parts to continue, if not to thrive. But when a jWPA takes the job,
the center of gravity shifts somewhat. The traditional tasks remain,
but the younger faculty member has less stake in tradition, in keeping
things running as they have been, in exerting authority over the program. Now the primary goal is likely to be, as Suellynn Duffey puts it
in her chapter, to establish "something very close to the teacher-scholar
atmosphere that many in academe consider ideal." With training in
management, often, and a career ahead in rhetoric and composition,
the jWPA may be more interested in challenging than maintaining the
way things are done. Research will play a larger part than heretofore,
since articles and books are part of the new agenda, and collaboration
rather than control become the modus operandi.

Thus Richard Gebhardt proposes the novel idea that the right
jWPA in the right English department will add healthy vigor to the
entire enterprise. It may be a rough ride for the individual but English
departments set in their ways will profit from some shaking up by an
up-to-date scholar in rhetoric and composition. The most poignant
experiences in—and out of—this book come from those who were
hired to maintain a writing program and were forced to leave because
they sought to improve it. But we also can now point to major uni-

versity administrators who not only began their careers as jWPAs but proclaim that their training and experience as jWPAs taught them all they needed to know to succeed as provosts, presidents, and higher education coordinators. There is a hidden moral behind such tales: English departments unwilling to listen to the new ideas of the new jWPA might well be on the way to relinquishing their hold on the campus writing program, while those expanding their vision and prospects under the leadership of the right jWPA are much more likely to thrive.

Anyone with an interest in college writing programs will find this collection a stimulating and challenging volume. It should be required reading for those seeking to work in and perhaps lead writing programs in American colleges and universities, as well as for senior faculty teaching graduate courses in rhetoric and composition. At the same time, those on hiring committees need to consider the issues brought up here, particularly if they are asking new and vulnerable members of the profession to take on the administration of a writing program.

Acknowledgments

We are grateful to Dave Blakesley of Parlor Press and the series editors, Catherine Hobbs and Patricia Sullivan, for supporting this project, and for their understanding of it as stepping beyond WPA narratives to look at substantive administrative issues in rhetoric and composition. We understand that readers may variously affirm or question the merits of our use of 'jWPA' to signify an alternate category of administrative work. With the lower case 'j', we signify a difference in rank and political positioning, while not diminishing the identities or credentials of those who actually occupy these positions nor the quality of their administrative work. If we are to critically examine the jWPA appointment as our primary aim here, we must first name it and thereby enable our readers to imagine that the jWPA appointment has been professionally naturalized as a legitimate, academic position. Finally, we are especially grateful to Professor Edward White for his generous preface and on-going support of this project.

Untenured Faculty as Writing Program Administrators

Introduction
What is Wrong with THIS Picture?

Alice Horning

A job ad: Rhetoric and Composition Tenure-track Assistant (three to five years' experience) or Associate Professor in rhetoric and composition. PhD, publications and administrative experience required. Will serve as Director of Writing, with responsibility for administering a large writing program, managing a well-funded writing center and providing leadership in general education initiatives. Teaching opportunities in both undergraduate and graduate programs [. . .]

***

Another job ad: [. . .] Center for Writing Instruction. Coordinates a new program for writing across the curriculum and also provides tutoring for undergraduate writers. We seek an Assistant Director who can contribute to both aspects of the Center's mission, preferably one who can also enhance our support of writers for whom English is a second language through tutoring, supervising other tutors, and designing workshops for ESL students. Responsibilities include helping faculty shape discipline-based writing courses, leading workshops for writing teachers, teaching a discipline-based writing course, and developing materials for ESL teaching and tutoring. PhD and teaching experience required; experience coaching writing teachers or tutors desirable. (NOT a tenured or tenure-track job)

Writing program administrators appear to be an unhappy lot; they come out of their PhD programs enthusiastic and energetic, ready to undertake the difficult job of writing program administration. They fill positions like the ones advertised here, a sampling of the common kinds of positions advertised on the MLA *Job Information List*, the

3

WPA discussion list, and in the *Chronicle of Higher Education*. They work long, hard hours for their programs and their own professional development. But ultimately, fatigued and enervated, they hit the institutional wall. War stories abound. They range from the difficulties of untenured WPAs who should not be where they are, to those who attempt to move a program from the status quo and find resistance, to those denied tenure. In addition, even those with tenure do fall into political disfavor and are subsequently released from their WPA duties, despite the success of their programs.

This edited collection arises from a discussion between the two editors, one who is junior faculty and a writing program administrator (jWPA), untenured, overseeing a writing program at a small state university, and the other, a tenured full professor serving as the WPA at a medium-sized public university. Despite our institutional differences, we share a number of administrative concerns. The issues we have in common are the need for effective leadership of writing programs in all sorts of institutions, the concern that the academic job market continually recruits junior faculty for administrative lines with little regard for the labor-intensive nature of administrative work, and the politics of junior faculty wielding administrative power without job security. WPA guidelines advise against junior hires, but few institutions recruit tenured faculty for the work.

By junior hires, we originally thought chiefly of those moving directly from a PhD in rhetoric and composition to a beginning tenure-track appointment that included WPA responsibilities. Those who responded to our call for papers broadened our definition of a jWPA to include graduate students, administrative professionals and everyone else who serves as a WPA *outside* of a regular, full-time, tenured WPA faculty appointment. Though diverse, these jWPAs commonly understand the difference that their "j" status makes.

The jWPA appointment regularly appears in academic job ads although the field has warned against it for decades, and thus the position is naturalized as a viable career path for rhetoric and composition professionals. Junior faculty are readily recruited because they are affordable, enthusiastic and largely uninformed about the professional risks of administrative work.

Junior faculty, and particularly graduates of programs in rhetoric and composition who are encouraged to think about and/or provided with training and experience in writing program direction, are often eager to answer the administrative "call to serve." They do so, however, at great peril to both their professional careers and their programs. Writing program administration requires a tremendous commitment of time and energy, and regularly puts junior faculty in positions where research and publication are difficult. In addition, untenured administrators risk much when, as their jobs demand, they define issues within the institution or the program that need to be addressed. jWPA status does not readily afford them ample authority to advocate for change, improvement and growth in the program. As doyen of writing program assessment Edward White believes, jWPAs must "use it [their administrative power] or lose it," because the "power game must [. . .] be played" whether or not WPAs have tenure (11).

This issue has seemed to us at times so hot as to be untouchable. For example, it was clear to the editors that, for a number of presses, our proposal for this collection touched a nerve, suggesting perhaps that a collection focused on junior faculty as writing program administrators is too risky, potentially offending senior faculty and administrators who might buy a publisher's books or who might send it their own book projects. It certainly was too risky for some of our original contributors. One of these people originally did submit a chapter, a reflective account of his "removal" from his jWPA appointment, asking for it to be published anonymously because of his difficult institutional situation. Subsequently, he withdrew his chapter, again because of future risks involved in a public *telling* of his political struggle and professional misfortune as a jWPA. Another contributor held his first jWPA position for one year, and then left the field entirely. Our topic is admittedly challenging and threatening then, for many reasons, especially in the face of recent renewed interest in the teaching and learning of writing spawned by the addition of a writing portion on the SAT and by widely publicized reports from the College Board's National Commission on Writing.

The chapters in this book have raised a variety of important issues for the contributors whose work does appear here. Some have turned to religion as a resource to shore up their arguments. Others raise concerns over gender: do male jWPAs get treated differently from females? As one contributor said, "This book really got me thinking!" Yet another contributor raises the question of his ethnic identity and its role in the work of WPAs, junior and senior. We hope it will provoke thought also among readers who expect to be jWPAs, who are jWPAs, and who appoint or decide the future of jWPAs.

WPAs nationwide know jWPA appointments are both widespread and problematic—professionally risky and rife with conflict. Most recently, our professional response includes the development of WPA seminars to train graduate students functionally for the work. But, the unwieldy scope of administrative training—curriculum development, assessment, TA training, as starters—has not yet opened up sufficient space for the treatment of jWPA politics and workload issues as an integral part of that administrative training. On the one hand, the Council of Writing Program Administrators, the national organization for writing program professionals, discourages junior appointments in its official position statements, and senior administrators advise against such appointments in forums such as *WPA: Writing Program Administration*. At the same time, more and more graduate programs are offering WPA seminars to train their doctoral students for administrative positions, understanding that such training is absolutely necessary and truly helpful.

As graduate faculty, we may invite our graduate students to answer the noble administrative "call to serve," but, we argue, our published resources and graduate training do not yet fully prepare us for the political challenges that come with the call. This collection sees the issue as one of competing professional interests—the need to protect junior faculty from political land mines and onerous workloads on the one hand, and, on the other hand, the need to promote our own WPA identities as legitimate and the desire to secure tenure-track positions for our graduates. We progress as we strive to train students to work in administration. At the same time, there is tension between our position statements sustained by an unsettling trail of jWPA "victim narratives" published in our journals, and the naturalization of jWPA appointments, which we ourselves sustain when we do not adequately address workload demands and jWPA politics.

The goal of this volume is to examine the politics of jWPA appointments given the demands of writing program administration, and thereby to fully admit and better reconcile the tension between the WPA position statement and current institutional practice. The chapters come from a range of contributors, including graduate students full of jWPA desire, jWPAs who actively pursued administrative appointments and are now ready to analyze their decisions critically, and from senior administrators whose experience authorizes their arguments for or against junior appointments. The collection brings theory to bear on the jWPA situation as the chapters move beyond the mere telling of victim narratives to examine the jWPA issue substantively.

It is interesting to note that even the chapters whose authors approve of jWPA appointments contain many, many qualifications and specifics set up before these writers are willing to support such appointments. jWPAs need to be trained; they should not simply be put into a leadership position without preparation for the responsibilities and demands they will face. jWPAs also need to be protected from the political risks these positions always entail. Senior faculty, department chairs, and other mentors need to help jWPAs negotiate the turbulent waters of running a program. Nonetheless, if the jWPA is the only rhetoric and composition professional on site, which is often the case, whose protection can she secure? Finally, jWPAs should be shielded from unreasonable expectations in terms of workload; no one should be running a large program with a single course release and then be expected to teach, do research, publish, present at conferences and so on. Our chapters suggest the ways in which jWPAs should first not be in these positions at all, the best of all possible worlds, or, second, should be protected in every possible way from the dangers of these vulnerable positions.

Our collection offers an in-depth analysis of jWPA appointments as it explores the following questions:

- What is a jWPA? Our collection is the first to offer the identity category of jWPA as a politically charged, professional location regularly inhabited by untenured rhetoric and composition faculty.
- What is the nature of jWPA desire? How are administrative lines marketed to our graduate students, and what is their appeal?
- What is the nature of jWPA work? How does the "j" significantly alter the appointment?
- Is the naturalization of the jWPA appointment ever appropriate—moral, useful, or "good?"
- What should the WPA Council, university administrators, and graduate directors do about the naturalization of jWPA appointments?

- How do we reconcile the competing professional interests that sustain the jWPA issue as *an issue?*
- What kinds of training do jWPAs, as "js," both want and need in their WPA seminars?

These are among the many issues and perspectives examined in the chapters that follow.

PART I: THE JWPA APPOINTMENT: YES, NO, OR MAYBE SO.

The first section explores the basic issues of the jWPA situation from both sides and provides definitions and distinctions in the terminology. This section offers a kind of counterpoint, alternating between arguments against and arguments for the position of jWPA.

"The Importance of Untenured Writing Administrators to Composition and to English Studies." Richard C. Gebhardt, Bowling Green State University

In this chapter supporting jWPAs, Gebhardt carefully defines the very limited circumstances where these appointments are appropriate. There is something unreasonable—and maybe detrimental—about limiting writing directorships to senior faculty. *Strong, young jWPAs* who do succeed in the *right institutions* can offer strong tenure cases that demonstrate the intellectual work of program administration and thus interrogate the "traditional models of intellectual work in English studies" rather than tacitly sustaining them. WPA work can lead to research and publication as well as "scholarship of teaching" kinds of projects. To succeed, jWPAs need to prepare carefully for tenure review, educating their review committees with help from chairs and mentors.

"Ethics and the jWPA." Alice S. Horning, Oakland University

Having untenured faculty serve as WPAs violates a number of ethical principles, based especially on "duty theory." Senior faculty in rhetoric and composition have an ethical duty to ensure that WPAs are fully qualified, tenured faculty who can do the needed work appropriately. Administrative decisions are ethical decisions, which require time, energy and the wisdom of experience. Senior faculty may more capably make such highly ethical decisions.

"Defining Junior." Suellyn Duffey, University of Missouri, St. Louis

We need to examine the widely publicized view that a *junior* faculty member in a WPA position is undesirable, one that ethical programs should neither create nor hire for. The material and cultural conditions of divergent institutions are so varied that current policy about jWPAs, in the form of policy statements, organizational positions, and so on, is inadequate: its reach doesn't extend to the multiplicity of institutional contexts in which writing programs exist. It oversimplifies the ethics of the jWPA position. The overall situation of the jWPA is more complex than it may appear. This chapter analyzes the varied cultural conditions in which jWPAs work and calls for increased attention to institutional differences in WPA policy-making, scholarship, and practice.

"Negotiating the Risks and Reaping the Rewards: Advice from a Former jWPA." Martha Townsend, University of Missouri, Columbia

This chapter argues that accepting a WPA position as junior faculty—even with a letter specifying the WPA's right to be evaluated for promotion and tenure based on her intellectual work with the program—can be risky. But at the same time, it shows that, with patience and persistence, work as a jWPA *can* lead to promotion and tenure even at a Research I university. As the shape of appointments and time to tenure review are modified in various ways, more flexible options may make this kind of path through the jWPA appointment a reasonable choice for some people.

PART II: jWPA DESIRE AND THE CALL TO SERVE

Part II examines the nature of jWPA desire and the administrative "call to serve." Authors analyze the nature of their own administrative desires theoretically and ask whether administrative appointments can fulfill such desire given their "j" status.

"jWPAs and the Call to Serve." Ruth Mirtz and Roxanne Cullen, Ferris State University

This chapter examines the "call to serve" or the desire "to be of service" that accompanies some jWPAs' decision-making. It considers whether WPA work, for junior faculty, can be defined as "good work" given the relatively powerless position of the jWPA. For many, taking a

WPA position is an intensely personal choice that may be motivated by practical, political, altruistic, or other reasons. Thus, thoughtful consideration of the WPA's motivation and personal views of the "good work" to be done in answering the "call to serve" is essential to a positive outcome.

"Labor Relations: Collaring jWPA Desire." Debra Frank Dew, University of Colorado at Colorado Springs

The promoting of WPA positions via the noble call to serve others dangerously sparks jWPA desire. jWPAs seduced by such calls naïvely understand administrative labor as sufficiently legitimate—tenurable—labor from an institutional perspective. Graduate training must enable aspiring administrators to conceptually reconcile the tensions between the selfless labor of program administration and the self-advancing labor of scholarship before they accept their appointments. Junior faculty who seek WPA work need cautious mentoring and much deeper training, even if the training warrants their delayed entry into the profession.

Part III: jWPA Efficacy: Matters of Location

This section presents views from alternative voices and locations, where the work of the jWPA often takes place: full-time, non-tenure-track faculty (NTTF) positions in the administration of writing programs filled by those who are effectively *junior* in terms of their job status, those who work from alternative identities, and graduate students who work as gWPAs in training for full-time faculty positions on completion of the PhD.

"The Center Will Not Hold: Redefining Professionalism in the Academy." Martha D. Patton and Jo Ann Vogt, University of Missouri

NTTF appointments place jWPAs in marginal or ambiguous positions, yet such seemingly "neutral" positions may enjoy influence. Writing consultants should alternately and productively define their administrative work as a new form of practice-based inquiry rooted in interdisciplinary relationships. These NTTF WPAs can succeed if they practice the key values of community, collaboration, and discovery. These values can give rise to cross-disciplinary allegiances and successful relationships and careers.

*"Demystifying the Asian American WPA: Locations in Teaching,
Writing and Program Administration." Joseph Eng, California State
University, Monterey Bay*

Non-native, nonwhite jWPAs must negotiate their identities, their "un-imagined roles" as English faculty and administrators. This chapter examines the interrelationships among one's identity, pedagogy, and administration. It calls for different administrative locations, and a more critically informed, field perspective on these faculty as WPAs.

Eng suggests that developing a critical consciousness about the Asian-American WPA location, supported by either theory or empirical research about WPA work, is about transcending existing definitions of race labeling, stereotyping, and the simplistic understanding of American democracy.

*"Graduate Students Hearing Voices: (Mis)Recognition and
(Re)Definition of the jWPA Identity." Brenda Helmbrecht, California
Polytechnic University, with Connie Kendall, University of Kentucky*

Graduate students in rhetoric and composition often find themselves in jWPA positions. On the one hand, these positions provide graduate students with good professional experience, but, on the other hand, gWPAs are in poorly defined, tense, transitory circumstances that are very difficult. The work is stressful and generally doesn't "count" toward a degree (just as it doesn't "count" toward tenure). Thus, gWPAs and faculty in rhetoric and composition should carefully consider the personal, professional and institutional ramifications of these positions.

PART IV: RHETORICAL STRATEGIES FOR jWPAS MEDIATING INSTITUTIONAL CONTEXTS

The fourth section offers yet another set of alternative voices, those of jWPAs who work in still other contexts, such as the small college, or the strange space of "betweens" where many jWPAs find themselves as they move toward tenure and promotion, and finally, a last counterpoint between a (former) WPA and a jWPA.

*"Redefining Our Rhetorical Situations: jWPAs in the Small College
Context." Rebecca Taylor Fremo, Gustavus Adolphus College*

Administrative training as situated within the large research university does little to prepare jWPAs to direct writing programs at smaller institutions. Theories of rhetoric and institutional histories of composition—rhetorical training—are most valuable because they enable the jWPA to construct an effective ethos. A multifaceted approach to rhetorical study best enables jWPAs to negotiate the demands of new rhetorical (administrative) situations often quite different from the PhD-granting institutions that trained them. The rhetorical situation of the jWPA at a small college entails both "gift" and "grind," requiring redefinition of the "complications [. . .] of professional ethos, institutional authority, and collegial acceptance."

"Administering Writing Programs in the 'Betweens': A jWPA Narrative."
Sandee McGlaun, Roanoke University

jWPAs work in the space between being "wanted" as resident expert and being "WANTED" for causing trouble and assigning blame. The author advises that jWPAs should actively *choose* a liminal, shifting space and claim the "betweens" as a space for securing their administrative agency. She argues that "in choosing to reclaim and negotiate the fluid, ever-shifting 'betweens,' jWPAs may transmute the often less-than-ideal conditions of our professional lives into transforming and transformational spaces of administrative agency."

"Fitness for the Occasion: How Context Matters for jWPAs." Paul
Ranieri and Jackie Grutsch McKinney, Ball State University

jWPAs need to know their *context* before choosing administrative appointments, and only doctoral training of a specific, rhetorical sort can enable them to make such a decision. Despite the widely held view that taking a jWPA position constitutes "career suicide," these writers suggest that such a choice can be positive if it arises from thoughtful consideration of overall context. We should not assume that such decisions are or need to be "risk-neutral" as no decision has such a characteristic. Following Isocrates, jWPAs are ready for administrative positions when they exhibit the skills to make, through language, the best decisions for the moment.

WORK CITED

White, Edward. "Use It or Lose It: Power and the WPA." *WPA: Writing Program Administration* 15.1/2 (Fall/Winter, 1991): 3–12.

Part I

The jWPA Appointment:
Yes, No, Maybe So

1 The Importance of Untenured Writing Administrators to Composition and to English Studies

Richard C. Gebhardt

During the year I started work on this chapter, I served on a committee developing recommendations for the dean about how my university's first-year writing director should be appointed and evaluated. Our director had been tenured and promoted to associate professor the year before, and then reappointed for another term. So the committee anticipated future appointments and sought ways to assure that strong rhetoric faculty would be attracted to the position and evaluated fairly for their work. Toward that end, the committee sought ways to describe the director's position as part of the work of a rhetoric faculty member, and it fiddled with language urging the appointment of "experienced assistant professors approaching tenure and, preferably, associate professors."

This last recommendation reflected, I think, the committee's intuitive compromise between what would be best for the writing program and its director and what the university would be likely to adopt as ongoing policy. For my part, I considered it essential not to hire brand new PhDs to direct writing programs, but I was skeptical whether the university would honor a senior-hiring policy over the years. And since untenured directors would be evaluated (as the present director had been, successfully) under guidelines that acknowledge the teaching and scholarly dimensions of writing program administration, I knew that the hiring of a strong third- or fourth-year assistant professor (if that is what the budget or the candidate pool required) would not prove as great a problem at my university as it might at some institutions. Indeed, as you can tell from my title, I think having junior rhetoric faculty serving as writing administrators—the jWPA appointment—can be important for departments and for English Studies, as well as for the faculty themselves.

Those words capture much of my point in this chapter, but I do not offer them as a general recommendation, either for our field or for untenured faculty considering administration. Indeed, I consider the Council of Writing Program Administrators' position that "[t]he WPA should be a regular, full-time, tenured faculty member [. . .]" ("Portland" 353) to be a good general rule. And I believe that the graduate students we mentor and the department personnel committees we serve on need to think carefully about the issues raised by Charles Schuster and by Gary Olson and Joseph Moxley in these passages:

> No departments I know would hire a beginning assistant professor of literature to chair the department or direct the graduate program. Yet these same departments choose freshly minted PhDs to direct writing centers and composition programs. Such a strategy undermines both the candidates and the programs they are asked to develop. [. . .] An untenured assistant professor who directs composition makes every decision with one eye glancing toward her senior colleagues and the other toward the dean. Moreover, administering a program drains away time best devoted to teaching, research, and publication. And it often makes enemies of certain colleagues, since the interests of a composition program inevitably conflict at certain points with those of the graduate or undergraduate literature programs. (Schuster 339–40)

> [I]t is exceedingly difficult to make unpopular albeit programmatically and pedagogically sound decisions when professional survival is at stake, and effective administration itself demands a great deal of time from the [writing] director—time the director might have spent on the types of scholarly activities that in most institutions are a prerequisite for tenure. No one

> should be placed in such a no-win situation. Thus if a
> department is unable or unwilling to grant tenure to
> its director *before* asking him or her to direct the writ-
> ing program, then it seems eminently reasonable [. . .]
> that the department appoint a director who already *is*
> tenured. (Olson and Moxley 57)

Given the difficulty junior faculty who are writing program administrators often have running the tenure gauntlet, it is reasonable, and
highly professional, for rhetoric faculty to work for the appointment of
tenured writing directors in their departments and to advise graduate
students and junior colleagues against premature administration. But
in a field in which administration is a subspecialty and a career track,
there seems something unreasonable about building a seven-year buffer
zone between the background and enthusiasm developed in graduate
school and the chance to put them into practice—and maybe extend
research begun in dissertations related to writing program administration—in meaningful writing program administration. Neither does it
seem reasonable for a department without senior rhetoric faculty (or
those who are able and willing to serve) to appoint a tenured person
in literature or creative writing in preference to a strong third-year
rhetoric faculty member interested in administration. Nor is it reasonable to assume that administration's competition for research time is
the same impediment, at all postsecondary institutions, that it often is
at research universities. Such issues, I think, call the tenure-first principle into question—for some junior faculty, some of the time. Indeed
there can be a number of benefits when strong assistant professors with
scholarly agendas related to the work of writing program administration take leadership positions at the right institutions.

Some of these benefits accrue to assistant professors, assuming
they are well prepared for and attitudinally-oriented to administration and that their scholarly interests relate closely to key duties of
the position. For such junior faculty, administration can give a venue
for research that builds on the dissertation or other work in graduate
school and contributes to a record of refereed publication. At the same
time, writing program administration can give a venue for the expression of scholarship in various kinds of workshops and in curriculum-
development documents, teacher-training materials, grant proposals,
and other kinds of "Program-Related Textual Production," which is

how "Evaluating the Intellectual Work of Writing Administration" describes texts a writing administrator might present for tenure review "in addition to conference papers, articles, refereed articles, scholarly books, textbooks, and similar products [. . .]" (98).

Beyond such local and personal complications to applying the tenure-first principle, there is something unreasonable—maybe even detrimental to rhetoric and composition—about limiting writing directorships to senior faculty. Or, to put it positively, there are values, for composition and English studies, when junior rhetoric faculty earn tenure and promotion while serving as writing program administrators. I will elaborate on this point in the next section and then, in the third section, I will offer some recommendations for junior faculty—and their senior rhetoric faculty colleagues—about preparing for tenure and promotion review while serving as writing administrators.

TENURE REVIEW AS CATALYST FOR RECONCEIVING TENURE QUALIFICATIONS

The difficulty junior faculty who are writing administrators often have in tenure and promotion review is the reason composition studies needs them to win tenure and promotion. As background for this paradoxical assertion, consider the view of the MLA Commission on Professional Service that a "dramatic shift in perspective" is necessary to escape "the power and apparent inevitability" ("Making" 170) of a model "of academic work as research, teaching, or service [which] does not simply differentiate faculty activities [. . .] but also implicitly ranks them in order of esteem" ("Making" 169). Think, too, about Jacqueline Jones Royster's analysis of a critical professional dilemma for composition studies:

> [P]robably only about a third of what we do in rhetoric and composition has been deemed through traditional models of intellectual work in English studies to be worthy of credit. So, in effect, we are measured by a habitually uninterrogated tape of value that does not permit our strengths as an area to show well in the company of other areas, which function differently. (1225–26)

The "strengths as an area" that Royster emphasizes include a number of matters important in the work of writing program administrators:

> We centralize students, teaching, and learning as subjects. [. . .] We are deeply committed to paying attention to the contexts of learning and to the delivery systems that will facilitate it. We are aware of the need for theoretically well grounded and conceptually well managed programs to address the problems in both [. . .]. (1226)

Such strengths, of course, typically fall low in the "order of esteem" the MLA Commission sees at the heart of the traditional view of academic work. So writing program administration has a special connection to the challenge I see in the words of the MLA Commission and of Royster—to significantly "shift the perspective in faculty evaluation" by interrogating the "tape of value" applied (among other places) in department tenure and promotion evaluations.

I stress the department, here, because such significant evaluation of rhetoric faculty takes place there, and because most departmental criteria for tenure and promotion do not yet reflect the significant professional recalibration that has been going on for years, in such recommendations and guidelines as the CCCC's "Scholarship in Composition" (1987), the "Report of the [MLA] Commission on Writing and Literature" (1988), the "ADE Statement of Good Practice: Teaching, Evaluation, and Scholarship" (1993), the AAUP's "The Work of Faculty: Expectations, Priorities, and Rewards" (1994), the MLA's "Making Faculty Work Visible" (1996), the Council of WPA's "Evaluating the Intellectual Work of Writing Administration" (1998), and the "Final Report" of the MLA Committee on Teaching (2001). That Royster's words about a "tape of value that does not permit our strengths as an area to show well" ring true today suggests that few perspectives and approaches of those documents have seeped into the departmental criteria used in reviewing junior faculty who serve as writing program administrators and other rhetoric faculty. Rather (as Margaret Marshall writes about the evaluation of writing center directors), by classifying administrative work as "service" or "teaching," the institutional process of "review regularly precludes submission of the very documents

that would demonstrate the intellectual dimensions" of writing program administration (Marshall 81).

Only a "dramatic shift in perspective" can move departments away
from approaches, like those, that leave rhetoric and composition's
strengths undervalued or unrecognized, especially in research departments. But that will not happen as long as the "habitually uninterrogated tape of value" *remains* uninterrogated. And I am afraid that the
reasonable cautions we give doctoral students and junior faculty about
administration may reduce the likelihood of this interrogation by low-
ering the pressure on departments to examine their expectations about
faculty work in light of compelling tenure and promotion portfolios
from strong junior faculty working as writing program administrators.

Clearly, we do not want to see promising new rhetoric faculty
get over their heads in administration too early in their careers. But
should we give our tacit approval to problematic evaluation criteria
rather than seeing them challenged by tenure cases that demonstrate
the intellectual work of writing program administration? And do we
want to encourage people whose work could help force a department
to rethink its tenure criteria to shun administration and go along with
"traditional models of intellectual work in English studies"? The professional answer to both those questions is "no," I think. For both
things are detrimental to rhetoric and composition and to the rhetoric
faculty (and those in English education, applied linguistics, and technical writing) who will continue to be evaluated unfairly as long as
departments need not recalibrate or reconceive their criteria for tenure
and promotion. Both things also are detrimental to English as a whole,
at a time when "the traditional triad of faculty rewards is attracting
criticism from both inside and outside academia" ("Making" 168) and
when many faculty across American higher education "get their great-
est focus and sense of accomplishment from working with students"
(Thompson).[1]

By itself, of course, reviewing jWPAs for tenure and promotion will
not change department criteria for evaluating faculty work. Indeed,
the effort to adjust formal and informal expectations can be undermined by negative recommendations resulting from weak tenure cases
or departments so inflexible that they resist not only the recommendations of major professional associations but also the explicit (and peer-
reviewed) evidence of the intellectual work one of their colleagues is

doing as a writing program administrator. But when *strong* assistant professors become writing program administrators in the *right* institutions, their work—and their successful tenure reviews—can help challenge traditional ideas of faculty work and expand departmental understanding of rhetoric and composition and of writing program administration as a venue for teaching and scholarship.

Since the benefits this challenge has for composition and English studies depend on strong and convincing tenure cases, the next section suggests approaches for assistant professors who are thinking about trying to demonstrate their qualifications for tenure and promotion through (rather than in spite of) their work in writing program administration.

APPROACHES FOR jWPA TENURE REVIEW

As most experienced rhetoric faculty know (and as the earlier passages by Schuster and by Olson and Moxley make clear), there are problems, even dangers, in becoming a writing program administrator before achieving tenure. Still, some new rhetoric PhDs are drawn to attractive faculty positions that include administration, and some are so committed to writing program administration that they consider taking it on before tenure. The following suggestions are intended for them, as well as for current writing directors who are approaching tenure review or looking toward further promotion.

It should go without saying (but I'll say it anyway) that the six approaches in this section come with no claim of comprehensiveness or guarantee of success. I would offer three other general notes about these approaches. Though this section reads like suggestions for untenured faculty thinking about or already involved in writing program administration, it assumes a crucial role for senior rhetoric faculty. A second and related point is that these six approaches are not intended for solo use by untenured faculty. Finally, the following approaches, while separately highlighted below, must work together in the thinking and planning that can lead to successful tenure and promotion review.

1. Seek Senior Rhetoric Faculty for Advice and Support

Whether you are thinking about writing program administration or whether you are already working as a writing program administrator, seek out senior rhetoric faculty who can help you with broad professional advice, insider information about institutional expectations, candid appraisals of your professional strengths and areas needing enhancement, and strategies you can use as you prepare for review. If you are thinking of accepting an administrative position but do not have supportive senior rhetoric faculty colleagues, the tenure-first principle may well be your best approach to administration.

If you are an untenured writing program administrator without senior rhetoric faculty colleagues to advise and support you, reach out to senior rhetoric faculty at other institutions—graduate school mentors, for instance, or people whose publications suggest that they might be willing to help a stranger in distress—and contact the president of the Council of Writing Program Administrators (wpacouncil.org). Also, let your department chair know that you need her advice and support, things chairs are expected to provide for all their faculty members. ("Mentor and Evaluator: The Chair's Role in Promotion and Tenure Review" in Gebhardt and Gebhardt may provide a context for work with your chair.)

2. Weigh Your Professional Interest in Writing Program Administration

Writing program administration (which can take place in first-year courses, writing centers, writing across the curriculum, service learning, distance learning, writing assessment, and other venues) is a subspecialty of rhetoric and composition and a potential career track for women and men in our field. But that does not mean it is a good career choice for every new rhetoric and composition PhD.

If you resent the time writing classes, student papers, and conferences steal from your research and writing, you are unlikely to be reading this chapter, let alone thinking seriously about writing program administration. But even if you derive a lot of satisfaction from working with students in writing classes and anticipate that undergraduate writing instruction will be a continuing part of your work as a faculty member, writing program administration still may not be a good choice. For the major work of many writing program administrators is not with undergraduates—to whom they may be nearly invisible—but with the teaching staff, curriculum materials, mentoring programs, committee meetings, budget requests, reports, and myriad other things that let a writing program work for students. Especially in the direction of a large writing program, administration is a kind of macro-level teaching. For instance:

> Rather than select the books for her own couple classes, the writing director may select books (or shape a process for selecting books) for dozens or hundreds of sections. Rather than try to understand and adjust for instructional problems involving her own students, she works daily with graduate assistants and others worried about such things in their classes. Rather than jump into trial-and-error innovation to shape her own sections around a promising scholarly trend, she may study how the trend might work with many sections and teachers and work to locate resources for the staff-development and public relations efforts to adjust the curriculum of her program. (Gebhardt, "Administration" 36)

If this sort of work is appealing, or at least interesting, to you, writing program administration may be a good career choice, at some point in your career. Whether it is a good choice for your pre-tenure years depends both on your institution's tenure expectations for research and publication and on your scholarly interests. Research and administration both are heavy drains on faculty time and energy. So you should probably follow the tenure-first principle about administration if your institution demands extensive research and publication *and* your scholarly interests are far removed from teaching, curriculum development, teacher-preparation, program assessment, and other aspects of writing program administration. However, early administration may make sense if your scholarly interests mesh with the daily work of writing program administration. Can research projects and scholarly publications grow out of the context of the position? Can your scholarship manifest itself in curriculum development, grant proposals, faculty workshops, and other aspects of writing program administration? Such synergies of research and administration give you something to think about—and to discuss with senior rhetoric colleagues and others—as you decide whether to take on writing program administration during your pre-tenure years.

3. Explore the Local Context of Faculty Evaluation and Writing Program Administration

Regardless of how strong the synergy between your scholarly interests and the work of writing program administration, you also need to consider the climate of research and faculty evaluation at your institution. It is one thing to submit a portfolio of research and publication related to your work as a writing program administrator when tenure guidelines value the scholarship of application, integration, and teaching (terms much used in American higher education since the 1990 publication *Scholarship Reconsidered*) or when the institutional climate is infused with ideals of the scholarship of engagement movement, which advocates "scholarship in the areas of teaching, research, and/or service" that "engages faculty in academically relevant work that simultaneously meets campus mission and goals as well as community needs" ("What"). But as the earlier section on "Tenure Review as Catalyst" suggests, you should not assume such a supportive climate for your research and publishing. Rather, you should be alert for hints about this during your interview, and later you should explore the culture of faculty work and its evaluation at your university or college.

Get copies of all policies and guidelines for faculty review (for tenure, promotion, annual reappointment, merit review) at your institution and discuss them with your chair and/or dean, and with senior rhetoric faculty colleagues. This exploration may be the single most important thing any new faculty member can do at the start of a career, so I would like to elaborate on it with these words from the "CCCC Statement of Professional Guidance to Junior Faculty and Department Chairs":

> After accepting a position, the candidate should discover and become familiar with any faculty handbooks, union contracts, and similar personnel policy materials. The new faculty member should know the practice, policy and philosophy on such issues as released time, rewards for grant seeking, summer school teaching, consulting with industry or other schools, and the relative weight given to teaching, service,

publication, and professional involvement in evaluations for reappointment, raises, promotion, and tenure. Candidates should know, for example, if there
is a systematic review process, and if so what criteria
and procedures are used. In any such review process,
both individual faculty members and the responsible administrators have specific responsibilities; the
new faculty member should understand these clearly.
(494)

If you are thinking about taking a specific administrative position,
find out as much as you can about it from "official" documents (job
description, evaluation forms, how or if the position is mentioned in
broader documents about faculty evaluation) and from conversations
with people—the WPA or a former WPA, for instance—who can tell
you how the position really works. This intelligence gathering might
be fairly cursory, if you are just thinking hypothetically about administration in the future. But if you are considering becoming a writing
program administrator within the next year, you should explore the
position in detail (in the context of the "Portland Resolution" and
other resources you have gathered—see the next approach). You also
should work with the chair or dean involved to negotiate a survivable
administrative job (see the later approach with this title).

4. Gather Resources on Faculty Evaluation and Writing Program Administration

As early as possible, start developing a library of resources you can
draw on during your preparation for tenure and promotion review.
You should seek suggestions from senior rhetoric colleagues (and be
grateful for their unsolicited suggestions) and look for useful ideas in
the journals you read and websites you visit. Here are four kinds of
resources I recommend:

*A. WPA—A Key Resource for Writing Administrators and Would-Be
Administrators.* Join the Council of Writing Program Administrators
(often called "WPA" for short) and look for useful resources in its
website (wpacouncil.org), its refereed journal *WPA: Writing Program
Administration,* its Summer Workshop for New WPAs, and its Summer
Conference.

B. Resources to Help You Understand a Position You Are Considering.
Seek guidelines and overviews (and get copies you can study and anno-
tate) that would help you better understand and evaluate the administrative position you are considering in light of institutional expectations. For example:

- The "Portland Resolution." A Council of Writing Program
  Administrators statement about working conditions and job
  descriptions for writing administrators.
- The "CCCC Statement of Professional Guidance to Junior
  Faculty and Department Chairs." Excellent, compact advice
  for rhetoric faculty members.
- David Schwalm's "The Writing Program (Administrator) in
  Context." Discussion, by a WPA-turned-dean, of a variety of
  local contexts of writing program administration and of how
  being a successful administrator requires changes in typical faculty member assumptions and values.

C. Professional Association Documents. Get to know—so you can use
them in the future—professional association recommendations and
guidelines that challenge the assumptions of many English faculty
that "scholarship" equals publication (though not about pedagogy
and other pragmatic matters) and that administration equals "service"
(with no connections to the "teaching" and "research" expectations
for tenure and promotion). Here are several documents that can be
useful as general background while developing evaluation portfolios
and as sources of quotes in tenure and promotion cases (and behind-
the-scenes advocacy by senior faculty colleagues).

- "Scholarship in Composition: Guidelines for Faculty, Deans,
  and Department Chairs." 1987 overview and recommen-
  dations from the Conference on College Composition and
  Communication.
- "Report of the Commission on Writing and Literature."
  Surprisingly forward-looking 1988 recommendations by an
  MLA Commission; for instance, much "important work [in
  composition] is dependent on forms of dissemination that are,
  in fact, not published" (74).
- "ADE Statement of Good Practice: Teaching, Evaluation, and
  Scholarship." A 1993 statement (republished by ADE in 2002),
  which, among other things, says that "[p]publication need not

be the only or even the most important measure of a faculty member's accomplishments" and that scholarship on teaching "should be valued on a par with traditional forms of scholarship" (87).

- "The Work of Faculty: Expectations, Priorities, and Rewards." A 1994 report from an AAUP Committee on Teaching, Research, and Publication which (among other things in recommendation 5) urges "a broader concept of scholarship that embraces the variety of intellectual activities and the totality of scholarly accomplishments" (47).

- The "Final Report" of the MLA Ad Hoc Committee on Teaching. A 2001 report which (in its Scholarship of Teaching section) recommends that "institutions and departments value the scholarship of teaching—of the methods, assessment procedures, and ways to improve teaching—as equivalent to traditional forms of scholarship, when it is subjected to equivalent scrutiny by the rest of the profession" (234).

- "Making Faculty Work Visible: Reinterpreting Professional Service, Teaching, and Research in the Fields of Language and Literature." An important, even radical, document from the MLA.[2]

- "Evaluating the Intellectual Work of Writing Administration." A Council of Writing Program Administrator's statement—essential.

- *Scholarship Reconsidered: Priorities of the Professoriate* (Boyer). Useful as background, since this 1990 book influenced the previous four items and much other recent discussion of faculty work and rewards in American higher education (including things in the next item).

- *Scholarship Assessed: Evaluation of the Professoriate* (Glassick, Huber, and Maeroff). A 1997 follow-up to *Scholarship Reconsidered*. Together, these Carnegie Foundation books influenced two recent developments relevant to the work and evaluation of writing administrators: a Scholarship of Teaching and Learning movement (see, for instance, Thompson and other articles in the *National Teaching and Learning Forum*) and a scholarship of engagement movement in which research "moves toward engagement as the scholar asks, "[h]ow can knowledge be responsibly applied to consequential problems?" and

"[c]olleges and universities [. . .] respond to the issues of the day
[. . .]" (Glassick, Huber, and Maeroff 9).

- *Good Practice in Tenure: Advice for Tenured Faculty, Department
  Chairs, and Academic Administrators.* This Web-available book
  from AAUP and the American Council on Education includes
  chapters on clarity in tenure criteria and procedures, consistency in tenure decisions, candor in faculty evaluation, and ways to
  improve tenure criteria and procedures.

D. How-To Resources about Tenure and Promotion Review. Look for articles, books, and other sources in which rhetoric faculty experienced
in administration offer strategies for developing evaluation materials
and otherwise pursuing tenure and promotion. Do not assume that
everything you read will work for you. But look for ideas that fit your
plans and your institution—particularly ideas recommended by several sources—and talk these over with senior rhetoric faculty colleagues.
Here are a few places you might begin your search.

- The WPA's "Evaluating the Intellectual Work of Writing
  Administration." Includes suggestions for writing administra-
  tors approaching review as well as for chairs and deans who are
  preparing to evaluate writing program administrators.
- *Academic Advancement in Composition Studies* (Gebhardt
  and Gebhardt). Among the fourteen chapters are "Preparing
  Yourself for Successful Personnel Review" by Richard Gebhardt,
  "Administration As Scholarship and Teaching" by Duane Roen,
  "Presenting Writing Center Scholarship" by Muriel Harris,
  "The Importance of External Reviews" by Lynn Bloom, and "A
  View from the Dean's Office" by Susan McLeod.
- Jeanne Gunner, "Professional Advancement for the WPA:
  Rhetoric and Politics in Tenure and Promotion." Discussion
  and strategies tailored specifically to the writing administrator,
  as well as a useful annotated bibliography of other resources.
- Duane Roen, et al., "Reconsidering and Assessing the Work of
  Writing Program Administrators." Discusses writing program
  administration—and offers a way to describe this work—In
  the context of two books (Boyer, *Scholarship Reconsidered* and
  Glassick, et al., *Scholarship Assessed*) that are well regarded by
  many deans and upper administrators.

5. Negotiate a Survivable Administrative Position. The demands of administration coupled with institutional criteria for faculty evaluation can make it hard for junior faculty in WPA positions to survive tenure review and, later, receive further promotion. So before you accept an administrative position, you should draw on the resources you have developed, consult with senior rhetoric faculty, and work with your chair or dean to make it a survivable job. There should be a clear and reasonable job description, as well as commitment of adequate support (budget, support staff, office equipment, professional travel funds, etc.) and a written statement about your evaluation, including how the scholarship and teaching of administration will figure in review for tenure, promotion, and salary increases. The WPA's "Portland Resolution" is a good place to start developing a position you are willing to accept. It has a long section on "Guidelines for Developing WPA Job Descriptions," and its section on "Working Conditions Necessary for Quality Writing Program Administration" includes such matters as evaluation, job security, resources, and access "to those individuals and units that influence their programs" (353).

Such issues are important to think about, even if your interest in writing program administration is more long-term or hypothetical. They can help you organize resources, give focus to consultations you have with senior rhetoric colleagues, and gradually sharpen your sense of the kind of administrative position that would work for you. The educational, financial, and political aspects of writing program administration are complex, and the personal and professional stakes for writing administrators are high. So thinking, over time, about your priorities and goals for administration will help you prepare to negotiate effectively in the future.

6. Plan Carefully for Tenure and Promotion Review. Preparation for successful tenure and promotion review should begin—for any assistant professor—in the first term (or even before signing a contract), with careful attention to department and institutional policies and guidelines about faculty work and its evaluation. The goal here, as the "CCCC Statement of Professional Guidance" puts it, is

> a clear understanding, in writing, of what activities
> will be considered important in evaluation for reap-
> pointment, raises, promotion, and tenure. Some insti-
> tutions base such evaluations solely on teaching and

> other locally assigned activities. Some institutions
> consider service to the profession and/or scholarship
> as well. Where service to the profession is a factor, a
> junior faculty member needs to know which activi-
> ties (e.g., workshops, committee assignments, offices)
> and which professional organizations are deemed im-
> portant by the institution. Where scholarship is a fac-
> tor, the junior faculty member needs to know which
> journals and types of publication will "count." (495)

The variety of tenure and promotion expectations at American colleges and universities makes it critical for you to understand what your
institution expects of you, to develop your plans accordingly, and to
follow those plans as you develop a record that, presented in your tenure and promotion materials, meets or exceeds those expectations. If
you have a written agreement with the chair and dean about how your
work as a writing program administrator is to be evaluated (see the
previous approach), that document will shape your plans and the case
you later make for tenure and promotion. Still, broad institutional criteria for tenure and promotion are important to understand, especially
if you are an administrator without an explicit agreement about your
evaluation or if you are thinking about becoming an administrator in
the years before tenure review.

Trying to understand departmental and institutional expectations
for tenure and promotion is not something for solo work. The same
thing is true of trying to decide whether your plans can lead to a record
that meets those expectations, and whether—given the institution's
criteria and the nature of the position—the writing program administrator's job you hold or are thinking of accepting is likely to advantage
or to derail your professional advancement. Such things are matters
for candid discussion with your chair, senior rhetoric faculty members, and the former WPA, as well as for careful reflection in light of
resources you are developing about writing program administration,
evolving trends in faculty work and evaluation, and strategies for preparing for tenure review (see the Resources approach).

If you decide that writing program administration will be an important part of the record you present for tenure and promotion review, this decision will shape the plans you make for scholarship,
teaching, and service (to use what are still the most common terms in

criteria for faculty evaluation), the way you follow those plans over the years, and the portfolio you eventually submit for review. Particularly in research-oriented institutions and departments with few rhetoric faculty, this decision also should influence the efforts you and your chair make to educate the faculty about distinctive aspects of scholarship and teaching in composition (see Gebhardt and Gebhardt 123–25 and 158–59) and the lobbying efforts senior rhetoric faculty mount on your behalf.

In all of these things—pre-tenure planning, "educational" efforts, and the development of tenure materials—you should draw on professional association guidelines (see Part C of the Resources approach). The WPA's "Evaluating the Intellectual Work of Writing Administration" can be particularly valuable as you keep records and collect materials for later compilation in your tenure and promotion portfolio. It describes five categories of intellectual work in writing program administration: Program Creation, Curricular Design, Faculty Development, Program Assessment and Evaluation, and Program-Related Textual Production—that is, "the production of written materials in addition to conference papers, articles, refereed articles, scholarly books, textbooks, and similar products that would be evaluated the same whether produced by a WPA or any other faculty member" (98). And it draws on earlier recommendations about faculty evaluation to show how such work of writing program administration can be

> viewed as a form of inquiry which advances knowledge and which has formalized outcomes that are subject to peer review and disciplinary evaluation. Just as the articles, stories, poems, books, committee work, classroom performance, and other evidence of tenure and promotion can be critiqued and evaluated by internal and external reviewers, so can the accomplishments, products, innovations, and contributions of writing administrators. Indeed, such review must be central to the evaluation of writing administration as scholarly and intellectual work. (94)

Besides aligning work of writing program administration with ideas of scholarship and peer review quite familiar to English faculty, deans, and college-level tenure committees, the WPA document offers (in Guidelines Two and Three) criteria for evaluating the intellectual work of writing program administration, and it suggests a framework for organizing the accomplishments of writing administrators and for viewing those accomplishments during personnel review.

You (and your chair and others working on your behalf) also should be aware of recommendations from organizations that have more credibility with literature faculty than do organizations within rhetoric and composition. In explaining your work during personnel reviews and developing a rationale statement for your tenure and promotion portfolio, you can use such guidelines to address, before they come up, issues that complicate the evaluation of writing administrators. Here are three examples:

- Tenure and promotion criteria that exclude publications about pedagogical topics violate principles in CCCC's "Scholarship in Composition" and WPA's "Evaluating Intellectual Work of Writing Administration." But they also are out of line with MLA's "Making Faculty Work Visible" and ADE's "Statement of Good Practice"—a 1993 document that was echoed in recommendations of the 2001 MLA Ad Hoc Committee on Teaching and republished in a 2002 "Chairs Reference" issue of *ADE Bulletin*—and the 2002 report of the MLA Committee on the Future of Scholarly Publishing, which sees the "devaluation" ("Future" 177) of textbooks by promotion and tenure committees to be part the problem facing faculty and the profession.

- Tenure and promotion criteria that rigidly limit "scholarship" to refereed books and articles contradict statements of the AAUP Committee on Teaching, Research, and Publication, the recently re-issued "ADE Statement of Good Practice," and reports from the MLA Commission on Writing and Literature, and the MLA Commission on Professional Service. They may even be out of synch with the flexibility the MLA Committee on the Future of Scholarly Publishing shows when it opens a brief discussion of book vs. article publishing and quantity vs. quality in tenure files with the words, "*If* peer review is assumed to be the ideal gateway to scholarly communication [. . .] "("Future" 179, emphasis added)

- Tenure and promotion criteria that identify all work of writing program administration (including curriculum development and staff training and supervision) with a "service" category that plays a minor part in tenure review are out of synch with recommendations by the MLA Commission on Writing and Literature—"administrative contributions should be given significant weight during tenure and salary reviews" ("Report" 74)—and the MLA Commission on Professional Service, that criticizes a "restricted conception of teaching, which focuses heavily on classroom events and other direct student contacts" ("Making" 182), and describes teaching in a way that includes much of writing administration (see endnote 2).

Quotations from recommendations like those can be used in various ways as you prepare for tenure and promotion—or as chairs and senior rhetoric colleagues work on your behalf. They can serve as background for or footnoted rationale within statements about evaluation that you negotiate with the chair and dean (see the previous approach). They can be used in statements you write about your work—and in evaluations written by your chair—during reappointment and salary reviews starting with your first year. They can be used to gloss the high-level generalizations most tenure and promotion guidelines use to describe faculty expectations in scholarship, teaching, and service—for instance, in proposals by senior rhetoric faculty or the chair to revise personnel guidelines so they more fairly evaluate the work of rhetoric faculty and writing administrators (I discuss the chair's responsibility for this in Gebhardt and Gebhardt 151–56). They can come up in the private conversations senior rhetoric colleagues have with other faculty members about your work. And they can be woven into the overview or rationale statement you write for your tenure and promotion portfolio, where they may prompt your external reviewers to include echoing statements in their recommendation letters.

CONCLUSION

Using guidelines from influential professional associations as part of the case for tenure and promotion is no guarantee of successful review, especially in research-oriented institutions and departments with few faculty in composition, applied linguistics, English education, and technical communication. But it is better for writing program administrators to use this strategy, as they explain their work over the years and prepare tenure and promotion materials, than to assume that the faculty who will vote on their tenure understand, let alone value, the nature of faculty work in composition and of the scholarly and teaching dimensions of writing program administration. This strategy gives jWPAs and their senior rhetoric faculty supporters a chance to convince skeptical department members, or to educate them in the years before the vote. It also encourages personnel committees and faculty members to evaluate the work of writing program administration within a context that has been developing for years in English studies, rather than applying, once again, an "uninterrogated tape of value that does not permit our strengths as an area to show well" (Royster 1226)—an activity which, as it is repeated by personnel committees and individual faculty members over the years, may lead to the development of fairer and more appropriate approaches to tenure and promotion in English.

This development, I believe, is important for junior composition faculty and writing program administrators of the future, for the professional status of rhetoric and composition, and for the health of English studies. But it is not something for which junior faculty as writing program administrators should sacrifice themselves, which is one reason I see such an important role for senior rhetoric faculty in the whole process of jWPA tenure. Those of us involved in doctoral programs should work, in our courses and mentoring, to help students see how their professional goals and scholarly interests align with evolving concepts of faculty evaluation upon which they can build strong cases for tenure and promotion. Those of us with junior rhetoric colleagues interested in writing program administration (or already involved in it) should work to help them see how—or whether—their professional goals, the quality of their work, the nature of the institution's expectations, and the demands of the administrative position make it feasible to pursue tenure while serving as a WPA. And when we find women and men whose administrative plans we can encourage rather than caution against, we need to support them strongly and consistently throughout the years leading up to tenure.

Notes

[1] I discuss these trends in "Evolving Approaches to Scholarship, Promotion, and Tenure in Composition Studies" (see Gebhardt and Gebhardt 9–13) and in "Scholarship of Teaching and Administration" (see the section on "A Critical Goal in Context"). The last source includes the following in-

formation about the important—and, for some, surprising—fact of wide-spread faculty interest in teaching and students:

> National surveys conducted by UCLA's Higher Education Research Institute show that "faculty increasingly are dedicating more time and energy to teaching students and less to research despite a common public perception otherwise" (Press Release, 1996). In the 1989 survey, 59% of faculty identified research as an essential or very important goal, and 23% said they spent more than twelve hours a week on research. By 1995, only 55% judged research essential or very important, and just 17% spent more than twelve hours a week on research (Magner A13). In that year, too, 75% of the faculty reported that their interests "lean more towards teaching than research"; and while only 55% considered research to be a top priority, 99% percent said that being a good teacher is a top priority (Press Release, 1996). UCLA's 2001–2002 survey revealed continuing faculty interest in their work as teachers, for instance efforts to use "a wider variety of teaching methods." Also, "[c]ompared with faculty in 1989, today's faculty indicate greater attentiveness to students' overall well-being. Faculty are more likely to view their colleagues as being interested in students' academic problems [. . .] and personal problems [. . .] . The study revealed an even larger increase [. . .] in the view that it is easy for students to meet with professors outside of their regular office hours" (Press Release, 2002). (Gebhardt, "Scholarship" 22–23)

2 "Making Faculty Work Visible" is a long and complex document. But it deserves the attention of rhetoric faculty members and writing administrators, as this excerpt from my "Scholarship of Teaching and Administration" may suggest:

> [This] 1996 report by the MLA Commission on Professional Service challenged the utility of using "scholarship," "teaching," and "service" as separate categories to describe and evaluate faculty work. In their place, the Commission recommended an approach (visualize a six-celled matrix) in which Teaching, Service, and Scholarship are *each* evaluated for the quality of its Intellectual Work and of its Professional Citizenship.

[. . .] It is a bold move to include, as the Commission on Professional Service does, not only teaching but also service (long "a kind of grab-bag for all professional work that was not clearly classroom teaching, research, or scholarship" [184]) within the same descriptive and evaluative framework as scholarship. Further, *Making Faculty Work Visible* describes as *applied* professional service some academic-leadership activities often relegated to an anemic service component in faculty evaluation (for instance, when "outreach activities" involve "demonstrating, training, and applying knowledge about educational practice in such external contexts as the public schools or colleagues in other fields at one's institution" [185]). And it emphasizes that "applied work in service, like teaching (also an applied or practical art), is not a mechanical [. . .] transmission or application of specialized knowledge" but an "intersection of academic knowledge enterprises with practical activity" in which practical activity "not only tests and refines academic ideas and predictions but also produces its own knowledge and skills" (185).

Just as significantly—especially for writing program administrators and others whose academic-leadership work often is undervalued in personnel reviews—*Making Faculty Work Visible* puts aside a "restricted conception of teaching, which focuses heavily on classroom events and other direct student contacts along with only the most immediate tasks of preparing for or supplementing these events (e.g., writing a syllabus, grading)" (182–83). Instead, it presents a view of teaching that takes "into account activities that enrich student learning or enable better teaching," a view that includes much of writing administration, for example: "running a writing center," "mentoring other teachers," "developing courses and curriculum sequences," "administrating a multisection course or teaching program," "designing and implementing the professional development of teaching assistants and professional instructors," and "offering faculty or student workshops in areas of one's professional expertise" (183). (Gebhardt, "Scholarship" 18–19)

Works Cited

"ADE Statement of Good Practice: Teaching, Evaluation, and Scholarship." *ADE Bulletin* 105 (Fall 1993). Rpt. *ADE Bulletin* 132 (Fall 2002): 85–87. Available http://www.ade.org/policy/policy_teaching.htm.
Boyer, Ernest. *Scholarship Reconsidered: Priorities of the Professoriate*. Princeton: Carnegie Foundation for the Advancement of Teaching, 1990.

"CCCC Statement of Professional Guidance to Junior Faculty and Department Chairs." *College Composition and Communication* 38 (Dec. 1987): 493–97. Available http://www.ncte.org/cccc/resources/positions/123791. htm.

"Evaluating the Intellectual Work of Writing Administration." Council of Writing Program Administrators. *WPA: Writing Program Administration*. 22.1 (1998): 85–104. Available http://wpacouncil.org/positions/intellectualwork.html.

"Final Report." MLA Ad Hoc Committee on Teaching. *Profession 2001*. New York: MLA, 2001. 225–238. Available http://www.mla.org/rep_ teaching.

"The Future of Scholarly Publishing." MLA Ad Hoc Committee on the Future of Scholarly Publishing. *Profession 2002*. New York: MLA, 2002. 172–86. Available http://www.mla.org/issues_scholarly_pub.

Gebhardt, Richard C. "Administration as Focus for Understanding the Teaching of Writing." *Composition Chronicle* 9.6 (Oct. 1996). Rpt. Ward and Carpenter 34–37.

—. "Scholarship of Teaching and Administration: An Elusive Goal for English Studies." *Teaching, Research, and Service in the Twenty-First Century English Department*. Ed. Joe Marshall Hardin and Ray Wallace. Lewiston: Edwin Mellen P, 2004. 17–39.

—, and Barbara Genelle Smith Gebhardt, eds. *Academic Advancement in Composition Studies: Scholarship, Publication, Promotion, Tenure*. Mahwah, NJ: Lawrence Erlbaum, 1997.

Glassick, Charles E., Mary Taylor Huber, and Gene I. Maeroff. *Scholarship Assessed: Evaluation of the Professoriate*. San Francisco: Jossey-Bass, 1997.

Good Practice in Tenure: Advice for Tenured Faculty, Department Chairs, and Academic Administrators. American Council on Education, the American Association of University Professors, and United Educators Insurance Risk Retention Group. 2000. 20 Oct. 2004. <http://www.acenet.edu/ bookstore/pdf/tenure-evaluation.pdf>.

Gunner, Jeanne. "Professional Advancement for the WPA: Rhetoric and Politics in Tenure and Promotion." Ward and Carpenter 315–30.

Magner, Denise. "Fewer Professors. . . ." *Chronicle of Higher Education*. 13 Sep 1996: A12–13.

"Making Faculty Work Visible: Reinterpreting Professional Service, Teaching, and Research in the Fields of Language and Literature." MLA Commission on Professional Service. *Profession 1996*. New York: MLA, 1996. 161–216. Available http://www.mla.org/resources/documents/rep_facultyvis.

Marshall, Margaret J. "Sites for (Invisible) Intellectual Work." *The Politics of Writing Centers*. Ed. Jane Nelson and Kathy Evertz. Portsmouth: Boynton/Cook, 2001. 74–84.

Olson, Gary A., and Joseph M. Moxley. "Directing Freshman Composition: The Limits of Authority." *College Composition and Communication*. 40.1 (Feb. 1989): 51–60.

"The Portland Resolution: Guidelines for Writing Program Administrator Positions."*WPA: Writing Program Administration* 16.1/2 (Fall/Winter 1992). Rpt. Ward and Carpenter 352–56. Available http://wpacouncil. org/positions/portlandres.html.

Press Release for *The American College Teacher, National Norms for 1995– 96.* UCLA Higher Education Research Institute. 20 Feb. 2004. <http:// web.archive.org/web/20030111123921/http://www.gseis.ucla.edu/her i/press_act95.htm>.

Press Release for *The American College Teacher, National Norms for 2001– 2002.* UCLA Higher Education Research Institute. 20 Oct. 2004. <http://www.gseis.ucla.edu/heri/act_pr_02.html>.

"Report of the Commission on Writing and Literature." MLA Commission on Writing and Literature. *Profession 1988.* New York: MLA, 1988. 73–74.

Roen, Duane, Barry M. Maid, Gregory R. Glau, John Ramage, and David Schwalm. "Reconsidering and Assessing the Work of Writing Program Administrators." The Writing Program Administrator as Theorist. Ed. Shirley K Rose and Irwin Weiser. Portsmouth: Heinemann, 2002. 157– 69.

Royster, Jacqueline Jones. "Shifting the Paradigms of English Studies: Continuity and Change." Proceedings of the Conference on the Future of Doctoral Education *PMLA.* 115.5 (Oct. 2000): 1222–228.

"Scholarship in Composition: Guidelines for Faculty, Deans, and Department Chairs." Conference on College Composition and Communication. 1987. Available http://www.ncte.org/cccc/resources/positions/123785. htm.

Schuster, Charles. "The Politics of Writing Promotion." *The Politics of Writing Instruction: Postsecondary.* Ed. Richard Bullock and John Trimbur. Boynton/Cook, 1991. Rpt. Ward and Carpenter, 331–41.

Schwalm, David E. "The Writing Program (Administrator) in Context: Where Am I, and Can I Still Behave Like a Faculty Member?" *The Allyn & Bacon Sourcebook for Writing Program Administrators.* Ed. Irene Ward and William J. Carpenter. New York: Longman, 2002. 9–22.

Thompson, Samuel. "Lessons Learned in Implementing Scholarship of Teaching and Learning." *National Teaching and Learning Forum* 10.5 (Sep 2001): 8–10. 20 Oct. 2004. <http://www.pitt.edu/AFShome/n/t/ ntlforum/public/html/v10n5/carnegie.htm>.

Ward, Irene, and William J. Carpenter. *The Allyn & Bacon Sourcebook for Writing Program Administrators.* New York: Longman, 2002.

"What Is the Scholarship of Engagement?" Scholarship of Engagement On-
    line. 2002. 20 Oct. 2004. <http://schoe.coe.uga.edu/about/FAQs.html>.
"The Work of Faculty: Expectations, Priorities, and Rewards." AAUP Com-
    mittee C on College and University Teaching, Research, and Publication.
    Academe. Jan/Feb 1994: 15–48.

2 Ethics and the jWPA

Alice Horning

From the perspective of a full professor currently serving as the writing program administrator at a medium-sized public university in the Midwest, it seems quite clear that the work of writing program administration can only be done by tenured, full-time faculty members. The reasons for this view range from the practical (who else has time and energy for this work?) to the professional (who else has the proper perspective?). More fundamentally, this position arises from philosophical reasons that have to do with ethical issues. It is unethical for junior faculty without tenure to hold WPA positions.

As a starting point, it will be necessary to explore what it means to say something is "unethical." The definition is not clear-cut by any means. However, a brief discussion of ethics from a philosophical perspective makes clear that a rethinking of the ethical operation of writing programs is in order. The Council of Writing Program Administrators, a national organization for those who direct college writing programs, and all who are associated with it, including other professional groups such as the MLA, CCCC and the AAUP, constitute a community whose ethical system urgently needs revision. Not much has been written about the ethics of junior faculty working as WPAs; a review of two recent collections edited by Ward and Carpenter on the one hand and by Brown and Enos on the other shows only one article on ethics at all. A variety of ethical definitions, drawn from philosophical, religious, and academic sources makes clear the nature of ethical employment and evaluation practices as well as the ethical use of power in administrative work; four specific functions that WPAs commonly assume provide examples of the ethical difficulties in having junior faculty serving in these roles and show why jWPA positions should be abolished.

A General Definition of Ethics

Here is a set of definitions that can be helpful to this discussion. It separates values, morals and ethics clearly and shows how these sometimes vague concepts fit together:

> In ethical terms, *values* are statements of worth or preference, that influence our thinking when we need to make choices. Our preferences reflect interests, attitudes, aversions, and affirmations. But not until conflicting claims on preference are put to a test do these preferences become and subsequently are called values. We use values to determine the way we want ourselves and others to live in society. Our values express what we really care about in relationship to our lives as human beings. "Good" and "bad" designate positive and negative values.
>
> To assure that our values affect our society appropriately, we join with others to develop rules of behavior to activate those values. The rules are called *morals*. Morals tell us what to do in specific situations, how to act when we have choices to make that affect other people. "Right" and "wrong" designate positive and negative moral directions.
>
> The prevailing values and morals held by its people represent the *ethical system* of a community. The term *ethics,* therefore, describes a shared system of values and morals commonly held by a group. (Schapiro, qtd. in Stern 26)

Turning to the situation of writing program administrators, both junior and senior, these terms have clear implications.

In general, the use of junior faculty as writing program administrators constitutes a problem despite the "desire" to serve in this role on the part of the faculty and the need for administrative help from the perspective of the institution. A number of jobs in rhetoric and composition entail writing program administration, so new PhDs may confront an unhappy set of choices: take a job with administrative responsibilities or nothing at all. English or writing program departments have an equally unappealing set of options: no senior faculty members have the time or energy or inclination or willingness to do the administrative work of running the writing program, and junior faculty already on board have either been denied tenure and are leaving or wisely refuse the task or are otherwise unavailable. Alternatively, the senior faculty with interest and ability to serve as WPAs have retired and because of the general declining budgets in academia, have not been replaced (Jacobson). So, for departments, the options are to hire a new jWPA with energy to serve or coerce some more senior person to oversee the program under duress. Neither of these is an attractive possibility.

Hiring junior faculty to work as WPAs, though, is not the ethical solution to this problem, as is clear in the ethical system proposed by British moral philosopher W.D. Ross (1877–1940) with his notion of "duty" theory. While Ross is only one of many moral philosophers and others dealing with ethics from Aristotle to Nell Noddings, he tries to set up a beginning, incomplete list of people's moral obligations to one another. Ross proposes that the way to make ethical choices is bound up with at least seven different duties, the first of which is fidelity (21). By fidelity, Ross means promises made explicitly or implicitly, that must be kept. Departments or programs make an implied promise to junior faculty when they are hired. The promise is to provide them with a good tenure-track position, reasonable teaching assignments in their areas of expertise, and support for their development as teachers and scholars. While no position promises tenure, I think most senior faculty would agree that we hope, when we hire, that we are choosing faculty to be long-term colleagues. If we set these junior faculty members up to spend so much time on administration that they cannot become effective teachers as well as complete and publish scholarly projects, we are exploiting their "desire" and not keeping our promises to them to help them have long and successful careers.

This exploitative hiring is a wrongful act requiring, in Ross's system, reparation. This is a second kind of duty: to make reparation, to correct "a previous wrongful act" (Ross 21). It seems to me that the Council of Writing Program Administrators and all national leadership have the duty to correct the present situation of having jWPAs at all by creating a statement of program ethics that keeps junior faculty out of WPA positions. There might be sanctions, such as those imposed by the AAUP for departments or programs that violate these ethical principles.

A third duty in Ross's scheme is gratitude or recognition of services performed by others. Here, the obligation of senior faculty can play out in at least two different ways. First, junior faculty should be recognized and rewarded for having served in WPA positions, both monetarily and in terms of their reviews for promotion and tenure. We already have the Portland Resolution and other guidelines for fairly evaluating WPA work. These documents should be brought to bear on reviews for those who have served as jWPAs. However, better or more fair evaluation does not make the workload or job description of jWPAs better. A stronger way to perform this duty is to make sure that junior faculty no longer serve in these positions.

The duty of justice is closely connected to the duty of gratitude. Ross says that this fourth duty is "the distribution of pleasure or happiness (or of the means thereto) which is not in accordance with the merit of the persons concerned; in such cases there arises a duty to upset or prevent such a distribution. These are the duties of justice" (Ross 21). Here, Ross is suggesting that we have an obligation to treat people fairly according to their merit. There is strong support for this claim in the Judeo-Christian tradition, which will be discussed later. But, here, it should be clear that the ethical requirement is that junior faculty be treated fairly; putting them into jWPA positions and then expecting them also to teach well and conduct and publish high quality research is not a just arrangement.

The fifth of the seven duties Ross sets up in his scheme is the duty of beneficence, which he describes as follows: "[. . .] there are other beings in the world whose condition we can make better in respect of virtue, or of intelligence, or of pleasure" (21). If programs and departments continue to hire young PhDs, exploiting their youth and energy by having them work as jWPAs, doing so can hardly fulfill the duty of beneficence. The narratives jWPAs write about their struggles in their work make clear that these roles are not beneficent work for junior faculty.

The last two of Ross's duties add to the list of reasons why hiring jWPAs is unethical. These are the duties of self-improvement and nonmalfeasance (21). The duties here are to improve our own conditions and to do no harm to others. These are clear ethical imperatives that apply to both senior and junior faculty who work in writing programs. All faculty have a duty, then, to do their best as teachers, scholars, and administrators (if they choose) and to perform these roles through processes of self-evaluation and improvement. But if those in leadership positions are going to fulfill the ethical duty to do no harm, they must protect junior faculty from taking on jWPA roles that will interfere with their ability to improve their work in teaching and scholarship.

Ross points out that some of his duties derive from the Decalogue, the Ten Commandments of the Bible (22). It is interesting that a philosopher would invoke the Bible, but doing so in 1930 would have produced a different reaction than any faith-based reference does now. The intention here is to bring in a wide array of sources of ethics, one of which is religion. The Bible, then, is only one of many religious texts that can be a source of guidance on ethical behavior. In several places (cf. Leviticus 19:35, Deuteronomy 25:13–16), the Bible speaks of using fair measures, and while the text refers to accurate weights for commodities, it is clear that the general moral principle intended is fairness in all kinds of evaluation. Is it fair to place untenured faculty into positions that often require workloads making successful research and teaching impossible, and then judge them on research and teaching, relegating their WPA work to the lesser category of "service"? Clearly, such judgments are unfair and hence, unethical.

A further Biblical point, not raised by Ross but pertinent in this discussion, occurs in Deuteronomy (22:10) where there is a law against plowing with an ox and an ass yoked together. Here again, if we are willing to look to the Bible as one of many sources of ethical guidance, we get advice on appropriate work and the ethical treatment of others. Commentary on this law suggests that the two creatures are uneven and that this is not appropriate for either animal. It is not ethical to ask the ass to do the work of the ox, as it is the lighter and smaller of the two animals and will simply get dragged along, making more work for the ox. My argument is not that jWPAs are asses, exactly (I'm quoting from Deuteronomy here), but that it is unethical to yoke jWPAs to work that is not appropriate for them to do because they are less experienced and vulnerable without tenure.

The Council of Writing Program Administrators was moving in the right direction on this matter when the organization issued the Portland Resolution document in 1992 (Hult). The Portland Resolution is a set of guidelines for WPA positions to address the need for fair evaluation and treatment of WPAs, especially those at junior rank. And, yet, the difficulties the Resolution is intended to address persist. The WPA Council also issued a statement on evaluating the intellectual work of WPAs in 1998, but it has not gone far enough either, in my judgment, to put a stop to the hiring of junior faculty for WPA positions. If these documents and the organization had taken a firm stand in the 1990s, we would not have jWPAs still resigning in protest or being fired unfairly from their jobs. A careful reading of the WPA-L listserv suggests that many, many jWPAs struggle to hold on to jobs that they should not, ethically, have been offered in the first place, and should not be in.

Before turning to specific examples of jWPAs' work and applying these ethical principles, there is one more preliminary point that provides a framework for the discussion, having to do with the appropriate exercise of power.

ETHICS, POWER AND THE WPA

Writing in the flagship journal of the Council of Writing Program Administrators, *WPA: Writing Program Administration,* Edward White suggests that WPAs must understand the power structure of their positions and how to use their own power effectively or lose it. But he notes that in order to have power within a program and across the campus, WPAs get their status in the usual ways, through achieving tenure and promotion to senior rank via successful teaching and scholarly publication: "[. . .] the WPA gains power as any other faculty member gains power, usually through publication and other professional activity" (10). He goes on to say that even if WPAs have not gained senior status and the security that goes with it, they must still exert their authority in directing their programs, protecting their faculties and budgets, and so on. However, if WPAs have families to support and might lose their jobs, exerting authority from a junior position may be unrealistic, as it may cause these junior faculty to be denied tenure and lose not only their jobs but possibly also their careers.

White goes on to recommend that WPAs be aware that their power is largely a matter of perception. Moreover, power accrues to WPAs (at least, to those of senior rank in such positions) because if their programs are good, both students and faculty are happy and productive and students actually learn to write. WPAs can use their power by demonstrating how many students they serve and using other kinds of data to show the effectiveness of their programs. They can draw on the professional network the WPA organization offers to gain outside support. They can use the WPA Consultant-Evaluator service to have their program assessed by nationally recognized experts. Finally, White says, WPAs have the power to resign, but he goes on to note that this way of exercising power is one "only the tenured are likely to contemplate" (12).

This article, then, by one of the most highly respected members of the WPA organization and of the profession generally, makes clear that WPA's power can only be exercised by those who truly have it, those in senior positions. The appropriate use of such power entails ethical behavior and ethical decision making of all kinds, in areas such as those White describes (in his own case, the loss of a budget for a WAC program he was overseeing [3–4]) and in areas like all the ones to be discussed in this chapter. The exercise of power, as White says, is crucial to doing the job of a WPA, "to use the considerable power we have for the good of our program" (12). That is, WPAs must use power ethically, but, as I will show, can only do so from senior positions. The national WPA organization and all who work in it must move to change national practice in an ethical way, so that no junior faculty are ever asked to serve in the WPA role.

The ethical claim I am making here is further supported by the writings of the Mishnah, the rabbinic law and teaching commentaries on the Bible (Strack and Stemberge 109). The Mishnah specifies a series of ages that people should reach in order to be ready to fulfill certain roles in life:

> [. . .] five years [is the age] for [the study of] scripture, ten for [the study of] mishnah, thirteen for [becoming subject to] the commandments, fifteen for [the study of Talmud], eighteen for the [bridal] canopy, [. . .]forty for understanding, fifty for counsel, sixty for mature age [. . .] (Mishnah 5:21, Judah ben Tema)

Notice that in this scheme, the ages for understanding and providing counsel are forty and fifty, well beyond the usual age for jWPAs. This scheme is not meant to be ageist, but to point out that jWPAs are often young both chronologically and in terms of experience, another reason it would probably be better to give WPA jobs to more experienced people. So White's points and mine are supported here by some ancient age guidelines: WPAs should certainly be of an age for understanding and counsel (i.e., they should be senior faculty).

WPAs must make decisions all the time, and administrators must also make decisions, especially about whom to hire in these decision-making roles. Sometimes, administrators look for guidance to professional organizations, hence the Portland Resolution and other WPA guidelines. If the national WPA organization sets its values in an appropriate way, then it can help administrators make moral and ethical choices in the hiring of WPAs. The right moral principles involving WPAs should clearly entail hiring only those who are already senior faculty members to do this work. Currently, our ethical system allows colleges and universities to hire junior faculty to serve as WPAs and doing so can cost these faculty members their careers and sometimes their marriages and families (Hesse), not to mention their emotional health (see Micciche). These outcomes point clearly to a systemic problem that is not ethical and that must be changed. Specific situations in the work of WPAs reveal the ways in which hiring and use of junior faculty in WPA positions is not ethical, based on Ross's duty theory and a few other philosophical analyses of ethics.

WPA Training in Graduate School

Many graduate programs in English and rhetoric and composition now prepare students to work in writing program administration. Some of these courses are taught by respected members of the discipline who have not only the experience of working as WPAs themselves but often also the additional perspective of having reviewed writing programs at many institutions around the country. I am thinking specifically of several of the authors whose work appears in this collection: Edward White, Richard Gebhardt, Gebhardt, Martha Townsend. They have taught graduate students how to be successful administrators and have created what other writers in this volume describe as the "jWPA desire" or "call to serve" as WPAs.

Surely, this training and preparation for administrative work is appropriate, just as it is appropriate to prepare graduate students to do research and write, contributing their knowledge, perspectives, and findings to the discipline. Surely, it is a good thing to help students understand the complex problems and challenges that writing programs face in colleges and universities. Surely, it is useful for students to have a national perspective on the shape of writing programs. And surely, it is appropriate for students to serve as administrative assistants in a writing program so that they have direct experience working with the issues they learn about in WPA-related classes.

However, simply because students have this training and experience assisting senior administrators does not make it ethical to give them WPA appointments. These young faculty members, filled with energy to assume jWPA roles, prepared with good training and experience assisting WPAs during their graduate school years, aware of the pitfalls of spending too much time doing administrative work and not enough time teaching well and writing for publication, must not be given such positions. Just as no parent would give children a steady supply of treats just because kids want them, no administration should give junior faculty members writing program administrator positions just because new graduates want them, notwithstanding their training, energy, and experience. The long-term chances of harm or damage are similar to the long-term risks of too many treats for youngsters, in terms of overall health. In terms of duty theory. as discussed earlier, departments and programs should do no harm to junior faculty members (Ross's non-malfeasance). The overall health and long-term careers of jWPAs are at risk if they are put into these positions; hiring new PhDs to do this work is not ethical.

The AAUP Statement on Professional Ethics helps to support this position. It says that professors' first allegiance is to "developing and improving their scholarly competence" and to "exercise critical self-discipline and judgment in using, extending, and transmitting knowledge" (qtd. in DeGeorge 130). In addition, it says that "As members of an academic institution, professors seek above all to be effective teachers and scholars" (qtd. in DeGeorge 130). Thus, faculty should be focusing first and foremost on research and teaching. No WPA, junior or senior, finds this a primary goal. Indeed, WPA work is so time-consuming that it is a wonder that WPAs *do* research and publish at all, in addition to teaching, often unreasonable loads of three or four courses. Surely, such expectations of those in the junior ranks contradict the AAUP principles as well as Ross's duties of beneficence, self-improvement, and non-malfeasance, and are thus unethical.

WPA RESPONSIBILITY FOR FAIR SCHEDULING

A further specific example of how the ethical concerns of the jWPA position play out arises in one responsibility that almost always falls to

WPAs: creating teaching schedules for all faculty working in a writing program. Schedule work can be very difficult since it involves balancing program needs against faculty members' personal preferences for teaching at certain times, on certain days, in certain rooms or buildings. It can also be overwhelming; the schedule and its issues can easily draw so much time and attention that it becomes difficult for the WPA to do much substantive work on the program itself. Moreover, scheduling may hinge on certain general principles that may or may not be overtly discussed and agreed to by the faculty. The WPA workshop, conducted every year prior to the annual conference and intended for new (though not necessarily junior) WPAs, spends a fair amount of time on scheduling issues and ways to manage this work.

In my own experience, too much of the work on the schedule looked to me like a set of decisions that were based either on my own personal whims or on something like patronage. I could decide to give or deny someone his or her desired schedule, a spring or summer course assignment, a class in the computer classroom and so on based on how I happened to be feeling about that person when I was drawing up the schedule. People who curried favor with me might easily be rewarded with the schedule they desired; those who annoyed me could be punished with 8:00 a.m. classes. It seemed to me that the needs of the program had little to do with my choices. Instead, my decisions were driven by precedent, seniority, and how cranky my senior colleagues would be about their assignments.

With the help of the current chair of my department, we have moved to a different and more ethical way of making scheduling decisions. For both regular semesters and spring/summer teaching, we have devised a set of guidelines for setting up the schedule. The principles address concerns about rank, personal needs, seniority, fairness, and other local issues. Negotiating these principles has been a complex and demanding task discussed over a number of meetings, emails, hallway conversations, and so on. It became clear that some issues would never be resolved among us and required an executive decision, which I made in consultation with the chair and with her support. I would not have wanted to be untenured during the negotiations over this issue and would not have wanted to make final decisions as a junior faculty member. Even if other programs do not have the level of contention I do in my group, it is not ethical to ask WPAs at junior rank to deal with scheduling issues. Exercising power they don't really have in the absence of tenure and senior rank is filled with risk.

One of the two different dimensions of ethics discussed by philosophers Kant and Hobbes that bear on the work of WPAs helps to explain why putting junior faculty in such positions is unethical. First, Kant's concept of the categorical imperative shows that the nature of the work of WPAs, on scheduling and other issues is such that it can only be done properly in an ethical context (Fieser and Dowden). The concept of a categorical imperative proposes that there is a core moral principle that is objective, rational, and freely chosen. One specifically relevant way in which the categorical imperative plays out is in the obligation to treat people themselves as ends, not as means to an end.

When junior faculty members work as WPAs, deans and department chairs are treating them as the means to an end, in this case, a fully staffed schedule of classes; asking for such work is unethical. This treatment is partly driven by economics; jWPAs constitute a relatively inexpensive labor force to do this very demanding work. Moreover, reaching ethical decisions requires time, energy, the wisdom of experience; ethical decisions must come from someone in a position to exercise authority and power as I did in creating the final set of scheduling guidelines. jWPAs should not be expected to meet these standards while they are also early in their teaching and research careers. The decisions that must be made in running a program are ethical decisions requiring the kind of judgment Kant suggests with the concept of the categorical imperative, and if we don't want to treat jWPAs as a means to the end of creating a fair and appropriate teaching schedule, they should not be asked to do this work.

The scheduling guidelines I created with my faculty and the chair of the department can also be seen as a kind of social contract. The social contract theory in philosophy was advanced first by Thomas Hobbes. According to Fieser and Dowden,

> Thomas Hobbes argued that, for purely selfish reasons, the agent is better off living in a world with moral rules than one without moral rules. For without moral rules, we are subject to the whims of other people's selfish interests. Our property, our families, and even our lives are at continual risk. Selfishness alone will therefore motivate each agent to adopt a

basic set of rules which will allow for a civilized community. Not surprisingly, these rules would include prohibitions against lying, stealing and killing. However, these rules will ensure safety for each agent only if the rules are enforced. As selfish creatures, each of us would plunder our neighbors' property once their guards were down. Each agent would then be at risk from his neighbor. Therefore, for selfish reasons alone, we devise a means of enforcing these rules: we create a policing agency which punishes us if we violate these rules.

The rules we created constitute the "policing agency" that provides me with a way to make ethical decisions about the schedule, without being swayed by my own selfish interests. Such ethical decision-making came about through a collaborative process under the leadership of the chair and myself. No junior faculty member could have arrived at this outcome alone, and possibly not even with the support of a good, popular chair. But it is an ethical and right outcome to which everyone has agreed. It is unethical to expect junior faculty to achieve such a goal.

WPA RESPONSIBILITY FOR TEACHING STAFF

Another responsibility that falls to writing program administrators is the hiring and firing of faculty, especially the part-time or adjunct staff who do much of the teaching in many writing programs. Here, the responsibilities include taking applications, interviewing, checking references, and orienting new faculty to the program on the hiring side. It may also entail mentoring new teachers and conducting reviews of them for continuing contract. On the firing side, the WPA must sometimes make a decision not to renew a contract. The work involved is enormously time-consuming. Moreover, it requires experienced judgments about whether candidates can do the necessary work, achieve program goals, set fair expectations for students and so on. To some extent, of course, these decisions are made on gut instinct and not on candidates' credentials. And occasionally, hiring errors get made. Many WPAs have had at least one faculty member, full-time or part-time, who was hired in error. So, then, that person must be asked to leave the staff. These are extremely difficult situations, and so much more so for a junior faculty member running a program.

In my own case, my only major hiring error occurred shortly after I started working as WPA. It was late in the summer and I still had unstaffed classes. I interviewed someone who had applied and had the right basic credentials, a Master's degree and college teaching experience. She interviewed well enough, too. When I called her two references, one was lukewarm in response to my general questions, and the other told me that I should not hire this woman. But it was close to the start of classes, and I didn't have many other options for staff, so I hired her anyway. For the rest of the year, I paid the price for this mistake in a steady stream of student complaints and various other problems with this teacher. This is not a good position for *any* writing program administrator to face, but it is especially difficult for someone untenured. The point here is that it is not ethical to ask untenured faculty to take on such roles and assume responsibility for hiring and firing.

It should be clear that lots of WPAs have responsibilities tantamount to those of department chairs. Hiring and firing, particularly of the increasingly common part-time or contingent or adjunct faculty is one big piece of it. A recent article in the *Chronicle of Higher Education* addresses the matter of untenured faculty serving as chairs (Jacobson). While exact figures on the numbers of faculty serving in such positions are not available, according to the article, this phenomenon seems to be increasing, particularly at private colleges and public institutions. On the whole, the *Chronicle* reports that most faculty think the idea of untenured chairs is a bad one:

> To be a chairman without tenure, critics say, is committing professional suicide, since you would be in charge of—and could therefore possibly alienate— the very people who would vote on your tenure [. . .]. Some departments have had no choice but to tap the untenured ranks for leaders. They've lost senior scholars to retirements but budget constraints have prevented many departments from replacing the retirees—thus shrinking the pool of potential department heads. (Jacobson)

So the risk is that junior faculty chairs or jWPAs could offend, annoy, or otherwise cause problems for colleagues who must then make a tenure decision. This situation puts those faculty members in a difficult spot to say the least. It is not ethical to run departments or writing programs this way.

WPA Responsibility for Campus-Wide Issues and Problems

For many WPAs, another role or area of responsibility has to do with addressing broad issues across the campus. Often, a writing requirement applies to all students in all programs at a college or university. Questions and concerns about a program may come from students, parents, administrators, advisers, or faculty in other departments. Students may be seeking exemption from course requirements, changes in placement, appeals for courses denied transfer credit, and so on. Parents may want to know why a student was placed in a developmental course or how AP or SAT exam results are used in the program. Administrators may need program information or sample syllabi to show to accreditors. Advisers may be seeking to help students with transfer, placement, exemption, or other issues. Faculty in other departments may want advice on writing assignments or requirements. Questions can come from anywhere and everywhere. The WPA is the person with the answers and solutions, or should be. But the WPA is also the person who speaks for the writing requirements, whatever they are, and may deny a student course exemption or revised placement as appropriate. If students or parents are dissatisfied, they are likely to go up the administrative ladder to the dean, the provost, and higher.

This situation occurred in my experience also. A graduating senior had waited until her final term to try to meet the writing requirement. She submitted a portfolio, including a paper that was plagiarized. Because she had received late notification of her failure to satisfy the writing requirement (never mind that it is always students' responsibility to know the requirements and whether they have been satisfied), the student had already been to visit the assistant dean of the college, who had alerted me that the student would be submitting a portfolio for immediate review. When I saw the portfolio, I had to deny exemption because of the plagiarism involved. The student went back to the dean's office and this time saw the associate dean of the college. This administrator, without even consulting me, overturned my evaluation, allowing the student to graduate. There was some flimsy excuse given for this behavior, but both my chair and I registered our intense dissatisfaction with the dean. Of course, my position was not threatened in this case, as I am a full professor. But woe to the jWPA who might come to the attention of senior administrators by this route!

Or imagine the poor junior faculty who is also the writing program administrator when the provost calls about a student complaint. Of course, one goal all WPAs have is to keep complaints from getting to that level. But inevitably some do go up through the ranks, and then a junior person is challenged with making a decision and making it stick. Even a senior faculty member like me has difficulty making a decision stick when it is challenged by a senior administrator. For a junior faculty member, such a position is even more untenable. But over-ruling the WPA may mean that the university's standards are waived, and that's not an ethical outcome either. We are obligated by our ethical duties to keep our promises, to be just, to do no harm. Putting junior faculty in WPA positions entails a failure to perform these duties on the part of senior administrators, programs, departments, and it is not ethical.

WPA RESPONSIBILITY FOR ASSESSMENT

A final area WPAs are commonly responsible for is program assessment. Assessment is always politically hot and has the potential to create many difficulties for a WPA. It is one way in which a program is viewed or analyzed across the campus. An assessment report is a public document that tells what the program aims to do and whether or to what extent it is achieving its goals.

In my own experience, assessment created two kinds of problems, neither of which I could have dealt with as a junior faculty member. First, I ran an assessment reading of final research essays from our second semester course, and wrote a report that the previous chair didn't like; I found that she changed the report but left my name on it before submitting it to the university's assessment committee. The changes she made didn't entail fudging the numbers, but did not, in my view, present an accurate picture of the program's status. While I was bothered that she changed the report, I was even more bothered by the fact that she left my name on it. In this case, had I been a junior faculty member, I would not have felt comfortable protesting the changes, which I did vigorously from my senior position.

The additional problem in our assessment scheme (another widespread issue I believe) is that it requires a fair amount of work on the part of the faculty that is unpaid or paid at an unprofessional rate. We have raised this issue repeatedly with administrators and the assessment committee. From my point of view, it is not ethical to ask faculty (especially part-timers) to do extensive assessment work for which they are not paid. I have always wanted to take an ethical stand on this matter and refuse to do any assessment in the absence of appropriate funding. Even from a senior position like mine, however, such a stand is very difficult to take in the face of possible loss of institutional accreditation.

This position creates an ethical quagmire: on the one hand, assessment can really help a program see where it has been and where it is going, but, on the other, there is a huge amount of work involved and no one can or should work for free. Junior faculty overseeing assessment, a common responsibility of WPAs, should never be asked to wade into a quagmire of this kind; such ethical dilemmas as these that are raised by assessment are best left to senior, experienced faculty serving appropriately as WPAs. Senior faculty have attained an age appropriate for understanding and counsel, they are not asses yoked to oxen, and they can perform all the duties involved while continuing to meet the duty for self-improvement and doing good. It is ethical for senior faculty to serve as WPAs, but not for junior faculty.

Duties and Ethics for WPAs

W.D. Ross's duty theory, mentioned earlier in this discussion, focuses on the seven duties involved in ethical behavior. Ross says that human beings are obligated to act in ways that are consistent with the duties of fidelity, reparation, gratitude, justice, beneficence, self-improvement, non-malfeasance (21–22). Each of these duties helps to show why having junior faculty serve as WPAs is unethical. Kant's categorical imperative tells us that people should not be treated as a means to an end; in the case of jWPAs, they offer a cheap means to the end of program management. Ethics, as defined at the outset of this chapter, is a shared sense of proper behavior, consistent with the values and morals of a community. The work of writing program administration is central to undergraduate education at every institution of higher education and should therefore provide a national model for fair and appropriate treatment of the people who do this work.

The community of senior faculty concerned with keeping writing programs in good working order should take on the responsibility of setting the ethical structure in which we all function. This group includes the MLA, CCCC, the AAUP and especially, the Council of Writing Program Administrators. Leaders of all of these groups should consider carefully the work that WPAs are asked to do, from their training and experience assisting in writing program administration work, to their day-to-day responsibilities in scheduling, staffing, campus-wide representation, and assessment. Asking junior faculty to take on this work is not ethical and the national leadership should put a stop to this practice as a matter of policy. Doing so would fulfill all the ethical duties described by Ross: keeping our promise, making up for years of bad treatment and exploitation of jWPAs, showing our appreciation for all those who have taken on these jobs and done them well, being fair to those joining the faculty, doing good by treating new faculty appropriately, helping new faculty with the duty of self-improvement as scholars and teachers first, and, finally, especially, doing no harm by keeping junior faculty out of WPA positions.

Works Cited

Brown, Stuart and Theresa Enos, Eds. *The Writing Program Administrator's Resource: A Guide to Reflective Institutional Practice*. Mahwah, NJ: Erlbaum, 2002.

Council of Writing Program Administrators. "Evaluating the Intellectual Work of Writing Program Administration." *WPA: Writing Program Administration* 22.1 (1998): 85–104.

DeGeorge, Richard T. *Academic Freedom and Tenure: Ethical Issues*. Lanham, MD: Rowman & Littlefield Publishers, 1997.

Fieser, James, and Bradley Dowden, Eds. *Internet Encyclopedia of Philosophy*. 2007. <http://www.utm.edu/research/iep/>.

Hesse, Douglas. "The WPA as Husband, Father, Ex." *Kitchen Cooks, Plate Twirlers, and Troubadours: Writing Program Administrators Tell Their Stories*. Ed. Diana George. Portsmouth, NH: Boynton/Cook, 1999. 44–55.

Hult, Christine, and the Portland Resolution Committee. "The Portland Resolution." *WPA: Writing Program Administration*. 16.1/2 (1992): 88–94.

Jacobson, Jennifer. "In Charge Without Tenure." *Chronicle Of Higher Education*. 6 Nov. 2002. 11 Nov. 2002. <http://chronicle.com/jobs/11/2002110601c.htm >.

Micciche, Laura. "More Than a Feeling: Disappointment and WPA Work. *College*

English 64.4 (March 2002): 432–58.

Noddings, Nell. *Caring: A Feminine Approach to Ethics.* Berkeley: U of California P, 1984.

Ross, William David. *The Right and the Good.* London: Oxford UP, 1930.

Stern, Jack. "Are Jews Ethical Enough?" *Reform Judaism* (Fall, 1991): 24–27.

Strack, H.L., and Gunter Stemberge. *Introduction to the Talmud and Midrash.* Trans. Markus Bockmuehl. Minneapolis, MN: Fortress P, 1992.

Ward, Irene, and William J. Carpenter, Eds. *The Allyn & Bacon Sourcebook for Writing Program Administrators.* New York: Addison Wesley Educational Publishers, 2002.

White, Edward. "Use It or Lose It: Power and the WPA." *WPA: Writing Program Administration* 15.1/2 (Fall/Winter, 1991): 3–12.

3 Defining *Junior*

Suellynn Duffey

> The worst way to begin an academic career is as a ju-
> nior administrator, one who does not know the cam-
> pus mores and history, the personalities, and so on; in
> other words, someone with a new PhD should NOT
> be a WPA or assistant dean, if that can be avoided.
> On most campuses, the WPA job has responsibili-
> ties way beyond the authority that comes with it, de-
> vours time that a new professor needs for teaching
> and writing, and has poor prospects for tenure and
> upward mobility. Some acquaintance with adminis-
> tration is important, since in time, that person will
> likely be a WPA. But not right away. Ideally, admin-
> istration should start after tenure, not before.
>
> —Edward M. White

Edward M. White's words (posted to a WPA-L discussion on new
PhD programs) are so clear and straightforward and his reasons so
strong that they seem irrefutable: Only problems, frustration, disappointment, and failure await a junior faculty member who is also a
writing program administrator, who *as such* begins his or her "academic career" in the "worst way" possible. Certainly, the pressures that
White cites are often (though not always) inherent in positions of writing program administration—directors have "responsibilities beyond
the authority" needed to perform effectively; they necessarily perform
time-intensive tasks and carry heavy loads; they function with a great
need to know and understand campus mores, history, and personalities; and they work under jeopardy toward "tenure and upward mobil-

ity." In conflating two positions, writing program administrator and assistant dean, White's post may skew his claim in a way he perhaps would not intend if describing only the WPA position, but he nonetheless lays out much of the received wisdom about WPA working conditions. The Portland Resolution, which also addresses workplace conditions for WPAs, in no way contradicts White's position. Given this congruence, why, then, is there any need for this book and the discussions we hope it will engender?

Let me start with one reason, an issue this chapter will approach from several perspectives. Taken together, White's post and the Portland Resolution explicitly or implicitly define the junior position as one in which the WPA is 1) new to the campus (White); 2) newly degreed (White); and 3) untenured (Hult 90). Using these three criteria, I can easily illustrate some of the definitional concerns this chapter will address. I do not wish, however, to hold White up as someone unaware of the complexities defining junior administrative positions. Instead, I use his post to show that a fairly well-accepted line of thinking about the junior faculty WPA position—that it is defined by a few criteria and is one about which it is easy to make clear and definitive statements—takes only a surface probe to undo.

For example, because I am new to my department and institution as well as untenured, I would seem, as director of first-year writing, to be "junior," or a jWPA. I meet two of the three criteria. But I am far from newly degreed, having held my PhD since 1987. In fact, I have directed writing programs full-time since 1985, roughly twenty years. While I am certainly junior now in terms of faculty rank and institutional longevity (having began my current directorship three years ago as an assistant professor, the reasons for which I will explain later), I am not junior in my intellectual and practical experience directing curricular change, creating collaborative work structures, mentoring new teachers and staff, handling budgetary matters, hiring and evaluating instructors, interfacing with other campus departments and offices, writing job descriptions, re-structuring instructor work-loads, and knowing how to "read" the rhetorical situation of my institution. Thus while this suit-jacket of junior may "fit" in the sleeves, it does not in the shoulder width and needs some alteration.

A simple alteration is to say that fitting the definition of junior to any given set of criteria is a matter of flexing both the definition and the criteria, fluidly. A reasonable rationale for doing so is that rarely is any concrete instance of a category fully defined by the general markers of the category. If we allow such a way out of the definitional problem, however, we fail to examine perhaps hidden assumptions that foster the notion many in our discipline seem to hold—that the position of a junior faculty WPA is ill-advised and perhaps unethical, either for individuals seeking employment or for institutions creating such positions. That stance fails, it seems to me, to take into account many complexities that we would do well to consider, perpetuates victim narratives and (self-) righteous indignation, and also risks transforming the definition of junior from the fitted suit jacket above into a loosely-hanging, relatively shapeless sweater, as maybe, in fact, the garment is.

Another approach is to argue that we make this suit jacket fit by isolating the job security conferred by tenure as the *sine qua non* by which one defines junior. Such an argument is reasonable because of the nature of WPA work and the hierarchical structures of academe, but doing so would also lead us to ignore a whole host of issues in the material realities of individuals and institutions. It oversimplifies the variety of WPA positions across institutions and departments, and ignores individuals' backgrounds, needs, and career paths. Thus at issue are the complexities of WPA positions and human lives and their relationship to professional guidelines and policies, a relationship it is difficult to draw monolithically, to hold onto for policy-making, and to guide individual choice.

Before I continue with the definitional issues surrounding the junior faculty position, let me point out certain other logistical and logical problems in White's post and the Portland Resolution that also push us to question perhaps unexamined assumptions. First, White's post seems to assume that a WPA would be chosen from within departmental ranks; otherwise, how could he or she "know the campus mores and history, the personalities, and so on?"

What would it require for such a possibility to be realized? A department seeking to fill a WPA position from within would, presumably, already include at least one faculty member with specialization in rhetoric and composition, preferably in the sub-discipline of writing program administration (unless, of course, the department is willing to appoint a director without specialized credentials). This already-on-staff faculty member is learning the "campus mores and history, the personalities, and so on," like a WPA-in-waiting. Unless this department concurrently has no one functioning as a program administrator (or has a WPA in a non-faculty line it wants to replace), the department would include two faculty specialists in writing program administration. And, yet, some departments can employ only one faculty specialist in rhetoric and composition, either because their small size or their internal politics dictate this stricture. Even departments with large numbers of faculty specialists in rhetoric and/or composition are unlikely to include two in the same administrative subdiscipline.

The Portland Resolution has similar logistical and logical contradictions about who should hold the WPA position. On the one hand, the Resolution is absolutely clear: Under Section I.3 ("Job Security"), it asserts that "The WPA should be a regular, full-time, *tenured* faculty member" (Hult 90, emphasis added). On the other, the Resolution takes great pains to claim the importance of employing departments to spell out the evaluative criteria WPAs will be subjected to for tenure and promotion (see Sections I.2, "Evaluating" and I.6, "Job Descriptions"). If the WPA is already tenured, then spelling out the criteria for tenure is superfluous; thus, the Resolution seems to reveal internal contradictions about how the ideal WPA position should be constructed. It could, of course, be counter-argued that the Resolution is concerned with other kinds of evaluation (annual performance reviews, promotion to associate or full, post-tenure review), but because the stakes for these reviews are not nearly as high as the ones for tenure, such an argument loses strength and the Resolution's internal contradiction stands.

Both the logistical and logical problems in White's post and the Portland Resolution would be of less significance if WPAs were hired at senior levels and tenured at point of hire. While some ads in the MLA *Job Information List* suggest some departments hire with just such luxuries (calling for a WPA-in-waiting or an associate or full professor), these ads are relatively few. If I extrapolate the conditions that would allow such hiring practices from the ads, I see departments that are ones in which the majority of the faculty members are well-acquainted with and respectful of rhetoric and composition as a discipline, where the institution is willing and able to hire at the more expensive senior level, where there is probably a long-established rhetoric and composition program, supported by institutional hierarchy and built by planning rather than contentious hegemony, and where the WPA position is highly valued. Such places probably exist, but I do not believe they are representative of the great majority of departments into which WPAs are hired and work.

As I have begun to illustrate and will continue to do, junior cannot be defined exclusively in terms of an individual's characteristics (e.g., newly degreed) nor the parameters of an institutional position (e.g., tenured, non-probationary). In addition, relatively invisible matters of perception figure significantly into defining junior. For example, the *perception* of junior helps construct the subjectivities and material realities within which a WPA operates and is judged. Perceptions are formed in complicated ways and construct, just as they are constructed by, those who might hold a position as junior faculty and WPA. Just as importantly, perceptions of junior (by the WPA and the department) do not necessarily correlate directly with an actual individual's experience, rank, or departmental standing. Narrating certain aspects of my career as writing program administrator in several different institutions will illustrate, more concretely, how perception defines the concept of junior and, as well, how it complicates an attempt to define junior in ways that are useful.

As I mentioned above, I have worked as a WPA since 1985, first directing the basic writing program at Ohio State University. I consider myself, at that point in my career, to have been most clearly "junior," especially when I realize how much I have learned since. But even then, my standing as junior is conflicted, if we compare my perception, my institutional rank, and the apparent definitional characteristics of junior. First, I had held administrative positions as a graduate student, a relatively uncommon occurrence in 1985, so I assumed my first full-time position with administrative experience. Since my degrees were from OSU, I was also familiar with the department and institution and thus knew some of the campus "mores," "history," and "personalities." By these measures, I was not junior—even though I don't believe these measures constructed my position as senior. I was, perhaps, something between. My position was further between or indefinable because I was not appointed to a faculty line. Instead, I was a member of the administrative and professional staff, on a yearly appointment, not eligible for tenure. My job was less secure than that of a tenured faculty member, even though the Portland Resolution seems to assume that an administrative appointment is as acceptable as a tenured faculty position, asserting in Section I.3, "Job Security," that "The WPA should be a regular, full-time, *tenured* faculty member or a *full-time administrator* [. . .] ." (Hult 90, emphasis added). Insofar as a tenured faculty appointment is equivalent to holding an appointment as administrative staff (a problematic equivalency, as my continuing narrative will demonstrate), I was not junior. But since I had not completed my dissertation, my academic "capital" was certainly low. For several reasons, it would be possible to argue that taking this first directorship was ill-advised, a bad career move, but the reasons cannot easily be explained by using the term junior.

I would argue, however, that taking that position was one of the best career moves I've made. This particular position—junior as I was in expertise at first, non-faculty in a department that did not, ultimately, respect administrative staff, and guaranteed no continuing employment—afforded me great opportunities and more authority than many senior positions do and was the most stimulating and satisfying directorship I've held in my twenty-year career. Because of the department's indifference to the program and geographic separation between the two, the program was largely invisible. This reality, while reflecting institutional problems, also gave me considerable freedom, the freedoms those on the margins have that those in the center may not. Thus, when I held the "invisible" position, in which I was initially "junior," and was for the duration non-faculty and untenurable, I also had professional and programmatic freedoms not always afforded to WPAs.

For example, I held hiring authority and so was able to shape the program's curricular and pedagogical aspects, as well as staff morale, in significant and positive ways. I was able to develop a vibrant teaching community. Its vibrancy eventually attracted graduate students, who previously had had little interest in basic writing, to teach and conduct research in basic writing. (Some of these students are now respected members of our profession whose names you would recognize. Their teaching and scholarship challenged the program to grow in exciting ways.) This program thus developed, under my leadership, into something very close to the teacher-scholar atmosphere that many in academe consider ideal (within, I might point out, a research-intensive setting).

It is possible to argue that my status as administrative and professional staff (which kept me invisible to the great majority of the department) actually worked *for* me. I could make decisions and choices that someone in a junior, tenure-line position might have been unwilling to make. Additionally, I might note, my first directorship also carried with it many accoutrements. I had an adequate budget, curricular authority, and autonomy in my work with placement practices and other programmatic concerns. I had an assistant director, two secretaries, and I even controlled my own travel funds.

When I began my WPA career, I thus found myself in a position that was stimulating, challenging, engaging, sustaining, and relatively well-funded. In addition, keeping it, rather than applying for tenure-line positions elsewhere (and thus enhancing my academic capital), allowed me to stay at Ohio State for the years my son was in school and thus live those years very close to my extended family, a fact that gave richness to my life and his. Thus my first job, a position clearly conflicted if we try to define it as either junior or senior, was very good for me. It was only in my last year at Ohio State, after I had left the basic writing program and directed all first-year programs, that things changed. At issue was not my status as junior or senior. My status as administrative and professional staff had become a problem because the department decided that administrative staff should not lead its first-year writing programs. I was faced with an unwelcome change in position (a demotion, essentially), but I was not, however, facing unemployment, so my job security was in no more jeopardy than if I had been tenured (when a department chair or vote, for example, might appoint a new program director or committee chair).

But Ohio State ceased to be a satisfying place to work and I left quickly to take a staff position at another university, one I held for three years. By then, I had accumulated ample experiential evidence of the difficulties and dangers in staff positions, such as faculty prejudice, restricted academic "capital," and unequal intellectual property rights, and so I searched only for a job with faculty status. Keenly aware of my outsider and compromised status, I believed I would be considered for and applied only for *assistant* professor positions, junior positions (a belief I am now less certain about). When I accepted my first *faculty* position, I thus found myself, again, with mixed junior and senior characteristics, as I had in my first directorship.

A mid-sized, public liberal arts university offered me a tenure-accruing assistant professorship, so my institutional rank was clearly junior, but I assumed the position with over a dozen years of administrative experience in complex and challenging programs, with a modest national reputation in basic writing, and with a repertoire of strategies for problem-identification and solution. What I lacked was an awareness of how different my perceptions and my department's were—about the breadth and value of my experience, about the tasks and roles appropriate for a WPA, about our constructions of both junior and senior, and about appropriate behavior. One could argue that my conflicted status was part of the reason I did not fare well at this institution, but more important for us to understand as a profession, I would argue, are the cultural differences among departments. These cultural differences account in great measure for my quite unhappy and isolating directorship there.

I expected to enter a congenial community in my new department, partly because of the professional friendships I struck up with members of the hiring committee and especially because all faculty taught first-year writing every semester. I believed, with good reason, that this community was one in which teaching writing was a component of departmental identify, professionalism, disciplinary knowledge, and coffee-room conversations. In addition, all non-tenure line instructors were full-time employees and were afforded many of the benefits of their tenure-line faculty colleagues. I thought, on these bases, that I would be entering a community of professionals with whom I would readily share professional concerns, a department whose professional definition and ethical standards I could be comfortable with.

My views, of course, were shaped by my years in Ohio State's basic writing program which had prepared me to expect a certain kind of vigorous dedication to pedagogical discussions, devotion to student success, antipathy toward deficit models of student performance, and demonstration of active and open collaboration on curricular and contributed to programmatic development. All of the instructors who worked in the basic writing workshop under my supervision, even if they were not scholars in rhetoric or composition, participated in discussions of teaching issues, pragmatic and theoretical ones. I thus assumed that the current of teacher-scholarship that ran through our working lives there would bubble equally strong at an institution where everyone taught first year writing. Even though I was quite familiar with the phenomenon of untrained instructors teaching writing, I knew more about such teachers as adjuncts than as faculty. I did not expect to find the same problems that an adjunct staff brings in a department whose full-time faculty were all, apparently, invested in composition instruction.

When my new colleagues began calling their common teaching assignment, first-year writing, "the great leveler," I experienced some degree of dissonance that I could not immediately define, nor could they
lessen it when I asked them to explore their term. "Leveling," it is clear
now, carried the suggestion of diminishment; it brought every one
down to size. I did not, however, fully realize the metaphoric under-
tones until I had already mistaken the degree of knowledge I expected
my colleagues to have about composition, rhetoric, and the profession.
Few faculty had any real knowledge of the field, and most of those
who did had knowledge only as current as the mid-1980s. Because
so many faculty had taught in the department for decades, many for
close to thirty years, the entire persona of the department was very
strongly that of the English department generation of the early 1970s
or perhaps early 1980s, highly masculinist, and largely uninfluenced
by faculty brought in from other regions of the country. Without the
groundwork of a theoretically informed, up-to-date, critical mass of
colleagues, my role could not possibly have been one that challenged
me to cutting-edge thinking and practice, as I had anticipated.

This absence of a critical mass of intellectually challenging colleagues impeded my success in another way, as well. At Ohio State,
I had worked in collaborative programs and perhaps because of my
gendered and intellectual predilections, a setting in which I work
alone—as a teacher, scholar, and administrator—settings I found myself in at this institution—is unsatisfying. I had an already well-developed professional management style that filled some of my intellectual
needs. Had I been junior in work experience as was this position, I
would have developed my management style in conjunction with this
particular culture and might have assimilated more easily, but I had
already moved farther along the developmental line toward a professional identity that was engrained, not because I resist change and not
because my professional identity is an essentialized "self" who collabo-
rates, but because one establishes her professional identity through the
interplay of contextual factors and individual predilections. I had already, in fact, proceeded along this developmental path in my previous
positions. The recursive interplay between my previous work settings
and my own needs and desires thus gave me reasons *not* to assimilate.

Holding a tenure-line position, *finally,* did not afford me any more
satisfaction than my first non-tenure-line job in which I was much
more junior, in my estimation; in fact, it offered much less. In retro-

spect, the rich, cultural knowledge I gained about this department on my odyssey's stop there renders unbelievably ignorant my assumption that I could find satisfying work there as a WPA. It seems obvious to me now that the mere fact that an entire faculty teaches composition does not mean the culture is congenial to a rhetoric or composition specialist. My ignorance, alone, though could not account for all the problems, nor did my status as probationary faculty. Thus it could be argued, counter-intuitively, that my prior professional life, that which conferred some degree of senior-ness on me, worked against me in this position. It set up unrealistic expectations as well as professional needs for collaboration and intellectual stimulation that could not be filled by repeating work that I had already learned how to do and by doing it without a team of colleagues.

As my cultural knowledge of this department accumulated, I eventually vowed to never again take an untenured WPA position, vowed, finally, to follow our discipline's advice and never again accept a WPA position as an assistant professor without tenure.

And yet. . . .

In March, 2001, without any intention of searching for a job, I went to CCCC where old and new friends "caught up" with my life. My stories led two of them to argue that I needed a happier work environment, and so with mild interest, I scanned the registration area for job announcements. The strength of my friends' arguments, plus the numerous job ads I found, led me to return home and, in a matter of weeks, fly off to interviews. One institution, Georgia Southern, had caught my eye, even in the preceding fall when I skimmed the MLA *Job Information List*. GSU had had several openings, with positions described in ways that my credentials and experience seemed to fit. Two of them were still open in March; and they offered the opportunity to work in a department of writing and linguistics, not English, an opportunity I found exciting. By the time I entered into the job search in earnest, my resistance to taking a jWPA job was weakening. And as I continued through the search process to the point at which I was offered and accepted my current position (assistant professor, probationary), I argued long and hard with myself about the choice I was making. Let me share with you some of my internal arguments—and the reasons I ultimately decided, in spite of personal experience, to go against what had seemed to be better judgment and the advice of my professional organization.

First, as I indicated above, I was not, on the basis of work experience, a junior faculty WPA and could never again be. Second, because of my conflicted first *faculty* position, I had learned the pitfalls I was subject to by failing to understand the wide divergence in departmental cultures, and I had gained considerable insight into how to investigate "culture" appropriately, knowledge I put to use during my interviews. Because in my first faculty position, I had experienced the insult of being considered "novice" when I thought I was not, I quizzed my prospective employer during the job search about how my past experiences would weigh into my performance evaluations and I was satisfied with the answers. I also quizzed my prospective department chair extensively about how the tenure process worked and whose evaluations "counted," something I had not known to ask during the interviews for my first faculty post. (In that department, all faculty voted, with each vote given equal weight, so my impressions of congeniality gained through the search committee misled me considerably about my fit with the department and my prognosis of its eventual assessment of my performance.) I also spoke privately with junior faculty about their sense of departmental culture. They, as well as everyone I spoke to, were open about the department's past conflicts which gave me insight both into potential problems (and my readiness to tackle them) as well as the department's willingness to acknowledge problems, knowledge my previous department seemed not to have access to or else denied.

I had grieved for many things during my first faculty job, and the loss of a congenial intellectual community figured significantly into my grief, so I knew that what weighed very heavily in my professional happiness was having a *community* of colleagues, something I'd lost when I left Ohio State and never found elsewhere, partly because I'd never again been among so many people trained in rhetoric and composition. Georgia Southern's Writing and Linguistics department offered roughly the same number of rhetoric and composition specialists as had Ohio State, and so once again—though on different evidence, I believed I would enter a congenial community. Further, I had much more evidence both that the department knew what it was getting in me (during the search process, I was greeted by faculty familiar with and interested in my scholarly work) and I knew, much better than I had previously, what kind of a culture I was entering and how to investigate its problems.

And so here I am, entering my fourth year of a (mixed) junior faculty WPA position. During that time, I have composed, collaboratively with the department chair, my position description; I have chosen the faculty members who would sit on the first-year writing committee. In slow and deliberate collaborative practices with faculty peer-teaching groups, the committee and I have developed new writing assessment policies that passed department approval easily. I have successfully passed my third year performance review and look forward with some confidence to a successful tenure and promotion evaluation this year.[1]

My stories and arguments thus far indicate many problems with defining the junior faculty WPA position and using it to make a prognosis of job success. In addition, I can't help but feel a kind of rankling paternalism in guidelines pronouncing the demerits of the junior position, and so I turn to Sharon Crowley's words, ones that validate my sense of paternalism in a way that makes my response less an individual quirk of personality and more an issue of academic class, privilege, and the complexities of the local and personal.

In *Composition in the University,* Crowley analyzes the work conditions of part-time instructors, but her observations pertain as well, I would argue, to the junior faculty WPA. Crowley explains what she learned by "talk[ing] with the temporary and part-time teachers and teaching assistants all over the country" and the accumulation of lived experience such interviews gave her (230). She came to understand not only the realities and complexity in the work lives many instructors have but also that it was "tenured academics who dictated the standards of professional instruction," just as it is privileged academics who, for the most part, have articulated admonitions against the junior position. Crowley asserts that these academics should not "presume to speak for others who do not enjoy [their] [. . .] privileges" (239), as she and the Wyoming Resolution had done.

Crowley goes on: "In my anxiety to preserve whatever academic privilege is enjoyed by the very few teachers of composition who are tenured or are on a tenure track, I wanted to upgrade the status of our profession by altering the fact that disrespect for it is reflected in the professional status of most of its teachers. Furthermore, in presuming to speak for temporary teachers and teaching assistants, I simply erased the reality that many English teachers must teach on a temporary basis if they wish to work at all" (239). Her work led her to believe that college teachers do not, as Richard Ohmann would have it, "possess 'the cultural capital and class resiliency to make lives for themselves somewhere other than the ghetto, prison, or homeless shelter' (1991, xiii)" (239). The reality of a jWPA position does not exactly replicate the realities of part-time writing instructors, but the realizations Crowley came to are certainly applicable to this book's discussions. At issue is who is authorized to speak for whom, who is authorized to represent the interests of the junior faculty, who is authorized to construct the subject positions of the *junior* and the *professional* (WPA), and where the agency for decision-making rests. My own decision to leave Ohio State was determined in large part because of a move to fill the WPA position with a regular, tenured, faculty member, something I was not. I left family and friends and paid high prices for the decision others made.

After Ohio State, I took a six year odyssey before landing in an institution where I am allowed to be successful. And the odyssey does not tell a single, clear-line narrative about the dangers of the junior faculty WPA and job satisfaction. Departmental cultures, professional credentials, and past histories of writing program administrators, to say nothing of personal needs, create too complex a mix for us to know just how the jWPA will fare.

So I am left with a conundrum: Organizations (like the Council of Writing Program Administrators) create policy because of a role they assume, often for very good and ethical reasons. They articulate ideal (working) conditions in order to influence decision-making in institutions. Insofar as this is the Portland Resolution's goal, the intent is understandable and the Resolution helpful, one might argue. But because the Council holds no official credentialing authority over institutions, the way engineering organizations do, for example, applying this argument to our discipline is problematic. The organization's power is only rhetorical—not insignificant but often far less key in guiding institutional change than budgetary constraints, inertia, and the historical conservatism of academic institutions in preserving the status quo. Even so, it could be argued that neglecting to articulate such policies would be ethically irresponsible.

Another layer of the conundrum occurs because it is people, human creatures, who relate to and make decisions about how to enact policy. How are we—both for individuals seeking WPA positions and the human beings determining a given department's configuration of faculty (or other) administrative lines—to relate to policy? Embrace it to the letter? Doing so allows one to assume a moral high ground, but how often does one ever have the institutional power to do so? If we don't have the power to embrace a policy to the letter, do we ignore it? Certainly we don't want to completely, especially when a policy such as the Portland Resolution is aimed to better the working conditions of WPAs. We do not, of course, relate in either extreme way (very often). We operate in some gray, middle ground, a wide expanse of territory where most of us (and most of our departments) find ourselves most of the time. The goal of this chapter, then, has been to illustrate a few of the complexities in this gray, middle ground, just as this entire volume intends to do so—to help us as individuals and departments think our way through to ethical, reasonable, and practical stances and choices regarding WPA work and the status, ranks, and conditions we find acceptable for it.

Note

[1] I should note that as of press time, my university has both tenured and promoted me.

Works Cited

Baker, Anthony, Karen Bishop, Suellynn Duffey, Jeanne Gunner, Rich Miller, and Shelley Reid. "The Progress of Generations." *WPA: Writing Program Administration*. 29. 1/2 (2005): 31-58.

Crowley, Sharon. *Composition in the University: Historical and Polemical Essays*. Pittsburgh: U of Pittsburgh P, 1998.

Hult, Christine and the Portland Resolution Committee: David Joliffe, Kathleen Kelly, Dana Mead, and Charles Schuster. "The Portland Resolution." *WPA: Writing Program Administration* 16.1/2 (1992): 88–94.

White, Edward. "Re: New Ph.D. program." 8 February 2004. WPA-L. 9 February 2004. <http://lists.asu.edu/cgi-bin/wa?A2=ind0402&L=wpa-l&D=1&O=D&F=&S=&P=17266>.

4 Negotiating the Risks and Reaping the Rewards: Reflections and Advice from a Former jWPA

Martha A. Townsend

INTRODUCTION

Midway through my doctoral program of study in rhetoric and composition, I made a conscious decision to aim for a career as a writing program administrator.[1] Early on in my MA studies, I had identified rhetoric and composition as my primary focus for graduate training. Instinctively, I felt at home with both the intellectual traditions of the field as well as the rigors of teaching writing and the satisfaction of preparing first-year students for their future writing experiences in academe. And, as a nontraditional student, I sensed that I had the skills, determination, and temperament to be a successful WPA. But my decision was also economically driven: as a single parent of two high-school-age children planning to go on to college, I was unwilling to subsist on an entry-level assistant professor's salary. I knew that administration would afford me a lifestyle more commensurate to my needs and those of my family. Fifteen years later, I am happy with the decision I made; my WPA work has been extremely satisfying. I am, now, a former jWPA who looks forward to going to work every morning. But I cannot say I felt that way each and every day that led up to this point in my career.

Two weeks after defending my dissertation at Arizona State University, I began my position as a "non-regular" assistant professor in the English Department at the University of Missouri-Columbia, a large, public, Research Extensive university. I was also appointed director of

MU's writing-across-the-curriculum (WAC) program. As a new PhD on a non-tenure track appointment, my situation was hardly unique within our field. But the specific nature of my appointment was—and that has made all the difference. Thanks to mentoring by generous senior scholars in rhetoric and composition, both at ASU and those I was fortunate to meet through CCCC and WPA, I was schooled in the field's unfair labor practices that my colleagues Marty Patton and Jo Ann Vogt write about in this volume. (See "The Center Will Not Hold: Redefining Professionalism in the Academy.") Thanks to many cautionary tales told at CCCC preconference workshops sponsored by WPA, for example, I knew that an administrative position in a large WAC program, especially at a research university, would be problematic at best for achieving tenure and promotion.

At the same time, my mentors had also taught me that a WPA with a professional staff title would not serve the program or my career well. So, the first two questions I put to my MLA interviewers were, "Why is MU considering a new PhD for an administrative job?" and "What is MU prepared to do to address the problems inherent in a non-tenure track assistant professor directing a campus-wide academic program?" Those questions, repeated multiple times during the hiring process, along with the ensuing answers and discussion they elicited, led the university to appoint me as WAC director and non-tenure track assistant professor—with the option of my activating the tenure clock when I felt safely grounded in the job and ready to undertake the traditional tasks that would lead to tenure and promotion. During the hiring negotiations, I did attempt to educate the vice-provost about WPA work as intellectual work so that I could be evaluated for tenure and promotion based, at least in part, on my WAC position, but it was clear that defining a new set of evaluation criteria as part of the offer was not going to be successful. "Sign the contract as it is," I was told, "or you may risk the possibility of losing the offer altogether. Trust that when the time comes, the university will do the right thing." The ensuing drama was simultaneously exhilarating and fraught with problems, but—to reveal the plot's final outcome—eleven years later, including four years of continuous negotiations to determine my tenure and promotion criteria, I received tenure and promotion in the English department.

This chapter takes a close look at the risks of becoming a non-tenure-track jWPA, using my own case as both a positive *and* negative ex-

ample; contemplates the potential rewards for persevering; offers suggestions for achieving success, including tenure; and cites sources from
rhetoric and composition's surprisingly voluminous, but little heeded
literature on valuing WPA work for tenure and promotion. In an era
of increasingly stringent fiscal resources, most colleges and universities are still mindful of their responsibility to offer a sound writing
curriculum for their students. WPAs are key to this enterprise. The
overarching message of this essay is that with preparation, patience,
persistence, tenaciousness, mentoring, and some luck, the transition
from jWPA to a fulfilling WPA career is possible.

RISKS

It's a truism to say that regardless of the kind of WPA one is—be
it writing center, first-year composition, comprehensive writing program, WAC, WID, or any other—the administrator's status, rank,
and title *matter*. As this entire volume shows, and Patton and Vogt
in particular, responsibility without rights is fundamentally unfair.
Even the vastly experienced jWPA will likely be perceived by senior
colleagues as lacking the authority to administer the program in her
charge. Fellow faculty may perceive the jWPA as uncredentialed.
Administrators may take the jWPA's work less seriously than that done
by her ranked faculty peers. Over time, the program will likely suffer
from a perceived lack of "authoritative" leadership. Administering a
writing program of any kind is challenging in the best of cases. The
impediments that all WPAs must address are exacerbated by jWPA
status. These claims seem so self-evident as to not require examples.
Yet, the reality of writing program administration in this country is
that in any given year, WPA responsibilities will be assigned to—and,
as I did, be accepted by—administrators of junior rank.

Even when the jWPA is a nontraditional person with substantial
teaching and/or lived-experience brought to bear on the position, and
even when the jWPA possesses rightly earned confidence and aplomb,
it can be extremely difficult to maintain a positive professional self-
image and self-identity in the face of the numerous assaults that come
with junior status. The uncertainty of renewed employment from year
to year, the label of "adjunct" in the institution's phone book or on
one's name badge at a conference, the effrontery of being assigned a
subordinate category on the department's publicly posted roster or of

having one's mailbox located in the basement rather than in the main floor office with the "regular" faculty—all take an understandable toll on the jWPA's self-esteem.[2] Individually and collectively, these and numerous other markers that confer inferior status can all too easily result in the diminution of professional self-identity, sometimes to the point of becoming self-fulfilling descriptors. If the jWPA suffers the effects, the jWPA's family life is affected, too. In my case, during the four-year process of my three "bosses" (provost, dean, and department) exchanging memos and phone calls to determine how I would be evaluated, I had to temper my husband's ire on my behalf about the length of time it was taking and his perception of senior officials' lack of decision-making ability. Every time he attended a university function with me, I had to remind him what *not* to say and *to whom* not to say it; unsurprisingly, this became a major exercise in marital diplomacy.

By far the most difficult burden to bear, though, is the risk of not having one's work *valued* by the department, the institution, and the academy. Unquestionably, academe's currency for valuing academic work is tenure. Receiving tenure signifies the ultimate recognition of one's work. With very few exceptions, tenure is the measure by which professionals in higher education know that their work means something and that their effort is formally acknowledged. For jWPAs who are not eligible for tenure track status, automatic *de facto* second-class status is ascribed. Without the possibility of tenure, jWPAs' work is seen as service rather than intellectual work, the work of the mind, the work that "real" faculty do. Knowing that my colleagues in English did not see my work as contributing to the university's tripartite mission of teaching, research, and service made for an unpleasant working condition, to say the least, particularly as I examined the amount of time I gave to it, the national attention my work was receiving, and the concrete accomplishments I was able to document. The conundrum, as many jWPAs experience it, is the lack of time afforded by "administration" to do the kind of work that typically leads to tenure and promotion juxtaposed with the inadmissibility of administrative work as "counting" for tenure and promotion.

This is the conundrum I had hoped to avoid, by asking at the time of being hired, to be evaluated for tenure and promotion based on my work as WAC WPA. Even though I was prepared to offer up the specific documents from my field that already at that time had begun to make the case for valuing WPA work as intellectual work, the vice-provost conducting the search was either not willing to entertain the idea or did actually believe that the search could fail if this new factor were introduced. (I prefer to believe the latter, inasmuch as the previous year's search had failed, and the university was eager to get the program back on track.) In retrospect, even though my tenure and promotion criteria were yet to be determined and even though the jWPA position I took wasn't ideal due to my non-regular, non-tenure track rank, the nature of the appointment the university created for me *was* innovative. To my knowledge, no previous nor subsequent hire has been given an offer of this kind at my university. And, although I have spoken about it widely in various contexts, I'm not aware of any other WPAs having been offered this kind of appointment. I would endorse the "start-the-clock-later" model in lieu of an appointment wherein the jWPA has *no* opportunity to achieve tenure—with the proviso that when the clock is activated, the appropriate parts of the jWPA's administrative work "count" in the evaluation process. (Guidelines for what might be appropriate appear in two sections below.)

But while the start-the-clock-later model might work as a stopgap measure in some cases, or for a short period in the history of WPA-dom while we make progress toward something better, I do *not* want to propose it as a preferred model. Institutions will rely on it to perpetuate the erroneous notion that WPA work is merely managerial. They will neglect to acknowledge the intellectual component that inheres in nearly every WPA's work. And they will refuse to grant tenure and promotion to jWPAs who are, therefore, not seen as doing work comparable to other, "regular" faculty. That lack of acknowledgment of intellectual work undergirded the appointment that I was initially offered at MU. Consider this language from my May 10, 1991, letter of offer:

> The position of Director of the Campus Writing Program is an eleven-month administrative position. [. . .] The position of Assistant Professor of English would initially be non-regular. Should you leave the directorship of the Campus Writing Program and wish to become a faculty member in the Department of English, this position will be converted to a regular (tenure-track) position on a nine month salary having

the administrative add-on removed. The tenure clock would not start while you are Director of the Campus Writing Program, thus assuring that your duties and the criteria against which you will be evaluated are consistent.

Although the specific words aren't there, the meaning is explicit: the duties of a writing director and the duties of a regular faculty member are not equivalent. Only the latter duties are worthy of tenure. In a subsequent phone conversation with the vice-provost about matters not covered in the letter (e.g., is spousal accommodation available? what is the moving allowance?), I reminded him that I sought a reward system that would value the work I was being hired to do. Surely, I posited, if the university values having a WAC program and a two-course writing-intensive graduation requirement for all undergraduates, it would want to make that value visible and tangible via tenure and promotion. I made clear that I did not want to leave the director's position in order to be evaluated. I pointed out that the majority of WPAs align themselves and their work more with faculty than with traditional administrators. And I referred again to the idea that some, *not all,* of a WPA's work is indeed similar to the intellectual work that other faculty do. I made my case to be evaluated on my WAC WPA work as strongly as I felt I could under the circumstances, knowing that I needed (and wanted) the job and that the power differential between him and me was vast.

When my revised letter of offer arrived a few days later, the language in the new letter revealed not only the departmental and institutional bias toward the nature of scholarship, but also a strong patriarchal approach:

> The statement in the original letter of offer (May 10, 1991) regarding the initial appointment in a non-regular position is for your protection. With such an appointment, you can concentrate on being successful as Director of the Campus Writing Program and not worry about producing sufficient scholarly work to meet the tenure requirement in the Department of English.

Disheartening as it was to see the discrepancy between "scholarly" work done by English faculty and the patently "non-scholarly" work done by WPAs carried through from the first letter, my argument had had some effect. The revised letter contained this new feature, immediately following the statement above:

> However, you may choose to turn on the tenure clock while you are Director of the Campus Writing Program, or to be reviewed for tenure as a result of your scholarly, teaching, and service efforts while serving as Director of the Campus Writing Program.

At this juncture, I phoned the vice-provost a second time to inquire about the specific evaluation criteria to be applied when I did turn on the tenure clock. And it was at this time that I learned that the complexity of hammering out those details with the number of people who would need to be involved could, in fact, derail the whole offer. I understood that this was the best offer I could hope for and I happily signed the letter, even as I wondered what it meant to trust the university to "do the right thing" some years hence.

The ensuing eight years passed with astonishing speed. Among other things, the Campus Writing Program conducted a year-long self-study culminating in an external review by Edward White and Lynn Bloom; implemented the university's second writing-intensive requirement, doubling the number of WI courses and students enrolled in them; and undertook a research agenda with international implications. While I was mindful of tenure and promotion considerations all along, it was the invitation to apply for an NCTE associate executive director's position that occasioned an inquiry from my new dean about why I was, in fact, not yet tenured.[3] That, plus the realization that the assistant professors who had entered the English Department with me had already been tenured for two years, jolted me into action. I began what was to become a four-year series of meetings, discussions, letters, memos, phone calls, and emails between two vice-provosts, two deans, two department chairs, and three chairs of the Campus Writing Board about how I would be evaluated. Not the least of these conversations concerned the placement of the comma after "Program" in "you may choose to turn-on the tenure clock while you are Director of the Campus Writing Program, or to be reviewed for tenure as a result of your scholarly, teaching, and service efforts while serving as Director of the Campus Writing Program." Following the English department's personnel committee meeting at which the chair opened a discussion of my case, a senior colleague told me confidentially that many questions were asked about procedure and precedent and that faculty felt that the language in the letter of appointment was "subject to different interpretation than [mine]."

The scope of this chapter does not permit a detailed accounting of my four-year campaign for tenure and promotion. But I can say that knowing the *intent* behind the letter's language; the conversations that led up to that language being added to the revised letter; the fact that, even though the primary parties behind the letter (the dean and the provost) had left the university, they were still in town and could be consulted if necessary; and the support of many senior faculty and my family sustained me.

Rewards

The rewards of WAC WPA work are many, and by no means did I have to wait until after tenure and promotion to enjoy them. They are all the more satisfying, though, for enjoying them from the other side of the transition from jWPA to WPA. I sketch here a broad overview of why I find this work so gratifying, with the caveat that this particular form of WPA work is richer and more meaningful than these few paragraphs can convey and that other WAC WPAs would undoubtedly add to these reflections from an even wider perspective.

First, there are documented results from our efforts at MU, in student writing, faculty teaching, and campus culture. Students affirm the value of WI courses and usually do not complain about "having" to take them. More often, they complain that non-WI courses have "too much" writing and thus ought to carry WI credit. We tell them that non-WI courses with "lots" of writing is a positive, normal phenomenon for a research university with a vigorous writing program. Faculty, even while shouldering a heavier burden due to WI teaching, affirm the need for writing across all disciplines. We've found that nearly fifty percent of the teaching awards on our campus go to faculty who have taught WI courses at one time or another. The 1993 Bloom and White external review confirmed a change in campus culture, a change that continues to hold more than a decade later. We have the satisfaction of knowing that our workshops, follow-up consultations, joint research with WI faculty, and other activities have helped to alter the way undergraduate education is offered at our university.

Because we try to ensure that as much WI instruction as possible is offered voluntarily rather than by conscription, we work with some of the finest, most dedicated, enthusiastic faculty on campus. We are exposed to their superb scholarship as they incorporate their own research and thinking into their courses. Listening to architectural studies professor Benyamin Schwarz lead students through a pictorial lecture on architecture's "vocabulary" or observing biological sciences professor Miriam Golomb conduct her unique version of Socratic dialogue in class is unfailingly inspiring. Our days are somewhat like entering an intellectual candy store as we review WI course proposals with our knowledgeable Campus Writing Board members, talk with teachers, visit classes, tutor students, and even read the occasional student request to waive a WI course, which requires submission of a writing portfolio. In other words, we get to keep on learning all the time, an attribute that drew us to higher education originally. We suspect that WAC educators in general are drawn to across-the-curriculum and in-the-disciplines work due to an innate curiosity about all manner of subjects, epistemologies, and problems that need solving. Not surprisingly, then, our WAC colleagues around the country are stimulating and intellectually vibrant. Moreover, as Toby Fulwiler noted years ago (most likely in a CCCC workshop or hallway conversation), one of the hallmarks of the writing-across-the-curriculum movement is the selfless sharing of information, ideas, resources, and research. We find this unequivocally true; the WAC community at large is generous to a fault. Such generosity begs for reciprocity, so sharing our resources in return is one of the pleasures of our work.

Not least, our institution values writing. As the campus culture shifted toward a greater recognition of the importance of both writing-to-learn and learning-to-write, the top-down administration and bottom-up faculty grass roots have diplomatically co-existed in the middle, a key factor behind the program's longevity. For twenty years, the provost's office has ensured that the WAC budget has been a recurring line item, so the program has not been forced to plead for resources. The eighteen-member cross-disciplinary Campus Writing Board provides strong leadership and faculty ownership for the program. And MU did, ultimately, "do the right thing" by granting me tenure and promotion based on my WAC WPA work. Lest this picture sound overly idealistic, I hasten to note that national and state fiscal problems of the past several years have impacted our university, and the WAC program has felt the impact along with other academic units. We were not affected disproportionately, however. At the moment, space is a hotly contested issue on campus. The offices we occupy have become increasingly desirable; the possibility exists that we may have to relocate. Still, we recognize that ours is not the only institution at which space is an issue, and we're trying to be simultaneously proactive and cooperative, a difficult stance.

In the meantime, our work continues. We have been privileged to represent MU at a variety of meetings, conferences, and workshops in fascinating venues, both in the U.S. and abroad. Our international research agenda has taken us to Canada, Romania, South Korea, South Africa, Thailand, China, and Costa Rica. We've hosted faculty from all of these and other countries on our campus. This aspect of our WAC WPA work was absolutely unforeseen and unfolded quite by happenstance. It has enriched our professional and personal lives many fold and often astonishes our colleagues in the English department for whom international travel is not usually as varied and far reaching. Despite the risks that all of us in the Patton/Vogt/Townsend triad have laid out in this volume, to a person we all agree that our professional lives have been—are—rewarding. My graduate school decision still holds me in good stead.

Suggestions for Getting There: How to be Your Own Advocate

The suggestions I offer here are a combination of the standard ones that any WPA might offer along with idiosyncratic ideas that I have found useful over the years but which may not be uniformly applicable. I share them, though, because they have worked for our program; if they aren't immediately adaptable, they might at least inspire some creative alternatives.

Become active in the professional venues. If you haven't already, join the Council of Writing Program Administrators (WPA), *the* organization from which you will derive valuable knowledge and mentoring. Attend the summer workshop at least once and the annual summer conferences as often as you can. Attend the annual WPA breakfast at each CCCC. Subscribe to the organization's journal *WPA: Writing*

Program Administration; submit articles for consideration. Subscribe to WPA-L and read it regularly. It's an active listserv (independent of the national organization, by the way) with an abundance of friendly, helpful members. It's an excellent place from which to collect precedents on how other WPAs are being evaluated, for example. Many WPAs have commented about how much they've learned just by following the various threads. Join the National WAC Network, housed at George Mason University. Join CCCC and attend the annual conference as you can. There are numerous WAC- and WPA-related sessions on the program as well as the WAC Special Interest Group hosted by the National WAC Network. Subscribe to *College Composition and Communication* and *College English.* Both journals feature articles on WAC and WPA issues from time to time. The online WAC Clearinghouse hosted by Colorado State University offers a wealth of resources, including *Across the Disciplines,* the new, online version of *Language and Learning across the Disciplines* which is also archived there. There are other organizations and journals important to rhetoric and composition, of course; those listed here are merely the basics for WAC and WPA issues.

Consider adopting an "If you don't ask, you don't get" approach. I owe this advice to a former MU department chair. I had asked the dean who he considered to be some of the campus's best administrators, and the head of psychology was on his list. I subsequently asked if I could pepper my colleague with questions over lunch; what I gleaned became invaluable, including the notion that well-supported requests are often granted. Over the years, this advice has resulted in such things as enlarged tutoring space, new hires for the program, and better starting salaries for staff. I recommend asking whomever you report to who she or he thinks are the most respected administrators on your campus and then seeking them out for advice. If the relationship isn't abused, most people are pleased to be consulted. Similarly, if you are traveling to a professional meeting and can afford a few extra hours en route that will take you near another institution's well-respected writing program, ask if you may spend a bit of time there, observing their operations and visiting with the personnel. Some years ago, when an awkward itinerary left me with a long gap en route to a WPA conference at Miami University in Oxford, Ohio, Barbara Walvoord graciously allowed me an afternoon's visit at her University of Cincinnati WAC program. The hours I spent there and my conversation with her were influential in many ways. When you feel suitably emboldened, and can solidly support your request, inquire whether funds can be provided for you to attend the Bryn Mawr Institute for Women In Higher Education Administration. This intense month-long event is held in July and features a series of successful adminis-trators sharing their expertise, case studies worked out in groups, and more reading assignments than you'll have seen since graduate school. Attending helped assure me that administrative work needn't be an exercise in futility and could, in fact, be rewarding. Ask why "x" isn't done or can't be done—so you have the basis on which to argue for change. For us, that played out by wondering aloud why our writing tutors hadn't received any of the college's graduate teaching awards. It turned out that no one had thought to ask they be included in the pool of eligible candidates, or to simply put the writing program on the list of offices receiving the call for nominations. For the following four years, WAC tutors received this recognition and had the honor to record on their *curriculum vitae*. At the same time, the corollary to "If you don't ask, you don't get" must be practiced, too: "If you don't get, don't take it personally."

Assemble, read, and know your institution's documents on tenure and promotion. Don't rely on lore or word of mouth for these im-portant topics. Get the actual, legal documents and become familiar with them. Be prepared to ask questions about how the statements and processes described in them have been interpreted. Be aware that you may get conflicting answers, so don't hesitate to ask for clarification from your chair and other knowledgeable administrators. Keep notes on these conversations, not to the extent that you become unduly fo-cused on them, but so that you have a record of the nuances that have been explained and of the precedents at your school. In my case, for example, it was important to know that although the department of English criteria state, "In regard to publication, we believe in the rule-of-thumb of a significant book accepted for publication [. . .]," they conclude with, "Our broad view is that the evidence of research by whatever measure should indicate an achieved significant contribution to knowledge and the prospect of more to come." Likewise, it was also important for me to know that the college of arts and science guide-lines read, "Promotion to associate professor (and the awarding of ten-ure) reflects a demonstrated *potential* for developing a national reputa-tion in the discipline. One promoted to professor shall have established such a reputation" (emphasis added). At the time I sought tenure and promotion, I had exceeded this criterion for associate and had actually achieved that required for professor. Had I not been aware of this provision, I might have been less likely to pursue my case as confidently as I did. With respect to the University Rules & Regulations, there was also language that worked in my favor. This document says, "Good researchers often are [. . .] members of site visit teams or [perform] other evaluative functions of the scholarly work of their peers. Any evidence of such contributions should be emphasized in promotion and tenure recommendations." Since at the time I sought tenure and promotion I had conducted external reviews of writing programs and had evaluated colleagues for promotion and tenure at institutions comparable to my own, these activities were important to my case.

Assemble your own *ad hoc* mentoring committee, if necessary, in addition to the one your department recommends. This is one of the idiosyncratic suggestions that may not apply broadly, but in my case proved extremely helpful. As WAC WPA, I report to the dean and provost and not at all to my department. Consequently, a departmental mentoring committee was never convened, nor even recommended. When discussions began to determine how I would be evaluated, it became clear that my work was much better known and understood by faculty outside the department than within it. Three people with whom I had worked over the years played key roles in advising me through the arduous process: a senior philosophy professor who had chaired the Campus Writing Board for two years; a senior food science professor who had taught WI courses and whose knowledge of tenure cases in Extension was informative; and the president emeritus of the four-campus University of Missouri system. Each of these scholars had a wider perspective on what was possible than did my department at the time, so their strategizing with me was beneficial. On the national level, the program's previous external reviewers, Lynn Bloom and Edward White, along with Susan McLeod, offered much needed counseling when necessary. None of these local or national advisors intervened in the department's deliberations, but all had excellent suggestions on how I could manage the process; more important, all of them provided encouragement when institutional forces seemed immovable. I am profoundly grateful to all of them.

Propose sample, alternative criteria which might be factored into your evaluation. Due to the differing nature of WPA work from that of other English faculty, items like the following probably haven't been considered, but might be taken into account if a case for them were made. A breakthrough of sorts happened in my case when someone (I wish I could recall who) understood and articulated that in seeking different criteria, I wasn't seeking a different *standard*. That is to say, I wasn't seeking to be evaluated on a lower level of performance than my other English peers, but I *was* seeking a different means of achieving it. That framing was helpful to everyone. Once the concept of alternative criteria is accepted, specific standards can be phrased according to the particular institution; what's expected of a WPA, for example, at a two-year college, a four-year liberal arts college, and a research extensive university will be different. The point is not to require and value the work another academician is doing, but to value and reward the work the WPA is hired to do. Phrased somewhat generically, for WPAs beyond WAC, some of the following suggestions for criteria might work as starters for your own thinking.

1. The program can demonstrate that it is well-respected.

2. The program explicitly addresses the institution's mission(s).

3. The WPA presents at professional conferences.

4. The WPA publishes in professional venues.

5. The WPA is professionally active beyond the home institution.

6. The WPA contributes to the institution's local and regional outreach efforts promulgating theoretically and practically well-informed pedagogies.

7. The program has multiple measures of assessment data it can provide on its activities and outcomes.

8. The WPA's own teaching, including syllabi and assignments, demonstrate that they are consistent with current theory and pedagogy could serve as models for the faculty and staff she oversees.

Maintain a record of the time and a paper trail of the correspondence related to your job. It was informative for me to learn that Barbara Walvoord kept a record of meetings and conversations with faculty, in half-hour increments, so that she could report this interaction periodically to her dean and writing committee. WAC WPA work typically requires a great deal of time spent this way; the hours add up quickly, they're essential to the job, and they should be counted. Not least, it helps you understand where your time goes. The paper trail should include not just communication pertaining to evaluation, but everything you do. Get into the habit of jotting notes with time and dates included and filing them in some fashion. Because I was already in this habit, keeping a record of tenure and promotion communication was more or less automatic, though because I knew early on that the case would be unusual, my notes are more detailed than some other documents. The chronology of meetings, phone calls, letters, verbal exchanges, memos of understanding that I sent after meetings and so on is revealing. I did not need them other than to substantiate an occasional detail, but knowing the record was available should it be needed was empowering.

Join the American Association of University Professors. Founded ninety years ago, AAUP is the professional organization that developed standards and institutional regulations governing fundamental aspects of higher education. Academic freedom, faculty governance, trends affecting faculty, legal and governmental affairs are some of the issues addressed by AAUP, which offers reduced rates for junior faculty. Its advice for all faculty, especially the under-privileged, is sound. The *AAUP Policy Documents and Reports,* now in its ninth edition, otherwise known as the "Redbook," is regarded as an authoritative source on sound academic practice. The organization has an informed, active legal staff that advises faculty on a range of issues, including tenure and promotion. On their advice, I surveyed other public universities belonging to the American Association of Universities, to which my university belongs, to collect information on how other AAUs were evaluating WPAs for tenure and promotion. While what I learned wasn't particularly promising, it was nonetheless instructive and provided the incentive for me to work for change. For example, it compelled me to write the following bibliographical essay so that this information could be easily available to jWPAs and the senior academicians and administrators who need to know of the extensive literature that argues for fair evaluation of WPA work.

LITERATURE TO DRAW ON

For almost two decades rhetoric and composition faculty, in conjunction with major professional organizations, have been striving to validate the intellectual work and scholarly achievements that WPAs contribute to the academy. Because the nature of WPA work within composition and writing-across-the-curriculum programs has historically been misunderstood, undervalued, or even invisible to the larger body of English studies faculty, numerous essays, book chapters, entire volumes, and policy statements have been written to inform our colleagues about what we do. In the main, this now substantial body of literature argues that WPA work is not managerial, but intellectual, in nature; is essential to the academy; requires well-developed scholarly expertise; produces measurable scholarly outcomes; and should be valued by institutions of higher learning for tenure and promotion.

All of the major professional organizations with which college composition is affiliated have issued policy statements or published guidelines showing how WPA work should be valued. The 1988 MLA Commission on Writing and Literature, for example, concluded that, "administrative contributions should be given significant weight during tenure and salary reviews" (74). The 1996 MLA Commission on Professional Service proposed a new model for valuing the traditional triad of research, teaching, and service which "proposes intellectual work and academic and professional citizenship as primary components of faculty work" (162). In particular, this Commission argued that program administration "presents major intellectual challenges and opportunities, and it should be evaluated for accomplishment in these terms" (210). The Conference on College Composition and Communication (CCCC) followed MLA's lead in stating that "postsecondary institutions should count seriously certain kinds of professional activity, sometimes undervalued within current measures of scholarly achievement, that are particularly important to this field. These activities include [. . .] the particularly demanding administrative service that is often a regular part of a compositionist's responsibilities" (*Statement of Principles*). Another CCCC document, addressed specifically to department chairs and deans, states: "[A]dministrative contributions should be given significant weight during tenure and salary reviews. Indeed, during these reviews, outside evaluators might be asked to study the applicant's administrative service and this review could be considered alongside reviews of research and reports on teaching" (*Scholarship in Composition*).

The Association of Departments of English (ADE) issued a 1993 policy statement reading, "In evaluations of scholarship, different kinds of activities should be given credit [. . .] and may include the presentation of papers, the development of instructional materials, reviews of others' scholarly work, and other forms of writing" (2). The Council of Writing Program Administrators' 1992 "Portland Resolution: Guidelines for Writing Program Administrator Positions" notes that "[t]he teaching, research, and service contributions of tenure-line composition faculty are often misunderstood or undervalued" (1). "Assessment of a WPA," the Portland Resolution continues, "should consider the important scholarly contributions each WPA makes by virtue of designing, developing, and implementing a writing program [. . .]. Requirements for retention, promotion, and tenure should be clearly defined and should consider the unique administrative demands of the position" (1–2). Building on the Portland Resolution, the Council's 1998 "intellectual work document" argues that "writing administration can be seen as scholarly work and therefore subject to the same kinds of evaluation as other forms of disciplinary production, such as books, articles, and reviews. More significantly [. . .] it is worthy of tenure and promotion when it advances and enacts disciplinary knowledge within the field of rhetoric and composition" (85).

A significant number of individual scholars affiliated with rhetoric and composition have made similar, clear cases for valuing WPA work. James Slevin, who served on the MLA Commission on Writing and Literature, extends the Commission's argument in a later essay on the politics of the profession. "[T]he larger cultural and social concerns of rhetoric and composition," he writes, "place it among a number of areas of the profession concerned with the ways in which intellectual work can critique and reshape the immediate institutional circumstances in which this work occurs" (141). Slevin notes that composition, feminist studies, African-American studies, colonial and postcolonial discourse studies, and American studies have in common "a sense that the work of research and publication is inseparable from the work shaping institutional structures such as the department, the university, and programs that connect the academy with the 'outside' world" (141). Lynn Bloom comments that in reviewing English studies candidates' work for promotion and tenure, she finds it quite possible to use a set of criteria "applicable equally to scholarship in composition studies and literature" (172). "Conventional literary faculty members," Bloom argues, "should derive their view of composition studies research from the major work—intellectual, theoretical, pedagogical—in the field" (173). In one of the earliest essays on the topic, Richard Bullock declares that WPAs "are not caretakers of a slice of bureaucracy; they are experts and scholars testing and refining their knowledge in the practical arena of application. The administration of writing programs under these circumstances advances our knowledge of the teaching of writing. No less than an architect's erection of a building or a playwright's successful directing of his or her own play, it is scholarship" (14). Similarly, Duane Roen argues that "[I]f the WPA's role is to innovate, to erect and maintain a program that embodies and tests theoretical principles and monitors the results over several years, that activity is scholarly and should be recognized as such, and the traditional disciplinary view of restricting scholarship to written publication must broaden to include performance in the artistic or theatrical sense" (52).

Richard Gebhardt, who has co-edited a volume of fourteen essays on the topic, notes that composition faculty coming up for promotion and tenure "often face a double task—to produce first-rate scholarship and to explain its nature and value" (51). His own essay in the book cites a number of ways and reasons for English departments to expand their definition of scholarly activity, to include such things as curriculum development materials and faculty development workshops (14–15). Christine Hult is plainspoken in her belief: "Rather than trying to force WPAs into traditional academic molds, institutions of higher education need to acknowledge the changing definitions of scholarship and to legitimize and reward WPAs for the scholarship of administration as reflected in the diversity of our work" (120). The "impacts and outcomes" of much of the writing that WPAs produce, she says, "are profound for programs and the individuals they serve; in fact, they are often greater and more far-reaching than those of any article in a professional journal" (127). Writing from the perspective of a dean, Susan McLeod points out that "[c]omposition scholars [. . .] are often viewed as other by their literature colleagues. Their scholarship often looks applied rather than theoretical. They publish in different journals, they sometimes do collaborative work, and they often have administrative duties that eat up their time but fall in the underappreciated category of service. The key to an effective review process [. . .] is for members of the English department to be educated about how the work of composition scholars fits into the larger picture of academic scholarship" (178).

Several of the scholars above invoke non-English studies sources for inspiration in finding models for new methods of defining and evaluating scholarly work. One of the most frequently mentioned is Ernest Boyer's *Scholarship Reconsidered: Priorities of the Professoriate.* In this widely discussed treatise, Boyer posits four "separate, yet overlapping, functions" that comprise faculty work: the scholarship of discovery; the scholarship of integration; the scholarship of application; and the scholarship of teaching (16). "What we urgently need today," Boyer writes, "is a more inclusive view of what it means to be a scholar- a recognition that knowledge is acquired through research, through synthesis, through practice, and through teaching [. . .]. [T]here is value [. . .] in analyzing the various kinds of academic work, while also acknowledging that they dynamically interact, forming an inter-dependent whole" (24–25). Boyer does not propose that the academy abandon its traditional faculty reward system, but he does suggest that new ways be found to describe and value the "great diversity of talent within the professoriate" (25).

Less frequently cited, but arguably more important, is the successor to Boyer's book, *Scholarship Assessed: The Evaluation of the Professoriate,* by Glasick, Huber, and Maeroff. Published seven years after *Scholarship Reconsidered,* this volume recognizes that "[t]o give the four kinds of scholarly activities the weight that each deserves, they all must be held to the same standards of scholarly performance [. . .]. [T]he academy must evaluate them by a set of standards that capture and acknowledge what they share as scholarly acts" (22). The authors posit a six-part heuristic based on their research which found that when faculty praise a work of scholarship they usually take into account: clear goals, adequate preparation, appropriate methods, significant results, effective presentation, and reflective critique (25). These six qualitative standards, they believe, can be applied equally to all four categories of scholarship and "taken together, they provide a powerful conceptual framework to guide evaluation" (25). The American Association of University Professors has also issued guidelines which could inform the evaluation of WPAs. "All appointments," the AAUP says, "[. . .] should have a description of the specific professional duties required. Complex institutions may require multiple models of faculty appointments consistent with the diverse contributions appropriate to the institution's needs [. . .]. Decisions on compensation, promotion, and tenure should be based on the specified duties of the position" (*Guidelines*). These citations from professional organizations, individual scholars, and sources external to the immediate field comprise, then, a compact—though still partial—bibliography of the literature on this topic.

CONCLUSION

When my case was presented to the department's personnel committee (all of the tenured faculty in the department), the vote was negative; they would have supported promotion, but not tenure. In our system, the department chair has a separate vote, and he supported both tenure and promotion, as did the college and campus committees, the dean (following an appeal), provost, and chancellor. Interestingly, after my tenure and promotion were official, my colleagues in the department welcomed me without prejudice, at least not any that I could discern. I sensed they perceived that I had properly earned my rank and that, if there were questions concerning my work, those are either resolved or just gone. Would I be as satisfied as I now am without tenure? Honestly, no. But then, I came up through the "old" system, in which tenure was virtually the only currency available. Times *are* changing. Nationally, a conversation is ongoing about valuing faculty work. A report was recently released by the *Creating Options: Models for Flexible Tenure-Track Faculty Career Pathways* project conducted by the American Council on Education and supported by the Alfred P. Sloan Foundation. Coauthored by ten prominent university presidents and chancellors, it calls for guidelines for multiple-year leaves and more time for junior faculty to complete research before tenure review (among other things). Locally, the MU faculty council passed a resolution on February 4, 2005, calling on the provost to require all colleges and schools to establish guidelines for annual review and promotion of non-regular faculty and to publish them on the provost's website by fall of the 2005–2006 academic year. A preliminary draft of the English department's guidelines appeared in our mailboxes almost immediately. At the four-campus university's system level, half-time tenure-track appointments, at double the usual time-to-tenure, are be-

ing considered. These developments and others like them around the
country could offer jWPAs new options for careers in writing program
work. Still, I predict the jury will be out for a long period before we
know whether these new options will provide fair and equitable treatment, including the possibility of rank commensurate with all of the
colleagues in our departments. In the meantime, the positive resolution to my own case leaves me wanting to encourage others to forge
ahead. Our reward practices still need to be improved, but our work
makes the perseverance worthwhile.

NOTES

 [1] I dedicate this chapter to my family and to the many faculty and colleagues (especially Marty Patton and Jo Ann Vogt) at the University of Missouri-Columbia and elsewhere who supported me throughout my lengthy
transition from jWPA to WPA. Their encouragement allowed me to continue the campaign.

 [2] All of these examples pertained at some point to either Patton or
Townsend at MU.

 [3] He was concerned that if I were to be hired by NCTE, my assistant
professor title would reflect poorly on MU.

WORKS CITED

Association of Departments of English. "ADE Statement of Good Practice:
    Teaching, Evaluation, and Scholarship." Modern Language Association.
    1993. 12 February 2007 <http://www.ade.org/policy/policy_teaching.
    htm>.

Boyer, Ernest. *Scholarship Reconsidered: Priorities of the Professoriate.* Princ-
    eton: The Carnegie Foundation, 1990.

Bullock, Richard H. "When Administration Becomes Scholarship: The Fu-
    ture of Writing Program Administration." *WPA: Writing Program Ad-
    ministration* 11.1/2 (1987): 13–18.

Conference on College Composition and Communication. "Scholarship in
    Composition: Guidelines for Faculty, Deans, and Department Chairs."
    CCCC Position Statement. 1987. 12 February 2007 <http://www.ncte.
    org/cccc/resources/positions/123785.htm>.

Conference on College Composition and Communication. "Statement of
    Principles and Standards for the Postsecondary Teaching of Writing."
    CCCC Position Statement. October 1989. 12 February 2007 <http://
    www.ncte.org/cccc/resources/positions/123790.htm>.

Council of Writing Program Administrators. "Evaluating the Intellectual Work of Writing Administration." *WPA: Writing Program Administration* 22.1/2 (1998): 85–104.

Gebhardt, Richard C. "Evolving Approaches to Scholarship, Promotion, and Tenure in Composition Studies." *Academic Advancement in Composition Studies: Scholarship, Publication, Promotion, Tenure.* Ed. Richard C. Gebhardt and Barbara Genelle Smith Gebhardt. Mahwah, NJ: Lawrence Erlbaum, 1997.

Gebhardt, Richard C. "Mentor and Evaluator: The Chair's Role in Promotion and Tenure Review." *Academic Advancement in Composition Studies: Scholarship, Publication, Promotion, Tenure.* Ed. Richard C. Gebhardt and Barbara Genelle Smith Gebhardt. Mahwah, NJ: Lawrence Erlbaum, 1997. 1-19.

Glassick, Charles E., et al. *Scholarship Assessed: Evaluation of the Professoriate.* San Francisco: Jossey-Bass, 1997.

Hult, Christine A. "The Scholarship of Administration." *Resituating Writing: Constructing and Administering Writing Programs.* Ed. Joseph Janangelo and Kristine Hansen. Portsmouth, NH: Boynton/Cook, 1995. 119-31.

MLA Commission on Writing and Literature. "Report of the Commission on Writing and Literature." *Profession 1988.* New York: MLA, 1988. 70-76.

MLA Commission on Professional Service. "Making Faculty Work Visible: Reinterpreting Professional Service, Teaching, and Research in the Fields of Language and Literature." *Profession 1996.* New York: MLA, 1996. 161-216.

Roen, Duane. "Writing Administration as Scholarship and Teaching." *Academic Advancement in Composition Studies: Scholarship, Publication, Promotion, Tenure.* Ed. Richard C. Gebhardt and Barbara Genelle Smith Gebhardt. Mahwah, NJ: Lawrence Erlbaum, 1997. 43-59.

Slevin, James F. "The Politics of the Profession." *An Introduction to Composition Studies.* Ed. Erika Lindemann and Gary Tate. New York: Oxford UP, 1991. 135–59.

Part II

jWPA Desire and the Call to Serve

5 jWPAs and the Call to Serve

Ruth Mirtz and Roxanne Cullen

> The pitcher cries for water to carry and a person for
> work that is real.
>
> —Marge Piercy

One of the questions this book attempts to answer is whether the position of jWPA should even exist in some form. It doesn't take many anecdotes or surveys to realize that the position is fraught with hazards to the jWPA's career, family life, and teaching. Even though many jWPAs have been successful and would call the experience rich and satisfying, just as many others would name the experience horrifying and debilitating. WPA positions can be a labor of love for the profession, a lucrative and tolerable career, or a series of power-plays that bureaucratize the very notion of writing. By examining the ways jWPAs (and experienced WPAs) see the mission of WPA work within their own sense of vocation and calling, we can see more clearly the kinds of work that WPAs do and why that work conflicts with their sense of self and with the notion of mission in other parts of the university. Because no list of job requirements can tell one whether a specific position is doable (even the most abusive-looking job description can be manageable for some), potential WPAs need to ask themselves what good work means to them, what kind of "call" they are hearing, and whether the answers make the jWPA position possible or impossible.

Nothing in this book will eliminate the jWPA position, but we hope, in this chapter, to show how the "call to serve" inherent in WPA work makes it more or less predictably successful or unsuccessful— something that individuals can think about before they take that first WPA position and for institutions and programs to think about before they offer the position. If a specific context allows the rewards of service in the position to equal or exceed the rewards of a teaching position, perhaps the jWPA position should continue. If not, then perhaps jWPA as well as senior WPA positions need to be called into question.

What is the Call to Serve?

The "call to serve" or the desire "to be of service" starts with our teaching careers. It is part of why most of us became teachers: we see ourselves having some influence on young lives; we see the power of writing and writing instruction to change attitudes; we feel we have special talents emotionally and academically that make us able to give something to others through our teaching. The call is rarely a voice, although our friends and family sometimes put voice to what we're hearing in their support for our decision to teach and administer. The call is more often a drawing towards, an internal pull or attraction. We might call it a vocation or a mission. The call to serve makes a job more than a series of tasks to complete; the call to serve gives a job a wider, stronger purpose that connects to our identity and sense of place in the world. Frederick Buechner describes it as "the place where your deep gladness meets the world's deep need" (qtd. in Towner 193).

The call comes from within for some people. They see things they value that are important for others and want to pass on those ideas and behaviors and enthusiasms and knowledge. Or they see a need to be of use in the world, and teaching composition is a good way to be of such use. As Marge Piercy's poem, "To Be of Use," reminds us, "But the thing worth doing well done / has a shape that satisfies, clean and evident"(50). Teaching can be inherently satisfying. Reading stacks of papers and writing lengthy responses, while knowing only a few of those responses will get much attention, pays off because of those students who do grow as writers and thoughtful human beings in our classes.

The call comes from without for other people. They see or feel great needs in the world and want to fulfill them; their existence in the world has meaning when they are serving a larger good or a common good. The Judeo-Christian tradition places emphasis on the call made by God, to serve God, in whatever way possible: "For many are called but few are chosen"(Matthew 22: 14). Edwin Hopkins, an instructor and WPA at the University of Kansas from 1889 to 1937, had a strong sense of calling to composition work that was spiritual as well as pedagogical. All the hours of labor required for teaching, according to Hopkins, was a "divine freedom," rather than imprisonment, to know "for what we are fit and prepare fitly"(qtd. in Popken 622). Eastern traditions might interpret the call as the path of sacred action associated with dharma, or socially mandated duty, and svadharma, or individual meaning (Bogart 14). Both currents of thought require us to use our gifts for a greater good. The incredible amount of unrewarded and unrecognized work required to teach writing well makes teaching easy to translate into a sacrificial act. We feel good about responding at length to student papers because it needs to be done, and there aren't very many people who would do it. We're special and specially chosen to be the ones who give more. The call to serve makes those stacks of papers an act of generosity and selflessness, whether motivated by God or by a sense of self.

Somehow the reward (psychological, not monetary) of teaching is greater than the sacrifice; somehow it pays off as "good work well done" for us as teachers. It becomes a passion or an art for us. Accordingly, many of us see the WPA position as an extension of the good work of teaching. Richard Gebhardt points out that graduate schools assist in the development of this pull toward administration by leading graduate students to see their work as a "fusion of interest in 'theory' and 'practice'"(34). Gebhardt goes on to explain that WPA work is actually "macrolevel teaching" and suggests preparing for administration by reflecting on teaching issues on a macrolevel (35).

Potential WPAs see administration as good work in the same way that teaching is good work. Gardner, Csikszentmihalyi, and Damon define the notion of "good work" as "work of expert quality that benefits the broader society" (5). They see good work as a flow experience, borrowing from Csikszentmihalyi's work, and claim that such experiences happen at work when "the job provides clear goals, immediate feedback, and a level of challenges matching our skills" (5). Good work, then, in theory, fits with our call to serve as WPAs. Even knowing the issues they will inevitably encounter, WPAs in particular keenly feel the call to serve their fellow teachers and their departments in the role of expert writing teacher, coordinator of writing instruction, and/or facilitator of teaching improvement, whether or not they see the call to serve as a religious or career matter. They want to use their acquired teaching skills to meet the challenges of the position; they see clear goals in a job description, and they imagine the immediate feedback of the classroom finding its way to their WPA offices. This pull of good work in the service of others may be strong, and has been strong enough to pull many WPAs over the mountains of known problems and obstacles they may encounter.

In contrast, the colleges and universities we work for have their own notion of the call to serve. Overwhelming amounts of negative feedback at the end of the semester, followed by a complete lack of feedback at other times, can make good work difficult. Serving the writing program sometimes means taking the blame for inept teachers, but never taking the credit for excellent teachers' work. Keeping the logic puzzle of scheduling and staffing under control, for instance, is in itself never a work of pure organization: the exhilaration one of the authors used to feel at completing a fall semester schedule and meeting at least three-quarters of the teaching staff's preferences was generally short-lived when that schedule was interpreted as a political act of betrayal by some colleagues. Many of our colleagues see administration as the antithesis of teaching and learning, which places the WPA in a position to be mistrusted, ignored, or attacked. These omnipresent negative forces mean that for WPA work to be good work, something has to outweigh or neutralize the oppressive work. The fact that WPAs can imagine administration as supportive of and necessary to good teaching means they see the university and their roles in the university more creatively and less antagonistically than the people they will be working with.

A potential WPA must realize the dual nature of the call to service. The definitions of the call described above are alike in their two-part nature: the call requires a desire from the individual to serve the community, and it requires a community ready and willing to receive that service, even if the server doesn't require recognition or thanks. The duality of self-in/as-community behind the call to serve will appear in different places and times for a jWPA than for a teacher. WPA work, in fact, requires a sense of the value of the work over and beyond the recognition and reward or acceptance from the community since the second part of the equation may be largely missing. Many of the recipients of our service never know about it; many of our colleagues and students wouldn't call our service helpful. WPA work thus requires more than the call to serve or at least a different definition of the call;

it requires, among other things, a thick skin, an ability to quickly re-prioritize, and a sense of humor (or a sense of the absurd) since the call to serve is antithetical to the produce-and-be-promoted system in place in most universities, despite the requirement of "service" in most departments. The very things WPAs are called to do will not be counted as "activity" by others.

May I Ask Who's Calling?

Potential WPAs can easily mistake the call to serve with the call to take the position. The phone call that comes with a job offer is a great prize in our competitive profession; even the phone calls for prelimi-nary interviews feel like validation of all those years of graduate school. One of the authors took a jWPA position partly because it was the only decent job offer she received by February after several interviews at MLA and several on-campus interviews. If a major research university was offering her a job, they must believe that she could do good work for them, she thought. Some of her new colleagues did indeed hope she could do some good work for them and for herself, but many more of them were hoping she would fail and thus prove them right about the needlessness of a WPA and the irrelevance of rhetoric and composition studies.

Figuring out why one wants a position as WPA isn't as easy as it sounds. The call to serve nearly always happens in a climate of change, and change is difficult for all parties. This makes interpreting the call more difficult. Whether the jWPA position is available because of a person leaving the position by choice or whether the person holding the position is being asked or forced to leave, stepping into the role as jWPA will no doubt add to a growing sense of uncertainty for the person answering the call and for those who will work with the new jWPA. In the case of one of the authors, the former WPA had been asked to leave her position. She had some supporters as well as some detractors. This split led to a very unstable position for the author upon entering a new position, a position full of uncertainty anyway by virtue of being new for her. Many jWPAs are making the transition from graduate student to faculty member as well, adding to the levels of change that they have to address.

The question then becomes, why do people answer the call? Is it out of a sense of superiority? (I know how this should be done.) Is it out

of a sense of responsibility? (I will do it for the good of the program.)
Is it out of a quest for power? (I will finally be able to do it my way!)
Or are there other motives? In the case of one of the authors, she had
left the call to serve unanswered several times. She did not want to be a
part of the ousting of the former jWPA because of a sense of loyalty to
her. However, when the department head who was responsible for fill-
ing the position became exceedingly desperate in the attempt to fill the
WPA position, the author could no longer stand on the sidelines. The
author had been quite vocal about how the writing program should
have been run, and when given the chance to put her talk into walk,
she had to face up to her responsibility.

Often the acceptance of the WPA position is made for sound
philosophical and pedagogical reasons; one wants to be the WPA to
provide better courses and better instruction for the students. These
are delightful aspects of the work: putting together a "best practices" guidebook for new teaching assistants and adjuncts that carefully
combines time-tested classroom assignments with cutting edge ideas
about student authority; pushing through a change in assessment procedures that treats basic writing students more fairly; removing a time-
consuming and worthless (and probably illegal) paperwork process by
showing the dean the latest NCTE policy statement and accreditation
requirements; clarifying and publishing previously unstated criteria
for hiring and for teaching awards. A jWPA can make a difference by
knowing more about writing theories, writing programs, and assessment and by making things happen. Sometimes a jWPA can be the
one person who can legitimately wonder and question, as in, "I'm new
here (or to this job), and I don't understand why we. . . ." When the
entire community can agree to act on what is good for the program,
the call to serve can easily translate into good work for the program.

We may answer the call because we know how we think the job
should be done. However, if we accept a jWPA position thinking we
can meet an ideal unattained by others, what we find are many constraints put on us that often prevent us from reaching our lofty goals,
constraints related to staffing, budget, administrative protocol, and
more. In the case of one of the authors, one perpetual complaint had
been the practice of the former WPA of overriding the cap on courses. It seemed like a simple task to say "no overrides." However, when
the first registration opportunity afforded itself, the department head
challenged the author's authority, and many of the instructors com-

plained that students wanted their classes but couldn't get in without an override. So while everyone agreed in principle with the idea of keeping class sizes to the prescribed number, in practice the upper administration wanted to stuff the classes full beyond the cap for reasons of productivity and reducing student complaints. The instructors fell victim to personal vanity, believing that they were the only ones who could help poor student A, so an override was preferable to having student A take a colleague's class that might have space. jWPAs don't often have (just as many WPAs never develop) the power, despite having the authority, to institute the changes they know are good or fair for students. These conflicts don't seem to have anything to do with our call to serve: though the motivation was clearly to follow a fair policy, the community had other motives. Therefore, if the call to serve feels like the call to "do the job right," a jWPA may have to make some adjustments.

We may answer the call because we have a sense of responsibility to our colleagues, to our students, or to the university. Answering the call because we want to "do it for the team" so to speak is a noble reason but also a dangerous one because it is very easy to become quickly disenchanted when one's self sacrifice goes unappreciated or is misinterpreted. Academics are not known for their sense of gratitude, even when the WPA has been a longtime colleague or friend. In the authors' experience, even though colleagues can often disappoint us in their selfishness or lack of appreciation, this is still a good reason to serve. If we take the job in order truly to serve, then others' ingratitude has to become less important because it isn't about us, it's about the program as a whole, even though others don't see *their* work as contributing to or detracting from the whole. WPAs have to see the willingness of TAs and adjuncts to return every semester to a poorly-paid job as a sign that they are doing something right. They have to look at the interesting, innovative teaching they see when they visit classes as a sign that they are having an impact. They have to look at student complaints, faculty ignorance, and upper administration's lack of support as challenges to face and as more teaching that needs to be done outside of the classroom.

Answering the call because of a desire for power is a disastrous reason because it takes a very short time to realize that there is very little power associated with the position and how easily the little power is subverted by personnel or political issues. An example of this happened to a friend of the authors at another university. When he took over the jWPA position, he devised what he considered to be a brilliant plan for preventing the lazy students from taking the professors perceived to be "easy" each semester. He submitted the course schedule to the registrar with "staff" as the instructor on all sections. He explained that he would not release the names of the assigned instructors until after registration closed. While it was technically within his right to submit the schedule this way, he was forced to abandon the plan. Everyone was up in arms, the registrar, composition faculty, the students, even the faculty across campus. He quickly learned that his power as WPA was ceremonial in this case, and his desire for power would not be fulfilled as a jWPA. In other cases, a powerless jWPA is a way of keeping the entire writing program powerless. jWPAs can be "used" by upper administration to keep adjuncts and first-year students in line, serving the bottom line, rather than to be "of use" to administration by solving problems to the benefit of teachers and students.

Answering a call that is only superficially felt is also a problem. Just about everyone who teaches can see ways to make a program run better. Just about everyone who can put a jigsaw puzzle together and alphabetize can schedule a hundred sections of first-year writing. Having the organizational skills or the creativity to imagine solutions to problems is only one part of the "good work" of a jWPA. The likely lack of "immediate feedback" and "clear goals," which Gardner Csikszentmihalyi, and Damon describe as necessities for good work, means the call to serve must be strong. Our advice is to answer the call only when you see fairly concrete evidence that the call is real, the call is possible to answer, and it's so strong it's likely to outshout the negative voices.

When the Call is Answered

Despite the array of reasons one might have for accepting the call, one can find a sense of satisfaction or completion in jWPA work. Sometimes the satisfaction comes from walking down a busy hallway seeing professors and TAs conferencing with students, or it may come from observing a teacher in the classroom putting into practice the theories and methods we propose. Seeing the assessment cycle come full circle with faculty reviewing the data from a recent portfolio project and then making subsequent changes to course outcomes or student evaluation forms can be very satisfying. However, more often than not the sense of satisfaction of a job well done is the absence of problems, a semester with no plagiarism cases to process or a semester without student complaints. A late Friday afternoon with the desk cleared and the office in order can create a moment of fulfillment in spite of the knowledge that Monday will fill the desk again and a new set of problems will be waiting. A year-end review or report on the writing program, whether required or not, is often an excellent way to create a record of, and thus see, one's accomplishment.

The call to serve can not only offer a reason for doing one's job but also bring coherency to it. One of the authors made it through many contentious committee meetings as a jWPA by reminding herself and her colleagues of their mission—how do we best serve students and teachers by solving this problem? Gardner, Csikszentmihalyi, and Damon point out that many factors such as technology pull our work out of "alignment" and that good work is more possible with a "coherent vision" of that work in the world (223+). A jWPA can find that kind of coherency by writing a mission statement, asking for feedback, keeping a journal, reading the WPA-L listserv, looking for what's going well, and so on. Edward M. White's story of his life in *Composition Studies* reminds us that the power of writing can serve us by allowing us to shape our experiences: "Writers control their reality by shaping the past, as I have said; they also have a hand in shaping the future, at the very least their own future"(189). Using writing to make administrative experiences coherent might be another use of "macro-level" reflection on writing instruction.

However, much of the work of WPAs doesn't fit the normal definitions of good work well done. The best work a WPA does is often invisible to others. It is the absence of problems, indicating that all is running smoothly, that is hard for others to appreciate. It is the quiet negotiations with complaining parents or students behind closed doors that make problems disappear. It is the subtle facilitating of faculty allowing them to feel that they have made the decision or resolved the issue to their liking that keeps the system rolling. It is the removal of an obstacle to assessment that no one afterward will ever remember existed. But it is just that invisibility of the work that can feed the sense of service for the WPA. Doing the quiet work behind the scenes, keeping the faculty engaged and empowered, seeing that the students'

needs are met, and providing all the needed data and answers for supe-
riors to keep the system running is the day-to-day work of the jWPA.

Not until long after accepting the call might a jWPA discover that,
while in the grander sense the struggles of the position are still about
the quality of teaching in the program, the majority of the work is
about personnel issues that seem only remotely related to the higher
cause. In other words, while answering the call may be a question
about "me," doing the job has little to do with "me" and everything to
do with everyone else. The WPA must put others first, others being
students and staff. One of the authors spent long hours on the phone
every week during one semester with a new TA who was convinced
she couldn't teach. Later, the author went through three secretaries in
as many years until finding one who could work independently and
speak to students respectfully. The author's definition of the call to
serve had not originally included interviewing secretaries or handling
basic self-esteem issues in teachers. The author had to make these parts
of the job fit, remembering that the secretary is part of the public face
of the writing program and that listening to a TA's angst is one way of
learning how to make more effective TA appointments in the future.

For jWPAs, the call to serve, alone, will not see them through the
semester. Perhaps the most frustrating job of the WPA is that of scheduling and staffing classes. In the case of one of the authors, upon first
attempting the job of scheduling the composition courses, she asked
for the faculty and graduate TAs' preferences regarding times and
rooms. She went to extreme lengths to accommodate everyone. A few
weeks later when the schedules were distributed, a number of individuals came in to complain, one even suggesting that the author "had it
in for" the person because of the terrible schedule he received. Showing
the person his written request for classes, which matched the assigned
schedule, stopped the blustering, but there was never a hint of an apol-
ogy. Other issues facing a WPA may even be even more difficult or impossible to reconcile with the call to serve. Hiring unqualified adjuncts
to meet the demands for seats from upper administration, enforcing
a teacher's written policy when you disagree with the policy, protecting incompetent faculty members when students complain—some of
the people we serve as WPAs simply don't deserve it. Unfortunately,
the WPA must be prepared to adjust to this and develop thicker skin.
Apologies and thank-yous are few and far between. Our colleagues'

sense of service is to their students, if we're lucky, or to themselves, not to administrators such as WPAs.

Thus, for jWPAs, the call to serve needs maintenance, since it is different from the call to teach. Yes, part of WPA work is "macrolevel" teaching, as Gebhardt says, but it is also scheduling, counseling, saying no, delegating, budgeting, hiring, firing, and a multitude of other non-teaching activities. The WPA feeds and nurtures her call to serve by adjusting her notion of where good work is located and finding ways to make the invisible more visible, as many recent publications about WPA work have pointed out. Institutions considering hiring a jWPA will have to adjust, too, and find ways to see, evaluate, and reward what previously may have generally been "good departmental service" for tenured faculty.

Conclusion: If You Really Hear The Call, Should You Listen to It?

The dual nature of the call to serve and the unique position of the jWPA don't tell us the best reason to take or continue in a WPA position. Most of the various motivations for becoming a WPA can be reconciled with the call to serve, including practical reasons, such as using the WPA position as a career steppingstone or taking the position because it's the only job offered; political reasons, such as knowing other candidates would run the writing program into the ground; or altruistic reasons, such as believing that WPA work is an even greater calling than teaching. We aren't suggesting every jWPA enter a position assuming great sacrifice of self will be required or necessary. Indeed, our profession needs no more martyrs. But rethinking why we take on jWPA positions may save us from some of the hazards. Our intent here is to make it clear that the call to serve and thus the nature of what makes WPA work "good work" are real factors in making honest decisions about jWPA positions. After all, if jWPA positions were as good as they sounded, they wouldn't exist because then senior faculty would be doing the job.

Unfortunately, the increasing professionalization of our field of rhetoric and composition can drown out the call to serve. Graduate schools emphasize learning the right theories, having the right contacts and the right publications, which to their credit are geared toward helping new faculty find a job and be successful at it. Some graduate programs have courses and seminars in WPA theory and practice. They attempt in good faith to give future WPAs the knowledge and skills they need to be successful. But these activities may focus us too specifically on what (what to do, what to say, what not to say), without asking enough why (why bother, why not bother). Our professionalization of WPAs needs to include attention to the sense of vocation and calling in administration, which includes the risky nature of caring about that which others despise.

The question this essay ultimately attempts to answer is: "Can the call to WPA work be reconciled to the call to serve?" Or, in other words, "How can WPA work, for a jWPA, be good work?" For many jWPAs, the question needs to be phrased thusly: "Can the relatively powerless position of the jWPA still provide enough 'good work' to make the job rewarding?" This question leads us to explore the problems of accurately interpreting the pull that WPAs feel toward their work. Can one reconcile the dual nature of the call to serve with the rather unreciprocal nature of the call to be a jWPA? While there are no "right" or "wrong" reasons for taking on administrative duties, these discussions help jWPAs define their roles within programs and departments, re-envision their work by seeing their greater overall goals more clearly and better preparing themselves for the realities of WPA work.

In the final analysis, potential WPAs have to ask whether they can do the job as offered and the hiring institution has to ask whether the job should be done by a jWPA. We want our colleagues contemplating jWPA positions to examine their motives and ask, "Why do I want this job? What will I need to accomplish to feel successful in the position?" The person contemplating the job of WPA needs to know that "good work" can be accomplished, but no leadership position consists solely of the duties on the job description. Fulfilling the call to serve involves the willingness to give beyond the job description. jWPAs must have room to make most of the administrative work "good work" for them.

WORKS CITED

Bogart, Greg. "Finding a Life's Calling." *Journal of Humanistic Psychology* 34.4 (Fall 1994): 6–37.
Gardner, Howard, Mihaly Csikszentmihalyi, and William Damon. *Good Work: When Excellence and Ethics Meet.* New York: Basic Books, 2001.

Gebhardt, Richard. "Administration as Focus for Understanding the Teaching of Writing." *The Allyn and Bacon Sourcebook for Writing Program Administrators.* Ed. Irene Ward and William J. Carpenter. New York: Addison-Wesley Longman, 2002. 34–37.

Holy Bible: Revised Standard Version. Minneapolis: Augsburg Publishing, 1971.

Peircy, Marge. "To Be of Use." *To Be of Use.* Garden City, NY: Doubleday, 1973. 49–50.

Popken, Randall. "Edwin Hopkins and the Costly Labor of Composition Teaching." *College Composition and Communication* 55.4 (June 2004): 618–41.

Towner, W. Sibley. "The Inner Self, the Word of God, and the Cause that Matters." *Interpretation* (April 2002): 192–95.

White, Edward M. "On Being a Writer, Being a Teacher of Writing." *Living Rhetoric and Composition: Stories of the Discipline.* Ed. Duane H. Roen, Stuart C. Brown, and Theresa Enos. Mahwah, NJ: Lawrence Erlbaum, 1999. 171–91.

6 Labor Relations: Collaring jWPA Desire

Debra Frank Dew

> Pedagogic action must always transmit not only a content but also the affirmation of the value of that content, and there is no better way of doing so than by diverting onto the thing communicated the glamour which the irreplaceable manner of communicating it secures for the interchangeable author of the communication.
>
> —Pierre Bourdieu and Jean-Claude Passeron

I have long been taken with the work of Charles Schuster, that is, the administrative idea of *a Schuster*—the charismatic WPA righting the world for the cause of effective writing instruction. My jWPA case is likely a common one, where a graduate student gets the WPA fever, relentlessly pursues the dream job, and never looks back. Administrative desire begins as an infatuation with a professional ideal, an ideal set before us at an early age in graduate programs of stellar repute across the country. The discipline of rhetoric and composition embraces an ideal of self-sacrifice and extraordinary service, and advances the notion that a truly noble path to embodying this ideal is through a WPA appointment. When one takes a WPA appointment as junior faculty, and is thus located as a jWPA, the professional ante is upped, just to fulfill one's dangerous desire. This chapter examines the allure of WPA labor to understand how junior faculty are drawn to the work and how our discipline markets administrative desire. Further, the chapter explores an administrative temperament to identify traits and tendencies that prove most vulnerable to WPA desire. Finally, the chapter disentangles the multiple and often competing dimensions of jWPA labor as hybrid work within the larger domain of academic labor. A useful and tentative, arguably false, separation casts jWPA labor as material, rhetorical, administrative, and scholarly. As hybrid labor with such multiple, often competing dimensions, the appointment by design can spur a crisis in professional labor relations if the jWPA does not conceptually admit their presence and secure enabling relations among them.

jWPA Desire: The Pull of Administrative Labor in a Specific Case

I had no more than a reasonable degree of confidence in my intellectual abilities as a PhD student, but my work ethic was strong, and my insatiable thirst for theories of effective writing instruction, and the rush of discovering more kept me pressing on. As a nontraditional graduate student, I had a few administrative assets: street smarts from my childhood, where blue-collar necessity sparked my rhetorical talents early on, diverse teaching experiences from travels with my career-Navy husband, and a passionate desire to right the wrongs of brutal writing instruction past. I had the work ethic, the love of teaching, and the cause all in place when I began graduate work in rhetoric and composition. At the MA level, I had also learned that WPAs had the agency to improve writing instruction, and writing programs were the grounds for such pedagogical change. Never once was the pursuit of a PhD about my career or earning a professional reputation. The PhD was the means to the ends of my desire to improve writing instruction for those developing writers behind me. My professional desire was clearly a need to advocate, to reach back and help struggling writers along. Administrative desire, the pull to serve others as just described, also risks a counter relation to scholarly desire, which is integral to graduate training and necessary for success as a tenure-track researcher and scholar in academia.

As a graduate student, I was keenly aware of scholarly desire, its impressive market value, its superior pleasure when satisfied via a publication. As a first-generation PhD student, I just did not then know, nor comfortably value, such work. In my context, the professional behavior and ethos of those who exuded such desire stood before many of us aspiring academics as a questionable model of "how to be." Graduate students keenly observe and evaluate their mentors, and simply put, the remarkable scholars were often less accessible, less prepared for class, and, even less redeeming, they squabbled over institutional rewards. (To be fair, the system of academic rewards largely perpetuates such a disposition.)

Scholarly labor, in fact, was easily set against excellence in teaching and service, so compelling choices arose—should one affect a scholarly posture like the *big dogs,* as we called them, or invest one's intellectual energy in teaching and serving the writing program? As graduate students, we knew explicitly that scholarly desire and subsequent publication were integral to our professional development, but it was always possible to labor otherwise, especially when other desires and their accompanying values were stronger. Administrative desire and scholarly desire are not essentially opposed, but culturally, I imbibed their political relations and accompanying values as less than complementary. As a graduate student, my administrative workload was both hefty and intellectually satisfying enough to justify an imbalance of time and energy. While I fulfilled research requirements for my degree, I did not essentially define myself as a traditional scholar. I naively believed that administrative work with its intellectual foundation was legitimate labor, not understanding that its intellectual legitimacy is an argument yet in the making for rhetoric and composition as a discipline. While a graduate student, I labored administratively and pedagogically, and excelled at both throughout my years of graduate training, and the best of my intellectual energy was spent on administrative work.

Importantly, this same competing dynamic of labor relations habitually constitutes jWPA work.. Many jWPAs are hired at an institution's point of need—the position is invented when a program needs deep review and when policy and practice relations are stressed. The jWPA appointment often responds to an urgent programmatic situation, and thus the frontloading of a hefty administrative workload naturally follows. Furthermore, administrative appointments by design demand multiple modes of production. A frontloading of pressing, backlogged programmatic needs along with the multimodal production inherent in the appointment compels jWPAs to choose among these labor demands, either by necessity or felt urgency. The push and pull among production demands and values must not be framed as either/or, or as a sequential prioritizing of first one/then the other; rather, an integrated both/and relation of multimodal production needs to be inculcated as the standard course for graduate training before one secures a jWPA line. What follows here is but one analysis of how tensions between scholarly desire and administrative desire may have transpired during my years of graduate study. My case is but one story of how the pull of administrative desire and the appeal of service to others may enable a prioritizing of administrative work.

In *Reproduction in Education, Society and Culture,* Pierre Bourdieu and Jean-Claude Passeron link the pedagogic work of schooling with the maintenance of social class hierarchies. From these theorists, we learn that an individual's "relationship to [her] social class of origin *dominates* and *informs* [her] relationship to the [educational] system," so the student comes to "school," even graduate school, with learned habits of work or labor linked to social class (160, emphasis added). The student's "behavior, aptitudes, and disposition to school bear the stamp of [her] whole academic past" (160). Bourdieu and Passeron identify "the principle underlying the production of the most durable academic and social differences [as] the *habitus*" (160), which they further describe as an inculcated "system of schemes of perceptions, thought, appreciation and action" (35). The student's aptitude for academic success is a "function of the distance between the primary habitus inculcated [. . .] within the different groups or classes and the *habitus* inculcated [taught via one's school work], (i.e., the extent to which education or acculturation is re-education or de-culturation, depending on [one's] group or class)"(45–46). From home and class, we are durably trained in our habits of work—labor relations—and schooling aims subsequently to enable the successful transfer of our work habits, or rather, requires a "re-education or deculturation" of original work habits if the work of school differs markedly from that of home and social class.

Graduate students in rhetoric and composition who undergo administrative training as jWPAs learn early on that administrative work habits are not easily aligned with the traditional mode of school work, the scholarly work we associate with PhD studies. WPA work with its material demands and mantra of "service and sacrifice" appeals to jWPAs with a home and class appreciation for blue collar labor. Consider, for example, Doug Hesse's administrative labor narrative, "The WPA as Husband, Father, Ex," where we see how the "durable training" (Bourdieu 31) of home and his father's blue-collar work ethic proved transferable to his administrative workplace (45–46). For Hesse, the distance between home and class and the work habits of WPA labor was eased. He ably transferred his learned labor relations to writing program administration, where an understanding of service and the value of sacrifice enable good work. Likewise, the jWPA's ability to produce "good labor" is linked to her ability to transfer and sustain, conceptually and practically, complementary labor relations across these contexts. The greater the distance between the labor of home and class, and the labor of program administration, the higher the risk for self-exclusion from administrative work itself. Further, the greater the distance between administrative labor as material production, "hard work and hard work alone" (Schuster 87) from academic labor as scholarly production, the higher the jWPA's risk of self-exclusion from the ranks of her tenured and promoted colleagues, for "career death at age seven"(Schuster 87). In the Hesse narrative, we see how the work ethic of home and class enabled him to successfully wield a heavy WPA workload and justify his administrative service and personal sacrifices.

As a graduate student, arguably already a jWPA, my blue-collar roots also fed my desire for administrative labor to likewise sustain home and class values (my father was a Norman Rockwell policeman) and imagine myself as capable of "good work." WPA work is scholarly, and it surely moves beyond the production of a General Motors assembly line. But, we must consider how our graduate WPA training inculcates blue-collar exertion promoted as noble service and self-sacrifice. Much of my administrative training inculcated working class labor relations—the good worker managed customer complaints, hauled oak desks on a dolly from TA offices on the first floor to the third floor, duplicated assessment essays, and ran campus errands. In this manner, I maintained a good portion of the program's material infrastructure. As a writing program assistant, I rolled up my sleeves, put my back into it, and regularly worked over time for the good of the writing program. Not only did I value the work, I shamelessly flaunted such *real* labor before the scholarly others who winced at my ability to fit any oak desk in any TA office on demand. The distance between these competing desires and modes of production was palpable, and my most urgent need was to quell my scholarly insecurity by teaching a very fine TA workshop, or delivering a few more desks to the adjunct bullpen.

I wanted two things most direly from my graduate studies—access to a WPA position where I would relish the intellectual oversight of a program to improve writing instruction, and the ability to labor, not for self, but in the service of others, a value integral to my primary *habitus* of home and social class of origin. My administrative desire—as it rewarded a transfer of home and class work habits to academia—was sparked. My labor in and for the program over-determined my graduate training, and effectively delayed the institution's demand for the more traditional mode of scholarly production. Beyond the pull of the familiar in WPA work, I also now more fully understand how I succumbed to the glamorous appeal of rhetoric and composition's professional ideals as marketed to PhD consumers across the country.

The Appeal of WPA Models Before Us

Graduate students, in particular writing program assistants, are quite prone to groupie behavior, defined as an urgent need to know, tout, and follow our field's administrative superstars. We first invoke their work among peers in the graduate seminar, where names linked to impressive initiatives and records of administrative labor of national repute constitute that which motivates our study, that which we revere. Groupies see only the glory and the glitz of WPA success. We do not grasp the dangers of our early desire as we are largely protected from the perils of WPA politics and the personal costs of WPA labor. We are WPA groupies, oblivious to the substantive trail of jWPA victim narratives inside our WPA research archives. Also, then, groupies are quite eager to flatter successful WPA professionals, both our local mentors, and national superstars, who deservedly appreciate the fawning of wannabe WPAs.

What follows lays no blame on a few superstars for promoting my administrative desire, but rather, I explore a disciplinary fuel source, which enables junior faculty like yours truly to blaze on with but a modicum of concern for the professional consequences of the administrative careers we choose. WPA desire needs to be admitted if we as a discipline are to do better both as graduate students choosing a career and WPA mentors who do want all their students to succeed if they dare choose a jWPA line right out of graduate school. WPA role models of excellence in our field abound, as do ample professional appeals to embrace the noble dimensions of a WPA identity.

I met Charles Schuster through his resonant assertion—"Composition is a dangerous business" (85), which we recognize as the opening claim of his "Politics of Promotion." In this essay, Schuster both defines our disciplinary temperament and locates himself inside the same. He rhetorically elevates writing professionals by punctuating their marginal identities through an institutional gaze. A few excerpts follow. As writing specialists, we are "not swashbucklers, or highwaymen," nor are we "the top guns of the academy"(85). In the institution's understanding, we are "incompetent, idiosyncratic, confused, valueless, [and] untenurable" (86). "[T]hose of us whose world is permeated with student writing are by definition among the expendable lower class; we are laborers, factory workers, piece workers" (89). The cumulative effect of Schuster's pejoratives, his diminishing of our professional esteem through rhetorical force, is an invited reversal—our familiarity with institutional name calling first sparks our Burkean identification, and then compels a full and confident rejection of these false terms. The appeal of these marginal terms lies in our insider understanding of the intellectual integrity of our work, and Schuster's strategic emphasis on our marginal location provides grounds for rhetorical action. We want to come out from under the institution's gaze, take control of our professional identities and advance the field.

Just as Schuster's "dangerous business" stirs our administrative desire at the start, so does institutional name calling move us to act, to resist and come together. Then, we imagine the professional risks of our chosen career path when Schuster beckons us deeper into the fold—"Most of us know stories of composition colleagues denied tenure and promotion" (87). Such failures have been endured by a "veritable Who's Who of composition," and "[m]any of the most famous faculty in rhetoric and composition" have "received some such professional setback" (87). To follow Schuster, we need to choose—do we want to be among "the most famous faculty in rhetoric and composition" or are we disciplinary weaklings and quitters? Such a reading surely presses on Schuster's aim, perhaps even against his aim, in an effort to track administrative desire as it circulates and rises in response to such a compelling textual analysis of our "dangerous business." Maybe Schuster does give fair warning, but jWPA groupies like me draw their swords intent on some serious institutional swashbuckling.

Everyone knows Kathleen Blake Yancey as she who twirls more administrative plates at one time than other WPA superstars, she whose professional success is humorously captured in WPA lore with the following insight: "I know I must be too busy when I no longer resemble myself." I first caught a glimpse of her in Kansas City back in the mid-1990s when I attended one of her seminars on implementing writing portfolios. To participate in her workshop, I drove up to Kansas City from Oklahoma with my family in tow. I recall her intelligent delivery, the packed room and appreciative applause. She dazzled us with her energy, her vision, and the promise of effective writing assessment. Her audience warmly embraced her values, and the promise of her service to others. Shortly after the main event, I caught sight of Kathi jogging out the main entrance of the hotel with a Walkman in hand. "She jogs, too! She has it together," I marveled reflectively.

I was three years out of graduate school before I could afford to attend the summer WPA workshop, where I learned what I should have known before negotiating my jWPA positions. By the time I arrived at WPA boot camp, I was less naïve about WPA stardom, but yet vulnerable to administrative desire. At the workshop, we were issued a copy of Doug Hesse's "WPA as Father, Husband, Ex," and the article sat silently in my binder for days. Not until the plane ride home did I pull it out and muse over its presence. Why this article? Why a copy of this one? Others were included in our WPA bibliographies as well, but Hesse's was copied and distributed. I read the article, and have read it numerous times since, and still I struggle to discern its aim—here is our ideal of sacrifice and noble martyrdom realized for the cause of writing, a model worth emulating. Hesse inculcates his model of work from his father, "a model driven by a sense of providership, characterized by stoicism and sacrifice," and his labor rewards him well—he makes full professor by his eighth year (44–45). Amazing.

Or, here is an unsettling victim narrative of the tragic familial costs of succumbing to the WPA ideal as marketed by our field. In Hesse's terms: "(H)owever noble our [writing] culture may make forbearance and sacrifice [. . .] it ultimately costs its practitioner an awful lot" (45). His long hours of WPA work distance him from his marriage, his children, and the absence is implicated in his subsequent divorce, and heartbreak at his son's artistic representation of his father as he who "stays at his office until nighttime" (55). As a WPA model, the Hesse narrative claims both of these conflicted aims, and thus captures WPA stardom.

How did I feel after reading his powerful account of failure in success, of shame in pride, of neglect in love? The horror of discovering a reckless pleasure in one's close identification with Hesse's WPA self penetrates deeply. Yet, I press on as do many other jWPAs, and we rationalize our sacrifices, personal and professional, as necessary to the noble labor we choose—I will be a *present* wife and *attentive* mother once the writing program is thriving . . . surely after I secure tenure. Pride in overproduction and personal sacrifices are integral to "good work" in writing program administration. When the discipline naturalizes these standards and makes them benign, even as they are truly debilitating, our drive to deliver the extraordinary blinds us to the dire circumstances within which ordinary junior faculty try first to survive their WPA appointments before they might thrive as magically as the superstars.

jWPA Desire and the Promise of Good Theory

As an MA student, I was seduced by the healing promise of early expressivist writing theory and drawn to rhetoric and composition's charge to save the writing souls of the damaged masses. I entered the field as a writing refugee, having had my own prose reamed most recently for a "pedestrian style." "Enough!" I asserted. I dropped Shakespeare and added a seminar on teaching writing, where I subsequently gave up literature for writing once I discovered one could teach writing without shaming the writer. I became a WPA groupie shortly thereafter by shadowing the WPA as her assistant. I observed her charismatic teaching, studied her administrative moves, and faithfully parroted her theoretical claims. I had run from writing throughout my undergraduate experience, but I confronted my anxiety and was academically born again under the promise of early process theory at the close of my MA studies.

My early expressivist zeal was sharply tempered at the start of my doctoral training, only to be reconfigured and fueled again under the license of the "critical," the "feminist," "the rhetorical," and the "liberatory," sufficiently appealing material for the administrative temperament. In the 1990s, any graduate student who paid attention absconded with critical theory enough for a lifetime of ideological bomb throwing and activist institutional critique. Activism. Critical literacy. Liberation. Empowerment. Critique. Who could not want to lay bare the institution's history of marginalizing or even excluding the masses from higher education? Who could deny their ethical obligation to put their privileged education to practical use via the empowerment of others? For graduate students like me, the writing program, again, afforded us a forum for such educational activism. Even the most scholarly students among us professed their desire to "take their schooling to the streets" if only as an intellectual exercise.

My theoretical training sparked my activist desire, and aptly furnished analytical tools which suited my administrative calling to improve writing instruction, and honestly, no better tool box could have been marketed more effectively. As Bourdieu and Passeron claim: "Pedagogic action must always transmit not only a content but also the affirmation of the value of that content, and there is no better way of doing so than by diverting onto the thing communicated the glamour which the irreplaceable manner of communicating it secures" for those who promote the work (125). I remain grateful for such "theory hope," the principles, strategies and beliefs which now enable the best of my administrative work. Useful theory (enabling the work), plus an appealing ideology (justifying the work), sustain jWPA desire and glamorize the labor like nothing else.

WHERE JWPA DESIRE MEETS THE INSTITUTIONAL ROAD

Thus, a timely confluence of appeals launched me into my line of administrative work—the jWPA appointment. My administrative destiny was starkly apparent: Blue-collar work ethic. An unsupervised academic youth. An impressionable professional innocence. An attraction to danger. A respect for service and self-sacrifice. A passion for truth, justice, and writerly empowerment through the WPA way. I so knew what I wanted and whom I would be.

I so did not know what a jWPA appointment would bring my way.

My jWPA desire and I hit the professional road without knowing we were looking to serve in all the ideal places—enabling contexts where rhetoric and composition enjoys a disciplinary presence and institutional critique and change are anticipated and warmly enabled. I had extensive experience in problem-solving matters of daily operations, excellent training in rhetoric and writing theory, and diverse pedagogical experience. What I did not expect was that rhetorical work (defining my discipline and enabling change) would be absolute-

ly integral, if not prior to, all other labor. Having written an historical dissertation, I also did not have a conceptually integrated research
agenda in administrative scholarship, where I now spend all of my best
intellectual energy. Finally, I would have benefited greatly from a mature understanding that overproduction is normal and necessary—the
expected output for jWPAs aiming to advance in their tenure-track
lines as rhetoric and composition professionals.

What follows is a definitional analysis of jWPA labor, offered as
an experience-driven model—what I have produced and how I have
labored as a jWPA on the ground. I define the work as multimodal,
always material, rhetorical, scholarly, and administrative (i.e., effectively coordinated *people work*). By exploring the multimodal nature of
jWPA labor, we may more responsibly see the work and then perhaps
redress the issue of how best to proactively prepare graduate students
for the unique demands of WPA work.

jWPA Labor as Material Production

Writing programs control their WPAs much more than the WPAs
control them. jWPAs need to know that the position asks them to con-
sign one's physical body to the program through a contractual charge
to sustain, grow, protect, and care for an academic unit which is actually a complex network of programmatic relations. The contractual
promise includes guaranteeing institutional access, both material and
intellectual, to the WPA's administrative body—the well from which
the writing program draws its life blood.

Lloyd Bitzer defines exigence within a rhetorical situation as "an
imperfection marked by urgency [. . .] something waiting to be done,
a thing which is other than it should be" (6). A writing program as a
complex network of institutional relations is essentially a rhetorical
network, where exigent situations arise naturally. As such, situations
arise at will, set their discursive constraints, and "so [control]" what
can be said that they become "the very ground of rhetorical activity"
(5). jWPAs encounter a slippage of agency from the graduate student
self to their program's recurring situations, which in Bitzer's terms—
dictate, impose and *demand* rhetorical mediation (5, emphasis added).
Upon appointment, programs determine what work is to be done and
urgently call us into their service.

When a programmatic event happens, the subsequent situation demands a response, perhaps rhetorical—in language—or maybe material, some physical action. In either case, the writing program compels an administrative presence to redress exigent relations. WPAs are hired to sustain the program's network of rhetorical and material relations around the clock. The institution's needs supersede others (i.e., the personal in Hesse's narrative) especially when the jWPA is the only disciplinary expert in the house.

Exigent events may warrant material action. As I edit this sentence, two instructors post their material concerns to our faculty list with a subject line—Dirty Rug!!! They compel me to respond to their message: "What facility takes care of the rugs in classrooms? The rug in 220 is *filthy!*" Followed by, "AMEN! I have been embarrassed by how filthy it is!"[1] Another situation. At 7:40 am on the first day of fall classes, a writing instructor cries out in distress as the IKON copier's error light comes on with its demand, "Add toner." Her class starts at 8:00, and our staff assistant arrives at 8:00. She needs to copy her ENGL 131 syllabi, so my administrative body is called into service. Up in the mailroom cupboard, we discover a Canon GPR-4 toner cartridge and follow the necessary ten steps as illustrated. The IKON beast is fed, and syllabi soon fly out of its satisfied mouth. And a third. I wash toner from my hands, return to my desk, and pull up the SIS enrollment database only to discover that our first-year caps are overridden in several sections. Faculty will shortly discover extra students on their rosters and in their classrooms. I need to discover the cause, intervene to prevent further overrides, and offer an explanation and justification to offset pending concerns that we are ignoring enrollment policies—a perceived or actual violation of the program's workload agreement. Writing-related events arise as they will. Material situations—insufficient toner, dirty rugs, too many student bodies in a classroom—stress programmatic relations as "things" that are "other than [they] should be" or "imperfections" marked by their "urgency" (Bitzer 6). WPAs employ their bodies to mediate materially "imperfect" situations. They do what needs to be done, and they figure it out on the spot if need be. They attend to the program with efficiency and silent grace, nonetheless. jWPAs seldom anticipate these material expectations for constant access to their administrative bodies because they are often unaware that the contexts within which we often begin our WPA careers seldom enjoy an infrastructure comparable to that of our degree-granting institutions.

Many WPAs spend much of their early work on site in producing a material infrastructure to give a full and functional presence to the writing program. One's first two to three years in a position may be devoted to securing resources and space enough to deliver the work. The material work of producing a programmatic infrastructure to deliver good instruction is also rhetorical work. The WPA must discover an audience capable of providing the needed resources, engage her audience via a credible ethos, and make an effective case for action. Advocating for offices, classrooms, and technology (material goods) always requires solid and savvy rhetorical work on the ground. Because WPAs understand that their program's material resources variously impede or enable effective writing instruction, they are called to advocate for relief whenever material issues arise and stress instructional relations. They advocate for immediate relief when material problems impede instruction; they further advocate for additional resources as they aim to enhance instruction in state-of-the-art facilities.

Even as rhetoric and composition has fully evolved as a profession, local arguments for disciplinarity must yet be advanced, especially if the jWPA is the only rhetoric and composition scholar on campus. In this context, the jWPA must *proceed directly to go* and make a defining case for the integrity of her work and legitimacy of the program's needs. Say a computer classroom needs reconfiguring because a rank-and-file layout isolates writers, impedes class discussion and works against a social-epistemic writing practice. Reconfiguring a classroom will not happen until an effective argument for the work is advanced. The WPA needs to present a disciplinary self to garner intellectual credibility and secure administrative authority for altering the space. She needs to reassure all stakeholders of her sound educational motives, build a consensus at multiple levels, and (as in my situation) maybe even muscle the argument by appropriating the authority of a few manly senior faculty. Much later, the full argument has been advanced, and the room is reconfigured. The WPA is then on site to theoretically reveal the logic of the new design, and secure understanding and confidence from the IT techies who do the actual labor. In this way, jWPAs discover that rhetorical and material work are integral to their administrative labor.

jWPA Labor as Rhetorical Production

jWPAs need to understand that the rhetorical work of defining our discipline and constructing an enabling context for change and growth is a necessary precursor to fulfilling any contractual obligations to administer the program. We need legitimate disciplinary grounds, and established working relations across multiple contexts—program, department, college, and institution—to authorize the work of our programs. The definitional work is fully rhetorical and always integral to establishing professional relations across all institutional contexts. The success of one's rhetorical claims for disciplinary integrity and its subsequent authority has everything to do with our ability to do the job. When we move to implement our work, we largely claim the following: "X is good, or X needs to be done to meet rhetoric and composition's academic goals." Our institutional supervisors and peer faculty shift the questions to one of definition, and compel us to answer: "What is rhetoric and composition?" and "Who exactly are you?"

Two years ago, I worked with writing faculty on a deep theoretical revision of our second semester course, Rhetoric and Writing II: Academic Argument and Inquiry. As customary, the revised course needed approval from the college of liberal arts and sciences' curriculum and review committee. Given our emphasis on academic research and argument, I imagined nothing but sheer appreciation for the theoretical infusion and raised standards. Sure enough, the majority of the committee members were enthusiastic and appreciative. Then came a direct challenge from Philosophy: "How can you claim curricular authority over critical thinking, reasoning, and academic argument, which surely resides with philosophy? And further, you admit no overlap, whatsoever. Your course competes for FTE with our introductory course in critical thinking." Philosophy did not know the disciplinary *me*, know *writing* as a discipline whose business included critical reasoning and rhetorical theory. I was compelled to define the field because faculty across the disciplines needed first to see and conceptually understand our discipline, before they could legitimately map our curricular terrain.

The committee tabled my proposal. Approval was delayed for months. As a jWPA, I proceeded directly to go and launched an extensive definitional argument. I accounted for the critical thinking subset of outcomes (those recommended by the Council of Writing

Program Adminstrators), defined rhetorical reasoning by delivering textbooks to philosophy, and edited course materials such that rhetoric and composition stood theoretically and materially apart from philosophy. Disciplinary boundaries were secured even as epistemological understanding can only be gained through sustained dialogue across time.

Curricular suspicions arose because rhetoric and composition lacked a local disciplinary presence, so producing my discipline—redressing the field's nondescript intellectual and epistemological domain—was my first charge. The insight here is that such rhetorical work, often invisible to our disciplinary peers, is peculiar and necessary to jWPA labor given our field's insecure disciplinary grounds. Again, rhetorically securing such grounds—a politically charged mode of discipline-specific intellectual production—is integral to the work, and it is this additional work I refer to when I define the jWPA workload as requiring "overproduction." In many contexts, jWPAs must first break disciplinary ground to enable them to work side-by-side with peers who work in fully established disciplines. Such ground breaking is also politically volatile work for junior faculty, who need to advance definitional claims of disciplinary integrity to an audience of senior faculty who likewise need to defend and secure their own disciplinary selves.

PEOPLE WORK: ADMINISTRATIVE PRODUCTION AS jWPA LABOR

The glamour or glitz of one's theoretical expertise in rhetoric and composition comes straight at you when a hiring institution taps the jWPA as a new hire who will solve problems and fulfill the institution's desire for curricular advancement and progress. Administrative hires happen when writing problems warrant expert solutions through the hiring of a professional someone to capably mediate the dissonance. Newly minted rhetoric and composition professionals imagine that hot-shot theoretical training is just what programs need, and that our smarts—compelling research, sound principles and strategies—are enough to solve local problems and produce a new and improved writing program. The jWPA just needs to put good theory into play.

Like our colleagues, jWPAs do bring disciplinary expertise into the workplace, and we are responsible for a specific area, but WPA work is not geographically bound as a historical period, nor a theoretical approach secured as the domain of an individual scholar as the resident expert. Rather, WPAs always enjoy the presence of others in our work. Ours is the material and intellectual responsibility for the collaborative development of curricula and the effective delivering of writing instruction as it encompasses the writing practice of faculty across the program. WPAs work with well-trained faculty, effectively linked in healthy and productive relations, to collaboratively develop and deliver instruction across the program. We sustain the program's intellectual argument, which both enables and accounts for everyone's instruction. In this manner, the company of others naturally shapes and determines, enables and constrains administrative production. Such administrative work is thus collaborative as we oversee, enable, and empower all faculty working within the writing enterprise.

Our administrative work demands the WPA's material presence to establish a healthy workplace climate and culture, and to oversee faculty training and curricular development. Furthermore, administrative work is again rhetorical as we first construct a credible ethos in-house among our faculty, and across institutional contexts. To administer collaboratively, WPAs must identify needs and advocate for institutional resources and policies, which enable and authorize our faculty's professional development with the subsequent aim of increasing faculty's intellectual control over their work, so they are empowered to participate more fully in the administration of our writing programs.

Much has been advanced about the ethical and professional appeals of a decentered or collaborative approach to administration. Jeanne Gunner faults WPA-centric models for their "anti-democratic cast," their tendency to exclude faculty from programmatic decision making and policy writing, and their disregard for the professional and instructional advantages of instructors securing theoretical control over their work (9–13). Writing instructors, in Gunner's preferred model of decentered administration, are "trained, theoretically informed faculty, [who work] together to develop a unified program that reflects their knowledge" (13). As stakeholders in the writing enterprise, faculty share "power, control and authority over the program"(14). Such administrative "democratizing" thus "gives all instructors a voice in governance and professional responsibility for the program" (14).

At the close of her argument for collaboration, Gunner admits the costs of a decentered approach—"It may be asking too much of already beleaguered WPAs to engage in such self-criticism and to cede to subordinates a share of whatever power they have attained, no doubt at high cost and through much effort" (15). They are always already *never* alone in their work, to be sure, but Gunner's decentered ideal, as ethically sound and ideologically appealing as it is, asks us to share power and influence which *first needs to be established* through rhetorical work at a local site. Furthermore, a fully collaborative design demands more administrative time and material production from all parties.

Christine Hult recognizes the limits of a fully democratic administrative model, which she classifies as a "constitutional government," known for its more egalitarian and representative approach. Hult points to the "downside" of the model: "It is often cumbersome and glacially slow," and then "the populace is not always necessarily as informed as their leaders and may be in a less advantageous position to make judicious decisions" (49). Given that writing programs still hire faculty who are in need of further theoretical training, the "novice writing teacher is no myth," and most WPAs train new writing faculty at the start of every academic year (49). Hult's concern here may be read as the absence of the necessary material conditions for the realization of a truly de-centered democracy, in her terms, a "utopian ideal" (49).

Most recently, Gunner invokes the central WPA "truisim" that "local conditions need to always inform program form and policies" to the ideal of collaborative administration (260). A collaborative leadership style does have "serious implications" for all stakeholders, yet "collaborative structures" remain "appealing in ideal form and effective in practice, in certain places, for certain times" (260). The ideal is set before us with the caveat that one's administrative situation, institutional setting, and the social relations therein have everything to do with the WPA's choice to implement a collaborative leadership model.

The decentered, democratic ideal holds sway as a standard for excellence in administrative labor even as our local, material conditions often obstruct, undermine and largely work against an immediate democratizing of relations. As jWPAs, we need to understand the inescapable ideological presence of the preferred standard in our work because our scholarly production will be assessed by peers who embrace the model and expect us to rhetorically produce the material conditions, which make a democracy possible. Awareness of the ideal sparks administrative desire, and thus the ideal remains on one's "to do" list of rhetorical initiatives. Our professional work records—annual reviews and tenure reviews—always include an account of our accomplishments in this area as embedded within the domain of faculty working conditions and development, a domain effectively defined in field documents.

Consider, for example, the administrative standards articulated in the "Guidelines for Self-Study to Precede WPA Visit," subsection III. Faculty, further noted as A. Status and Working Conditions (Ward and Carpenter 390). In this subsection, the local WPA prepares for an external review by accounting for the current status and working conditions of resident writing faculty. Requested data include faculty rank, qualifications, salary, evaluation procedures, and professional development. When the WPA's administrative work is reviewed (perhaps by primary peers and external reviewers in a jWPA's tenure and promotion case, or perhaps solicited via a WPA self-study), someone is held accountable for progress in this administrative domain. Given the profession's strong statement of acceptable standards on faculty status and working conditions, the WPA's workload thus includes the rhetorical production of improved working conditions.

Furthermore, faculty working conditions and development have everything to do with instructional effectiveness. The administrator may design an extraordinary curriculum only to have substandard working conditions (i.e., high faculty turnover, heavy workloads, low pay) undermine its delivery. Eileen Schell's resonant claim—"Teacher's working conditions are students' learning conditions" (198)—compels the WPA to pursue improved conditions as integral to her ongoing administrative charge to improve writing instruction.

To be sure, no WPA needs to be pressed to embrace such standards—ethically, theoretically, or professionally. That is not the concern here. Rather, we need to see how it is that the democratic, decentered ideal of collaborative administration as pressed upon WPAs compels our administrative production and increases our workload in largely invisible ways. At this point, we might remember Schuster's use of George Orwell's Boxer to represent the "good" administrative worker, whose ideological faith in the "farm's" ideal compels him to rise earlier and work harder (86–87). The WPA self-study represents our administrative workload with its exhaustive definitional framework. The frame advances our understanding of WPA work and carries with it our field's values and ideals. The document, with its embedded vision of a fully democratic administrative workplace, serves the cause of good writing, authorizes the WPA's work locally, and lends credibility to the program. Still, the institutional reality is that the onus for fully realizing its scope, its values, and ideals falls largely upon the WPA, as she who initiates institutional critique and advocates for the program she is explicitly hired to administer. Institutional critique and advocacy for improved faculty status and better working conditions are integral to WPA labor because our work is ethically bound and materially determined by the presence of others. In this manner, the rhetorical production of an administrative democracy is fundamentally integral to the daily operations of a writing program. Upon their appointment, jWPAs seldom see the scope of their professional work as a liability for realizing a fully democratic writing enterprise on such a grand scale. jWPAs need to recognize the determining presence of this disciplinary ideal and understand how significantly the responsibility impacts the WPA's workload.

jWPA Labor and Scholarly Production

Given the demands for material, rhetorical and administrative production, WPA scholarship, and the publication of intellectual work as defined by one's local tenure criteria risk being deferred or neglected. As already noted, the writing program controls us more than we control it, and the forcefulness with which the program demands our labor impacts our distribution of time and intellectual energy. The issue is not whether the jWPA has the ability or desire to write and publish in the traditional vein, but, rather, whether the administrative scholarship manifests itself credibly for peer review across the disciplines. Effective arguments for the intellectual nature of administrative scholarship have been advanced within WPA research. Most notably, we now have definitional standards articulated in the WPA Council's "Evaluating the Intellectual Work of Writing Administration." My aim here is not to rehearse the field's arguments for administrative work as scholarship, but to describe and analyze this mode of production as integral to the jWPA position.

The WPA line has existed longer than it has been recognized as a disciplinary specialization worthy of tenure-track or tenured faculty. Administration is gaining a substantive presence as an emphasis in graduate rhetoric and composition programs. Some programs now offer a seminar or even an actual concentration, where one gains a deep intellectual understanding of the work. Considering the breadth and depth of administrative labor (perhaps as mapped in our WPA self-study framework[2]), we clearly have not yet established graduate seminars enough for a specialty in program administration. Charles Schuster captures the scope in his claim: "No WPA can work effectively without knowing the theories and practices that underlie basic writing, invention, pedagogy, collaborative learning, [WAC], assessment, portfolios, computer classroom, radical pedagogy . . ." ("Forward" ix). As WPA work gains disciplinary depth through research and publication, we discover just how much foundational knowledge and practical experience the WPA professional need amass. Given that we are just now building graduate curricula on WPA research, it is surely true for many current jWPAs that our graduate work afforded us ample experience in the trenches, but little access to administrative scholarship in our seminars. Thus, we necessarily build our foundational knowledge while on the job—at the point of need. Unlike our colleagues whose areas of expertise have long been established, the intellectual baseline for WPA understanding and, in particular, research and publication, is now being written. Future WPAs will surely enjoy earlier access and deeper exposure to administrative scholarship.

For their scholarship, jWPAs first need to grasp WPA research generated before them and then generate new administrative knowledge in the company of senior WPAs in rhetoric and composition, who have established the intellectual baseline in administrative research. What kinds of scholarly work do WPAs produce? Materially, rhetorically, and administratively, we employ our best intellectual training and creative energy in producing our writing programs. I need here to invoke Joan Mullin's compelling claim, which she shared with me at a past WPA event in Delaware—"My most extraordinary publication is the Writing Center I direct." Or, alternately, Christine Hult defines the scholarship of administration as "the systematic, theory-based production and oversight of a dynamic program (as opposed to the traditional scholarship, which is generally defined as the production of "texts") (126). Hult also claims a scholarly presence within "the day-to-day written work of the administrator" given that these texts (i.e., course curricula, program guides, and in-house publications) all reflect "the rhetorical skills and the professional knowledge and the expertise of [their] writer" (127). WPA scholarship and the representation of such work remains an issue which we continue to address. As producers and publishers of writing programs, we need to successfully represent such scholarship to colleagues across the disciplines. The task is both to represent the program itself as a scholarly product and to garner traditional publications wherein we advance new administrative knowledge. WPA scholarship incorporates such multiple modes of intellectual representation.

For WPAs, the scholarship of producing a writing program is inescapably a collaborative enterprise. Our production timelines have less to do with the individual scholar's efforts than the nature of the work and the readiness of local conditions for such work. In my case, our program's innovative first-year curriculum, a fully collaborative effort (as integral to a decentered, democratic model) was researched and written across a period of three years. After three years of whole-faculty production, I had an administrative product—a revised program and new knowledge—enough to submit for peer review. Thus, I oversaw the scholarly re-production of our first-year program, and later secured a traditional publication in the *WPA: Writing Program Adminstration*.

As WPAs identify gaps and intellectual problems in the context of their programs, they need to road test strategies at their specific sites and actually gain material, rhetorical, or administrative ground before they can submit the work product for peer review. Under pressure to produce new administrative work and publish, jWPAs encounter political and material obstacles, some beyond their control, and these local challenges may impede production or stall it completely. The jWPA victim narrative of the political foibles and fatal efforts of the struggling "j" has also emerged as a subgenre in our field. These narratives are published accounts of jWPA efforts to review, revise, and produce scholarly programs in specific contexts. When context-specific variables impede the production of programs, jWPAs produce accounts of such struggles because one *must* progress, one *must* publish whether or not the local situation generously enables or dangerously impedes our intellectual work. Aspiring jWPAs need to anticipate the distance between their theoretical expertise and a publishable record so essential for academic success, especially in institutional contexts where day-to-day, in-house publications are not enough to scaffold the jWPA's tenure case as the first of its kind on campus.

jWPAs must understand the multimodal nature of administrative production. They need to anticipate the challenges of such work, both in terms of total workload and the constraints of producing in complex institutional contexts, where both material and political variables over-determine both the when and the how of their intellectual production.

By further delineating the dimensions of our work through this analytical separation of the material, rhetorical, administrative, and scholarly modes of WPA labor, we may better predict and proactively prepare aspiring administrators to mediate labor relations while yet undergoing their graduate training. To successfully establish complementary relations among the material, the rhetorical, the administrative and the scholarly, one may never imagine that we may pick and choose or that all enjoy equal legitimacy in academia. For jWPAs, overproduction is essential and making a case for our administrative scholarship exacts production beyond other career paths, both because rhetoric and composition remains a nondescript and untested academic enterprise in many contexts and because administrative scholarship departs from academic norms. Making the invisible intellectual work of program administration effectively visible to peers across the discipline is a greater charge, and thus jWPAs need cautious mentoring and deeper and more exhaustive scholarly training, even if such responsible preparation delays one's entry into academia.

DESIRING LABOR AND LABORING UNDER JWPA DESIRE

Mine is both a self-reflexive account of WPA desire having fueled my professional journey to a jWPA appointment as well as a latter-day mapping of administrative labor as I have discovered it. In the summer of 2004, at the WPA conference in Delaware, I defined institutional critique and advocacy—rhetorical work—as necessary if not prior to other modes of our WPA work. Unlike our disciplinary peers who produce more traditional scholarship, jWPAs must speak up and advocate if they are to produce intellectually respectable programs as scholarly products worthy of latter-day publications. After my impassioned talk, I was generously admonished with the following question, "Why are you working so hard? Woman, you need to slow down!"

Still reeling from my delivery, I laughed and replied, "Hmm. I want to keep my job." My immediate response registered the ever-present urgency with which I work to satisfy my administrative desire and fulfill my commitment to field standards and ideals, and to meet local contractual standards of excellence in teaching and research. I work in passionate pursuit of all that, but my answer reduced it all to one compelling need—keeping my job. More fully now, this chapter responsibly answers the question. Much like all other jWPAs and WPAs by design, I work this hard because I still desire administrative work this much, because multimodal administrative production is absolutely integral to the work, and because scholarly administration in rhetoric and composition in the year of 2007 naturally requires me to.

NOTES

[1] No, I do not intend to clean the rug. That said, I need to answer the call for material labor and identify venues for addressing the problem.

[2] The WPA self-study framework surely does not recommend that any one individual deliver all the work it represents. Rather, its fullness serves any WPA and any program as it makes all we do visible for local understanding and appreciation. In this manner, the document intends very good things for the local WPA. I only need offer the following insight—many jWPA appointments by design do assign the work to one individual. Consider the ads posed within our introductory chapter as well as jWPA experiences explored in individual chapters. Many jWPA appointments charge us with actual responsibility for the whole enterprise. Others delimit responsibilities and forecast areas for future growth or latter-day contributions. Because jWPAs do imagine and value a fully realized writing enterprise as mapped in our self-study framework, their administrative desire moves them to further invent, supplement, and extend their programs. A heavier workload is seldom cause enough to check their desire to grow their programs, and serve more fully.

WORKS CITED

Bitzer, Lloyd F. "The Rhetorical Situation." *Philosophy and Rhetoric*. 1 (1968): 1–12.

Bourdieu, Pierre, and Jean-Claude Passeron. *Reproduction in Education, Society and Culture.* 2nd ed. London: Sage Publications, 1990.

"Guidelines for Self-Study to Precede WPA Visit." *The Allyn & Bacon Sourcebook for Writing Program Administrators.* Ed. Irene Ward and William J. Carpenter. New York: Longman, 2002. 388–94.

Gunner, Jeanne. "Collaborative Administration." *The Writing Program Administrator's Resource: A Guide to Reflective Institutional Practice.* Ed. Stuart C. Brown and Theresa Enos. Mahwah, NJ: Lawrence Erlbaum Associates, 2002. 253–62.

Gunner, Jeanne. "Decentering the WPA." *WPA: Writing Program Administration.* 18.1–2 (Fall/Winter 1994): 8–15.

Hesse, Douglas. "The WPA as Father, Husband, Ex." *Kitchen Cooks, Plate Twirlers, and Troubadours: Writing Program Administrators Tell Their Stories.* Ed. Diana George. Portsmouth, NH: Boynton/Cook, 1999. 44–55.

Hult, Christine. "Politics Redux: The Organization and Administration of Writing Programs." *WPA: Writing Program Administration* 18.3 (Spring 1995): 44–52.

Hult, Christine. "The Scholarship of Administration." *Resituating Writing: Constructing and Administering Writing Programs.* Ed. Joseph Janangelo and Kristine Hansen. Portsmouth, NH: Boynton/Cook, 1995. 119–31.

Schell, Eileen. "Part-time/Adjunct Issues: Working Toward Change." *The Writing Program Administrator's Resource: A Guide to Reflective Institutional Practice.* Ed. Stuart C. Brown and Theresa Enos. Mahwah, NJ: Lawrence Erlbaum Associates, 2002. 181–202.

Schuster, Charles. I. "Foreword." *Resituating Writing: Constructing and Administering Writing Programs.* Ed. Joseph Janangelo and Kristine Hansen. Portsmouth, NH: Heinemann/Boynton-Cook, 1995. ix-xiv.

—. "The Politics of Promotion," *The Politics of Writing Instruction: Postsecondary.* Ed. Richard Bullock and John Trimbur. Portsmouth, NH: Boynton/Cook, 1991. 85–95.

Part III

jWPA Efficacy: Matters of Location

7 The Center Will Not Hold:
Redefining Professionalism
in the Academy

Martha D. Patton and Jo Ann Vogt

Our university telephone book identifies no one by the title of "junior writing program administrator," yet the term aptly describes many of us who play second fiddle in first-year writing programs, writing across the curriculum programs, writing centers, and other writing-related initiatives. The two of us addressing you here take the liberty of using the term somewhat differently from the way other contributors to this volume have used it; we use the term "junior writing program administrator" to describe a narrower population (non-tenure-track faculty and professional staff who are in some sense writing program administrators) to address a larger problem: the character of professionalism in the modern university. We two work in the University of Missouri Campus Writing Program, a nationally known writing across the curriculum program;[1] one of us has held a professional staff position for fifteen years; the other has held both professional staff and adjunct professor positions before recently taking a tenure-track position. Both of us believe that the junior positions we hold are more junior than they ought to be, that this university and others across the country are overdue for change.[2] Nonetheless, we believe that from our marginal and sometimes ambiguous positions, junior writing program administrators may have unique opportunities to be productive. We challenge the center to redefine itself more like the margins: we challenge the entire university to more substantively celebrate community, collaboration, and discovery.

In a 1999 issue of *Writing Program Administration,* Kenneth Bruffee critiques WPA identity metaphors based in dualities and self-pity, claiming that there are more nuanced and collaborative ways of viewing power, scholarship, and opportunity (6). Tom Amorose agrees and, quoting David Bell, reminds us that those individuals holding the most power and authority are not necessarily those who have the most influence on the internal operations of a program (89). With important qualifications, we agree. There are some very real dualities that cannot be ignored—namely, the disparities between the tenure track and the non-tenure-track track. That said, we argue that all university professionals eventually need to get beyond existing dualities and create a new standard of academic professionalism for the twenty-first century.

What we want on behalf of all jWPAs and non-tenure-track faculty, then, isn't simply an invitation to climb the existing university ladder, only to find more individual power and better benefits and paychecks; what we want is to change the ladder, to redefine the core values of being an academic in the modern university. We advocate not elimination of all hierarchy, but *elimination of double standards;* we advocate not a rejection of professional standards, but a *redefinition of professional standards.* Specifically, we advocate professional standards that more centrally celebrate community, collaboration and discovery; we advocate professional standards where responsibilities and rights are evenly held in check.

We want first, though, to see the current standards of professionalism with open eyes. By virtue of our ambiguous positions, we non-tenure-track WPAs can paint in broad strokes the strengths and weaknesses of traditionally understood "professionalism," as well as the strengths and weaknesses of traditionally understood "junior status."

"Professionalism" Through the Eyes of Two jWPAs

Professionalism is a term that generally carries a host of connotations (Bledstein, Jarausch, Friedson). On the positive side, professionals are valued for their expertise, advanced education, certification, autonomy, ethical code, and social responsibility. On the negative side, professionals have been criticized for their domination and control of market monopolies, for their cultivation of privilege and self-interest, and for their exclusion of laypersons.

With little difficulty, we can see how these general characteristics of professionalism apply not only to doctors and lawyers, but also to the professoriate, at least tenured faculty. Most large U.S. universities have a two-class system with a regular class of tenure-track faculty and an underclass made up of professionals who often hold credentials and responsibilities more similar to than different from those of their tenure-track colleagues. The rights of this underclass, however, are more different from than similar to those of tenure-track faculty, for professionals in the underclass usually have limited job security, disproportionately lower pay, limited benefits, and, perhaps most of all, little recognition or voice ("A Collaborative Study"). Those in the underclass are likely to hold any number of non-tenure-track or "professional staff" titles.

The problems associated with a two-class system are multiplied for those of us in writing programs since professional staff and non-tenure-track positions are disproportionately associated with writing—with administering writing programs and with teaching, tutoring, and/or consulting within writing programs. Moreover, the problems associated with a two-class system are more keenly felt by women than by men. Those of us who might be called junior writing program administrators are likely to be women and are likely to be part of this academic underclass.

We suspect that most non-tenure-track jWPAs clearly identify with and try to demonstrate the positive qualities of being a professional, but non-tenure-track jWPAs are also keenly aware of the exclusionary tendencies of professionalism, as is evident from the lively, charged discussions about adjunct faculty carried out on listservs and in conferences throughout the country. The authors of this chapter recognize the double-edge to "professional" and wish to re-examine what the term means in the twenty-first century; we especially wish to infuse with new meaning the value of professional responsibility.

We find the current two-track system in academia with its inherent double standards parallel to the postcolonial situation in the late 1770s, at least in one important respect. (We recognize many ways in which the comparison fails.) Certainly, our slave-owning founding fathers were sheepishly aware of their hypocrisy when they failed to accord their slaves citizenship. They knew they were creating a system with double standards that violated the very principles they were espousing for their own class of landowners. They simply did not see how they could afford to buy their slaves' freedom. It would be too expensive. A bloody century or two later, U.S. citizens realized that expense was no excuse for failing to right a fundamental wrong. We call upon leaders of the modern research university to admit the same: cost-savings is not a legitimate excuse for academic slave labor, for professionals who have the responsibilities but not the rights of their tenure-track counterparts.

"Junior Status" Through the Eyes of Two jWPAs

Just as "professionalism" has both positive and negative connotations, "junior status" is a double-edged condition. If *junior* simply means less experienced, non-tenure-track jWPAs should have little to quibble about. In some cases, that's all there is to it: The non-tenure-track jWPA is new and green, someone who will over time earn greater respect and more opportunities. Many non-tenure-track jWPAs, however, are veteran teachers of writing, seasoned by years of working closely with faculty, GTAs, and students, and wise beyond their paychecks. When "junior" is a function not of limited experience, but, again, of double standards in the institution, something is very wrong.

As we see it, this is the problem: Tenure-track faculty tend to have both the rights and responsibilities of professionals, while non-tenure-track faculty and professional staff have, in large part, the responsibilities without the rights. Furthermore, in most writing programs, graduate students are given preference for teaching and administrative assignments over non-tenure-track faculty, suggesting that expertise, advanced education, and certification count little for non-tenure-track faculty. Ironically, then, one marker of a professional "certification" can function as a liability for non-tenure-track faculty. "Junior" signals a problem when it is a code word for someone given professional responsibilities without professional rights.

The Injustice of Double Standards

In a university environment where tenure is the cache for recognition, the lack of material benefits is only part of the problem for non-tenure-track faculty and professional staff. Certainly, most writing instructors and junior writing program administrators want to make a living wage and have decent benefits. But many who work in writing programs weren't drawn to rhetoric and composition by the lure of future pay-checks. Most of us working in rhetoric and composition have an intellectual commitment to the teaching and theorizing of writing and, on some level, wish to be recognized for our intellects. Being ignored or taken for granted is almost as destructive as being underpaid. Who wants to pretend to play second fiddle to some director of record who may not be anywhere near the fiddle? Who wants to work to sustain a program while remaining invisible to the profession beyond the walls of the university?

It might be noted that at a time when approximately one-third of the teaching at many research universities is done by non-tenure-track faculty and professional staff ("A Collaborative Study"), such faculty have little voice in their affairs, literally having no vote in departmental decision making. The disparity between the rights and responsibilities of individuals points to an ethical problem in the larger system. If tenure-track and non-tenure-track faculty have similar credentials (PhDs, MDs, etc.), similar experience (years of research or of teaching) and similar responsibilities (levels of teaching, research, or clinical expectations), but vastly different rights (voting, status, pay, benefits, security), there is a double standard—an unjust and unethical double standard. Something is grievously wrong when universities have two entirely different systems, tenure-track and non-tenure-track, for employing individuals whose credentials are more similar than different. In this respect, the under-recognition of jWPAs is the tail of a much larger beast, of a larger crippled system.

In writing programs, exploitation is most likely to occur when the jWPA has a professional staff position. Almost axiomatically, most staff positions are understood within a labor model, with a sharp division between decision-makers (directors) and workers (everyone else). Job descriptions for professional staff positions must conform to university procedures, which for the most part are premised on a labor model, not an academic model. That is, human resource job descriptions for most "junior" personnel imply that the "junior" staff are workers who report to bosses and merely carry out the assignments defined and mapped out for them. This is far from the reality for most WPAs in professional staff positions, professionals whose credentials are similar to those of their directors but whose rewards and recognition are far different. Often, the work is collaborative, but the recognition for it is not. Even if the tenure-track WPA recognizes contributions made by professional staff, the university is predisposed to credit the fruit of any collaborative effort as the result of good supervision on the part of the director. (Justifiably so, some of the time, but not always.)

While many "professional staff" are in reality autonomous and self-directed (because they are professionals, recognized or not), their self-direction may not be reflected in paychecks or in institutional procedures. Many people in "professional staff" positions are not reviewed by promotion and tenure committees and have few advocates for salary increases; many professionals are neither evaluated nor valued. They must keep electronic if not actual time cards; they must report hours away from the office, and they have no voting rights in the institutions they serve. Ironically, then, people in positions dubbed "professional" are treated as if they in fact are incapable of the self-governance accorded professionals such as tenure-track faculty. In short, the oxymoron "professional staff," like the term "junior" is a coded expression for someone given professional responsibilities without professional rights.

Unsatisfactory Solutions to a University System with Double Standards

Vexing as the labor issues of the modern university are, we don't see the solution as simply a matter of eliminating the tenure system or a matter of eliminating writing program administrators, for we are arguing for a radical reassessment of collaborative productivity. Whether or not tenure is maintained, we would argue that all faculty and professional staff should have the opportunity to be evaluated and rewarded by the same standards—everyone is tenure track or no one is tenure track.

We find unsatisfactory any solution that would only reify a two-class system of senior and junior professionals, with labor unions fighting for better material conditions for the non-tenure-track junior professionals without opening any doors for recognition or influence. (That is, while the authors of this chapter advocate organizing, we caution against organizing along traditional labor lines, which would only reinforce and perpetuate the status quo.) To break out of the current two-tiered system, we advocate radically redefining what it means to be a university professional, perhaps using as a model something like the government G-scale as a basis for restructuring a graded set of expectations and rewards that is still common to all employees.

Others have called for similar kinds of reform, including Glassick et al., researchers who produced a special report for the Carnegie Foundation entitled *Scholarship Assessed: A Special Report on Faculty Evaluation.* Among the professional organizations re-evaluating faculty roles and rewards is the American Association for Higher Education. Consider, for example, Eugene Rice's featured address at the AAHE's January 1996 meeting in Atlanta. We hope to build upon these discussions, but would like to see more sweeping reform.

Before turning to a discussion of professionalism redefined, though, we wish to acknowledge what has been perhaps the most incendiary of recent publications about labor practices in writing programs, Marc Bousquet's "Composition as Management Science: Toward a University without a WPA." We find unsatisfactory any solution that simply dismisses the important work that WPAs do. To address the contemporary management problems in writing programs, Bousquet turns to materialist critical theories—modern-day Marxism—and points to the efforts of teacher unions at New York University, Michigan, and in the California State University system to boost working conditions for writing teachers. He further makes a case for spreading the responsibility for the teaching of writing beyond disciplinary borders.

While Bousquet credits the sincerity of many WPAs, he discredits the ability of WPAs—bosses or managers, as he views them—to lead the charge for "change." This is in part because Bousquet believes that WPAs identify less with the "we" of the rhetoric and composition underclass and more with the "we" of "real faculty" and "faculty-wannabes." As he says, "To that end, my ultimate claim will be that 'change' in composition depends primarily upon the organized voice and collective action of composition labor" (494). This is, in our view, shortsighted, although we agree with Bousquet that something needs to disrupt the status quo and demand the attention of the entire university before material conditions will be changed. Perhaps that "something" will be teacher strikes, but we seek ultimately an attention-getting action that reaches beyond material conditions and attempts to redefine, not reinforce, academic professionalism. To us, organized labor is likely to perpetuate—not eliminate—the double track and double standards that plague the university system right now. Rather than buttress the dividing line between "professor/manager" and "non-tenure-track quasi-professional labor," we call for a new standard

of professionalism that eliminates the double standards of a two-class
system and better rewards collaborative productivity.

The Values of Non-Tenure-Track jWPAs: Community, Collaboration, Discovery

Whatever model is used for restructuring university hierarchies, with
or without tenure, we believe that a new model of professionalism has
much to learn from those of us who have had the privilege of working with colleagues in other disciplines. Those of us who are WPAs
in writing across the curriculum programs often find ourselves at the
crossroads of intellectually stimulating and personally rewarding interdisciplinary work. Our work requires professional self-direction, expertise, and informed judgment, but it is conducted in an atmosphere
that celebrates community, collaboration, and discovery.

jWPAs in WAC programs are naturally positioned to raise questions about stale assumptions in any one discipline; we are positioned
to be the intellectual gadflies that keep academic inquiry alive. For instance, disciplines seldom question their own axioms, but jWPAs can
create discussion forums involving faculty from different disciplines,
who, in that setting, must address the outsiders' questions about foundational assumptions. For example, logicians might not question their
own disciplinary assumptions about the relevance of formal logic to
writing, but jWPAs can create the settings for cross-disciplinary conversation that might generate alternative ways of viewing reasoning,
critical thinking, and informal logic.

Many of us in junior-status positions, whether in WAC programs
or in other writing-related programs, are doing conventional research,
but even when we aren't doing conventional research, we are regularly
collecting and disseminating information. We are regularly making
observations about student writing, other teachers' syllabi and assignments, teachers' writing, teachers' philosophical assumptions, teachers'
presentations, student reception, tutoring, and so forth. In making an
argument that these activities constitute important intellectual work,
we draw on Ernest Boyer's *Scholarship Reconsidered,* the MLA document, "Making Faculty Work Visible," Joseph Janangelo and Kristine
Hansen's *Resituating Writing,* the WPA document describing the intellectual work of WPAs, Charles Glassick, Mary T. Huber, and Gene I.

Maeroff's *Scholarship Assessed,* and, most importantly, Shirley K Rose and Irwin Weiser's *The Writing Program Administrator as Researcher.*

But we would like to stress that this intellectual work is collaborative and only indirectly serves the WPA or jWPA. To be effective, we must be trusted to subordinate our own personal research agendas to a larger institutional good. (We do not need to subordinate "research" broadly and collaboratively understood; we only need to subordinate "research" individually and traditionally if doing the conventional form of research undermines our colleagues' trust in us.) If we aren't trusted, important dialogue and problem-solving will not take place. That is, in our positions as jWPAs, professionalism too narrowly and individually defined would hamper us in doing the very work we need to do. We suspect that professionalism too narrowly defined in the larger institution all too often hampers inquiry there as well, at times fueling turf wars, low faculty morale, and departmental dysfunction.

Several characteristics distinguish much of our less-conventional jWPA research from research that counts for promotion and tenure. One is the genre of communication; another is the venue for "publication"; and still another is who gets the credit for our work. We may write conventional articles for peer-reviewed journals, but in addition, we write arguments in e-mail, in policy reports, in survey designs, in presentation or workshop materials, on web pages, in re-worked assignments, or in conversations and consultations. Our arguments are heard, and they are often documented. But they tend to function locally; they might not be published outside the walls of the university. Our arguments occur in the halls of the English department (or biology department), in university conference halls, and in individual faculty members' offices. Most of our research, whether formal or informal, conventional or unconventional, is intimately related to raising questions and to helping others make discoveries for themselves, if possible. We are directly or indirectly agents of academic inquiry, a kind of inquiry that is rarely recognized outside our local settings despite its benefits for faculty and students.

REDEFINITION OF "PROFESSIONALISM": LEARNING FROM THE MARGINS

Certainly much good research begins when an individual recognizes a problem and continues as that individual works to address that prob-

lem in writing. Clearly, solo-authored papers have a place, and competition and self-interest can contribute to productivity and quality academic research. That said, it is possible to pursue research that serves
an individual's interests without benefiting the common good. And
even when solo-authored research does serve the common good, it's
often more collaborative than meets the eye. For example, to acquire
research time, a researcher may buy out his or her teaching responsibilities by having another professional teach his or her classes, adjuncts
who have professional credentials but not professional pay. WPAs may
do profitable off-site program and departmental consulting, but with
the knowledge that other competent professionals, often non-tenure-
track WPAs, are carrying on the program in their absence, under inferior working conditions and pay. To some degree, constructions of
individual research, individual teaching, and individual administration belie a much larger collaborative debt.

The issue, though, isn't simply a matter of giving recognition where
recognition is due, or for instance, of recognizing the intellectual work
of jWPAs when it is embedded in the intellectual work of WPAs. The
issue also is a matter of celebrating the intellectual pleasure and the
superior results when a group of professionals work together, even if
not in exactly the same ways. It is especially stimulating when several
professionals come from different disciplines and challenge each other
on the level of foundational assumptions. Increasingly, government,
corporate, and nonprofit funding agencies privilege projects that demonstrate this kind of teamwork, and we hope that the university white
papers and promotion and tenure guidelines begin to follow suit.

To illustrate what "professionalism" looks like from the margins,
we offer two case studies, one of Mary Licklider, an administrator of
a grant-writing program, and the other of the authors, assistants in a
WAC program. We hope to show through these two cases that tenure-track professionals often understate their debt to their non-tenure-
track colleagues; that is, we hope to show that most academic professionals tend to work collaboratively, whether or not they acknowledge
it. We also hope to show that openly recognized collaboration can be
joyous and personally rewarding.

THE CASE OF MARY LICKLIDER IN MU's OFFICE OF RESEARCH

Mary Licklider is an University of Missouri (MU) colleague who fits
the oxymoronic definition of a professional staff member. She admin-

isters a writing program of her own making in the office of research; she oversees a staff of ten other grant writers, all of whom she hired and trained according to her own standards. Mary's staff grew by developing a funding plan whereby her office of research set aside a 50 percent FTE salary one year and offered to match funds for any unit or department interested in having its own grant writer. Faculty in medicine first wondered what good a grant writer with limited scientific training would be. As faculty started to see the results that Mary's team was getting, more and more units started applying for their own writers. As her reports indicate: "In 2002–03, grant writers supported over 100 proposals requesting over $89 million. Awards during 2002–03 for proposals supported by grant writers totaled $30.6 million. This represents over a 150-fold return on the Office of Research investment of $175,000 in the grant writing part of the Office of Grant Writing and Publications."

Mary is a professional with a PhD. She is "junior," though, given that she holds a professional staff position. Mary's advice is sought after, but the respect accorded her is despite her professional staff appointment, not because of it. She earned her respect.

Mary doesn't function as a gofer, matching faculty with recent calls for proposals. She is actively engaged in academic inquiry. She writes; she consults; she delves into subject matter. She is a master rhetor who helps faculty throughout the university become more adept at analyzing calls for proposals and writing purposefully and convincingly for specific audiences. Mary is not officially credited with teaching or research, yet she teaches and researches every day, and her intellectual work is embedded in the teaching and research of scores of faculty members who are credited with teaching and research.

She and her staff meet and work with faculty in disciplines ranging from medicine to engineering to education to biology. They collaborate internally as well, teaming up in different combinations for various purposes.

Mary does advocate actively for better pay and working conditions for her staff of grant writers, and she does feel the injustice of the current two-track system with regular faculty on one side and non-tenure-track and professional staff on the other. Nonetheless, Mary knows that her work is part of a larger research cause. Her intellectual output is enormous; nonetheless, it is motivated less by self-interest than community interests.

The Case of Jo Ann Vogt and Marty Patton
in the Campus Writing Program

We in the Campus Writing Program believe that our own intellectual work is embedded in the larger teaching and research community, too. We would like to think that a number of MU faculty publications about writing (in natural resources, nursing, environmental design, journalism, and mechanical engineering) were at least encouraged if not inspired by our work in the Campus Writing Program. From time to time, we have gladly served as behind-the-scenes editors for faculty publications, from peer-reviewed journal articles to scholarly books. We note that a majority of the recipients of our campus's most prestigious teaching award, the Kemper, have been affiliated with our program. Over the years, many of those Kemper winners have sought our help with assignment design, paper grading, peer review—even, occasionally, with the public addresses they have delivered at the ceremonies honoring their contributions to MU.

We pay attention to our colleagues' experiments with writing; we notice and call further attention to important teaching initiatives. The brown bag sessions we regularly sponsor not only recognize faculty achievements but encourage idea exchange and collaboration across departments. One exceptionally fruitful session immediately prompted math department faculty to schedule follow-up meetings with one another; within forty-eight hours of another brown bag, a teacher from consumer and family economics adapted a biology professor's goldfish-bowl discussion technique to enhance both participation and understanding. Our efforts to ensure equitable grading across multiple sections of some writing-intensive courses have led to revised evaluation criteria, clearer assignments, and one-to-one training sessions for graduate TAs assisting in writing-intensive courses. At least one department on campus has "adopted" one of us, allowing a warts-and-all view of a large-enrollment writing-intensive class and encouraging participation in the planning and execution of the course. Not only is our WPA work embedded in other faculty members' work, we relish what we do.

The joy of collaborative work at the Campus Writing Program wasn't born overnight, but it is something that we feel is integral to the CWP and something that visitors frequently comment upon. Faculty dropping by hear laughter and conversation in our suite of offices; they often find our quarters a friendly refuge where someone is always eager to listen to teachers talking about teaching. While the WPA, Martha Townsend, and we two jWPAs have different talents, we recognize and build on each other's strengths. The effectiveness of one of our traditional workshop segments is tied to the delight one of us takes in leading a wide-ranging discussion of using writing as a teaching tool. Other segments are rooted in other staff members' gifts for generating practical, easy-to-use handouts that summarize years of hard-won classroom know-how.

After faculty workshops, participants frequently note that we obviously work as a team and that we play well together. That collaborative spirit infuses everything we do. None of us is comfortable sending out significant writing without subjecting it to each other in our own in-house peer review. We serve as each other's mentors, prodders, critics, encouragers, and writing coaches. We trust one another to ask the hard questions that demand honest, sometimes uncomfortable, answers. We mull over each other's ideas and to a large extent subordinate personal advancement to the wellbeing of the writing program and the university. Collegiality, confidentiality, and professionalism trump selfish interests when we might have a personal stake in a researchable question. In short, our in-house interactions and our collaborative, supportive work with faculty model exactly the kind of cooperative, mutually beneficial relationships that we believe should replace the competitive, segregated, almost universally accepted academic model.

IMPLICATIONS FOR THE SHORT AND LONG TERM

While non-tenure-track WPAs model an ideal of social responsibility, we cannot sacrifice ourselves in the process. One way to protect ourselves in the short term is to offer a corrective to simplistic representations of WAC and first-year English programs. Most books on WAC, for example, have done an excellent job laying a foundation for WAC principles and have provided a much-needed overview of selected WAC programs. Among the visionary and pioneering texts that have made subsequent theorizing of WAC possible are Susan H. McLeod's *Strengthening Programs for Writing Across the Curriculum*, Toby Fulwiler and Art Young's *Programs that Work: Models and Methods for Writing Across the Curriculum*, and Susan H. McLeod and Margot Soven's *Writing Across the Curriculum: A Guide to Developing*

Programs. More recent titles include McLeod and Soven's *Composing a Community: A History of WAC* and Bazerman et al.'s *Reference Guide to Writing Across the Curriculum.* Nonetheless, as Jeanne Gunner argues in both "Decentering the WPA" and "Identity and Location: A Study of WPA Models, Memberships, and Agendas," most literature on WAC inadvertently perpetuates the myth that writing programs are individual constructions. Furthermore, even when the WAC literature explicitly acknowledges that writing programs seldom are the work of one director, there is usually a gap between the public perception and program reality. WAC consultants must speak up to close this gap.

Among those who have been speaking up are Jeffrey A. Jablonski, whose dissertation describes and analyzes the scholarly work involved in academic writing consulting, and Joan Mullin, Neil Reid, Doug Enders, and Jason Baldridge, who complicate reductive ideas about writing program administration and scholarship in "Constructing Each Other: Collaborating Across Disciplines and Roles." Their arguments about writing professionals follow in the vein of other arguments about the scholarship of teaching and administration, such as that of Boyer, the MLA and the WPA mentioned previously.

We must continue to make visible the intellectual work of administration. We may need to brace ourselves for short-term crisis since "creative tension" is sometimes necessary to call sufficient attention to a problem, particularly the massive problem of under-recognized and underpaid adjunct teachers. But the long-term changes we advocate are ones that involve making the center more like the margins rather than the margins more like the center. From our perspective, jWPAs have something to celebrate: We not only wish to retain our values of community, collaboration, and discovery, we pressure the larger academy to participate in our professional ethic. To the degree that the larger academy already participates in communal and collaborative activity, it needs to disclose more of the collaborative activity and to reward the contributors according to their contributions. To not do so is to perpetuate unjust labor policies and a questionable portrait of professionalism.

NOTES

[1]The Campus Writing Program at the University of Missouri was recognized as a successful writing program in its 1993 external review, was cited

as one of sixteen best writing in the disciplines programs in the *US News & World Report*'s "America's Best Colleges 2005," <http://usnewscom.usnews/eu/college/rankings/acadprogs08_brief.php>, and received the 2004 CCCC Writing Program Certificate of Excellence.

[2] We write from two perspectives. As two members of a three-member team, we feel fortunate to work in a warm, mutually supportive environment, something we hope to make abundantly clear later in this chapter. If we are under-recognized, it is not because Martha Townsend, our program director, fails to support us. All three of us, though, are situated in a larger institutional context that acts through and upon us. It is toward this larger system that we direct our criticism.

WORKS CITED

Amorose, Thomas. "Work at the Small College or University: Re-Imagining Power and Making the Small School Visible." *WPA: Writing Program Administration* 23.3 (2000): 85–103.

Bazerman, Charles, et al. eds. *Reference Guide to Writing Across the Curriculum*. West Lafayette, IN: Parlor P, 2005.

Bell, David V. J. *Power, Influence, and Authority: An Essay in Political Linguistics*. New York: Oxford UP, 1975.

Bledstein, Burton J. *The Culture of Professionalism: The Middle Class and the Development of Higher Education in America*. New York: Norton, 1976.

Boyer, Ernest L. *Scholarship Reconsidered: Priorities of the Professoriate*. The Carnegie Foundation for the Advancement of Teaching. San Francisco, CA: Jossey-Bass, 1990.

Bousquet, Marc. "Composition as Management Science: Toward a University without a WPA." *Journal of Advanced Composition* 22.3 (Summer 2002): 493–526.

Bruffee, Kenneth. "Thoughts of a Fly on the Wall." *WPA: Writing Program Administration* 22.3 (1999): 55–64.

"A Collaborative Study of Undergraduate Faculty." Coalition on the Academic Workforce, a Group of 25 Academic Societies: Who Is Teaching In U.S. College Classrooms? 2000. 5 April 2007 <http://www.historians.org/caw/pressrelease.htm>.

Council of Writing Program Administrators. "Evaluating the Intellectual Work of Writing Administration." *WPA: Writing Program Administration* 22.1–2 (1998): 85–104.

Friedson, Eliot. *The Professions and Their Prospects*. London: Sage, 1973.

Fulwiler, Toby, and Art Young, eds. *Programs that Work: Models and Methods for Writing Across the Curriculum*. Portsmouth, NH: Boynton/Cook, 1990.

Glassick, Charles E., Mart T. Huber, and Gene I. Maeroff. *Scholarship Assessed: Evaluation of the Professoriate.* San Francisco: Jossey-Bass, 1997.

Gunner, Jeanne. "Decentering the WPA." *WPA: Writing Program Administration* 18 (1994): 8–15.

—. "Identity and Location: A Study of WPA Models, Memberships, and Agendas." *WPA: Writing Program Administration* 22.3 (1999): 31–54.

Jablonski, Jeffrey A. *Reconceiving Interdisciplinary Collaboration: Locating the Intellectual Work of Writing Across the Curriculum Consultants.* Diss. Purdue U, 2000.

Janangelo, Joseph, and Kristine Hansen, eds. *Resituating Writing: Constructing and Administering Writing Programs.* Portsmouth, NH: Boynton/Cook, 1995.

Jarausch, Konrad H. *German Professions, 1800–1950.* Ed. Geoffrey Cocks and Konrad H. Jarausch. New York: Oxford UP, 1990.

Licklider, Mary. "Grant Writing Services." MU Office of Research Brochure. Columbia: University of Missouri, 2004.

McLeod, Susan H., ed.. *Strengthening Programs for Writing Across the Curriculum.* San Francisco: Jossey-Bass, 1988.

McLeod, Susan H., and Margot Soven, eds. *Composing a Community: A History of Writing Across the Curriculum.* West Lafayette, IN: Parlor P, 2006

—. *Writing Across the Curriculum: A Guide to Developing Programs.* Newbury Park, CA: Sage, 1992.

MLA Commission on Professional Service. "Making Faculty Work Visible: Reinterpreting Professional Service, Teaching and Research in the Fields of Language and Literature" *Profession 1996.* New York: MLA, 1996. 161–216.

Mullin, Joan, Neil Reid, Doug Enders, and Jason Baldridge. "Constructing Each Other: Collaborating Across Disciplines and Roles." *Weaving Knowledge Together: Writing Centers and Collaboration.* Ed. Carol Peterson Haviland, Maria Notarangelo, Lene Whitley-Putz, and Thia Wolf. Emmitsburg, MD: NWCA Press, 1998. 152–71.

Rice, R. Eugene. "Faculty Caught Between the Times: Making a Place for the New American Scholar." Fourth AAHE Conference on Faculty Roles and Rewards. Atlanta, GA. 20 Jan. 1996.

Rose, Shirley K, and Irwin Weiser. *The Writing Program Administrator as Researcher: Inquiry in Action and Reflection.* Portsmouth NH: Boynton/Cook, 1999.

WPA Executive Committee. "Evaluating the Intellectual Work of Writing Program Administrators: A Draft." *WPA: Writing Program Administration* 20.1–2 (1996): 92–103.

8 Demystifying the Asian-American WPA: Locations in Writing, Teaching, and Program Administration

Joseph Eng

Rhetoric and composition and my own professional experience of two decades continue to reveal how our critical discussion of authority and voice is rarely situated within the Asian-American academic sphere (Chiang "Insider/Outsider/Other?" 159; Braine). It is imperative that we as a field develop a critical consciousness of the nontraditional professionals crucial to the discussion of identity politics as a post-process interest (Tobin, Chiang, Sciachitano, Johnson, Prendergast). I observe that, first, just as WPA as a professional category stands for the great variety of college writing program or center coordinators, the esoteric Asian-American WPA could represent a growing number of nonwhite or nonnative English PhDs now serving as writing program administrators. Very different people occupy the WPA camp, just as very different people make up the nonwhite, nonnative group. While recent threads on the WPA-L listserv continue to problematize the location of WPA as an issue of authority, the Asian-American WPA remains largely an unknown location.

The increasing number of nonwhite, non-native-speaking students most noticeable in the 1980s and 1990s complicates our understanding of authority. What seems surprising is that nonwhite students do not necessarily accept their nonwhite English professors as their legitimate teachers; these instructors are still regarded as not native, trained, or reliable enough to be teaching them English (Chiang "Insider/ Outsider/ Other?" 159; Braine). Not unlike Sansei in America (Mura), non-native, Asian-American roles as English faculty are unimagined. Such a phenomenon becomes interestingly complex in writing instruction and, hence, writing program administration.

Following earlier advocates involved in the Bay Area Writing Project and its outgrowth, the National Writing Projects, NCTE has asked writing teachers to practice the art and craft of writing and to write alongside their students for personal and pedagogical purposes. According to research in basic writing, composition students writing in the margins struggle to emerge in contexts of academic discourse. Therefore, non-native, nonwhite writing professors might occupy a crucial position; at the same time they begin to chart unimagined roles as English faculty, their own reading and writing could, in turn, help students develop their voices and further engage their learning interest. From this vantage point, the Asian-American WPA—as a teacher and curriculum coordinator—could play an even more influential role.

Responding to feminist WPAs' critique of rhetoric and composition as dominant culture (Dickson) and the need for body-mind unification (hooks), this chapter explores how specific locations are necessary to enable, collectively and holistically, an agency for the Asian-American WPA. Based on the increasingly significant interrelationships among teacher identity, writing pedagogy, and writing program administration, I will argue for a positioning of the Asian-American WPA within the writing, teaching, and administrative spheres as preferred locations.

Lived Experiences of "Other"

As "lived experiences of 'other,'" the following narrative captures what might be *commonly* shared by Asian-Americans teaching college English or administering college writing programs. If personal, together they seem to suggest broadly discipline-based and admittedly awkward moments. Eschewing the victim narrative, this chapter presents these experiences as just the opposite—as small victories at preferred locations.

Twenty years ago when I was a beginning MA student in English in a large southern university, a professor in the department told me that a better major for me would be "something in international relations." I would "benefit more [from such a major]," he said, at a writing lab where I worked as a tutor. When I began teaching college composition in the Midwest as a graduate teaching assistant, most people on and off campus assumed that I was pursuing a degree in TESOL (or applied linguistics, an entirely different specialty) instead of any other subspecialties within English Studies. Other assumptions were actually contradictory to each other, including my assumed expertise in grammar and my need for further education in grammar and usage. Still, to many of these people, I was an "assistant" instead of the "instructor of record."

In 1992, when I began my first full-time position at a community college in the upper Midwest, a student mumbled, "There is your teaching Ching," as I quietly walked past the crowd. In an otherwise favorite class of mine, a seemingly well-intentioned student told me during break that he really thought that I should work in fields such as "translation" or "international business." (It certainly brought back memories of the southern university professor's comment.)

In several English classes I have taught in the Midwest, West, and Northwest, it was not unusual for a few students to ask me, as they walked into the room on the first day, "Is this an English class?" Apparently good-natured colleagues wonder if I had a good "reception" in class.

Having been writing program administrator at two different institutions, I sometimes wonder how issues regarding my communication, authority, and career choice in general might be shaped by my ethnic identity or identities perceived. For instance, some colleagues or graduate students seem to scrutinize every memo I send out—even under informal circumstances—for usage or idiomatic perfection. To many new acquaintances, why and how I have become an English faculty member are their only greeting lines. (Now I realize the irony that I am either regarded as a trained grammarian by some or an ESL learner who really needs to be corrected by others.) Then, of course, there are always well-intentioned people wanting to "fill me in" before I make every administrative decision.

Returning to the United States from a trip abroad in 1999 (a pre-September 11th era), I proceeded with my wife through customs at L.A. International Airport before connecting back to Spokane, Washington. Exhausted from the long flight, I did not think twice when answering the question from a customs officer: What do you do for a living? A well-built Caucasian man in his forties, uniformed, he sat rather casually on a stool while processing the line of "Permanent

Resident/Citizen" at an average of a person per minute. I, wearing an olive-colored suede jacket on top of a white T-shirt, answered matter-of-factly, "I teach English." He seemed surprised, then continued, "How about this?" pointing at the two printed letters, my (original) last name as "Ng," on the customs declaration form. Without waiting to hear what I had to respond, he said, "It's a joke. You have a nice day." I quickly proceeded for the connection. But, in my mind, the typical question reappeared, almost expectedly, regarding my name and my declared profession.

Would all these encounters have been the same had I been native and white? Probably not. From all these places as "other," nonetheless, I have been given several forums, including this one, to explore the topic of identity. There must be a reason for my more legitimate professional existence in the twenty-first century. Within rhetoric and composition, it would be meaningful if, as a WPA, I could also theorize my identity as a series of locations within contexts of writing, teaching, and program administration. Strategically, they position the nontraditional teacher-scholar-administrator as an agent for change.

THE WRITER LOCATION: THE ASIAN-AMERICAN WPA AS WRITER

There is very little doubt that a WPA should also be a practicing writer. Whether compositionists like Elbow could convince us further about the necessary twin identity, such as the hyphenated student-writer or the teacher-writer, the WPA-writer is a useful location. Professionally and privately (in body-mind unification), the writer location seems to have demystified my identity as an Asian-American WPA practicing writing and helping others with writing.

Despite the long line of immigrant relatives I did not discover until my late teen years, "Asian-American" was a literary term or identity category introduced to me by my Minnesotan professor within an undergraduate literature course. In other words, the frequently anthologized fiction of Kingston, Tan, and other writers and poets of non-European descent became my first Asian-American images or even heroes or heroines. Asian-American remained mostly a literary or writerly interest throughout my college education. This intellectual construct, instead of a visual marker, obviously continued as I finished graduate school and later developed myself as an English professor and then a WPA. Naturally, then, there has always been an interlocking relationship among my professional identity, literary studies, and, ultimately, writing.

As an Asian professional, my writerly role positions me rather expediently within and outside the classroom, and I share my writing, both topic-wise and process-wise, whenever and wherever I can. "So what did you write about?" A colleague's friend asked at the recent Christmas party, and I answered, "Well, given my job where I wear many hats, I tend to write about professional topics such as assessing and teaching writing, but lately I have been able to finish a couple of pieces on identity politics and its pedagogical implications." (She seemed genuinely interested, even though her interest finally waned when I offered to copy her once the pieces go to press.)

Like many WPAs at work, I have perhaps written too many memos, reports, and statements; unlike some of them, perhaps, I continue to monitor how bureaucratic writing, too, is a long-term learning process for me regarding its "American" conventions and rhetorics. If sounding more native now, my memos and reports have become terser, with mechanics and idiomatic issues perfected. As with more serious academic writing, I use drafts and benefit from feedback. After all, I remember clearly how my very first WPA memo, a page-long arrival statement introducing myself at a small school in southern Ohio, was taken home by a new fellow colleague to share with her unemployed husband and later became a topic in her private circle. She found it unnecessarily personal, long, and, of course, at times unidiomatic. I had thought it was meant to be a personal introduction to my composition colleagues, who were mostly adjunct faculty, seldom interacting with an Asian person before. And I was partially right, given the only question one long-term (i.e., respected) adjunct had asked was about whether Asians continued to consume different herbal medicines for sexual prowess. But, I learned my lesson.

I have also learned to share my academic manuscript experience as a social, professional, and sometimes politicized process, so that my students (and colleagues) could view me as *a practicing writer*. In order to produce an effective text, the manuscript writer assesses and reassesses the task, experiments with words, and meets topical and rhetorical demands based on perceived conventions and targeted forum. This writer transacts among parties, going through stages of revision from author-based, to peer-based, and finally to editor-based as the result of a blind-review process. My ethnic appearance or demeanor, then, reemerges as *a fellow writer* who evolves in the common space broadly called composition and writing about composition.

This ongoing process of rhetorical revision is reinforced in a visible WPA-modeling environment—with an identity twist. For the experience essay assignment in English 101, for instance, I bring my draft (summarized in the following) as a teacher-modeling piece for the very first peer-review session of the pre-fall teaching workshop. As we will see, such a practice facilitates a multifaceted introduction: I, a non-native born Asian, WPA; their fellow E101 instructor, "teaching coach"/ colleague; they, mostly native-born caucasians, graduate teaching assistants (GTAs defined by the contract), professors of E101 (perhaps "young" and "inexperienced" by their students' observation), emerging scholars in our field, or unemployed persons in the challenging economy. (Over the year, some GTAs have replaced the sign "teaching assistant" with "writing instructor" on their doors.)

For the draft I brought to my composition classes and the TA workshop last year, I recaptured a "moving" experience in southern Ohio. As newcomers looking for a house to buy, my wife and I were greeted with subtle and uncomfortable remarks on race. During an open-house visit, the owner cheerfully boasted her premium, quiet neighborhood, but casually injected that the house across the street was occupied by a black family, adding "*but*" they were "nice too." "And you know how sometimes you don't see people's color," she continued. And my wife and I wondered if she saw us as "Asian," and, if we did not intend to buy her house, were we "nice" too? Beyond the obvious newcomer's experience in nearly rural southern Ohio, my personal essay aimed at unveiling the ever-existing race factor in our thinking.

Anonymous copies of the draft were made for the class workshop. These new instructors or GTAs then marked up my writing as a peer draft for further discussion. Many seemed to appreciate the racial understatement lurking in the essay, which they found truthful in the twenty-first century. "No name-calling or yelling across the street, and yet it happens daily in our society," Carla, a white student, noted. Jenna, her black group member, agreed. Many asked that the author elaborate the concluding line, "The year was 1996, about 30 years after the civil rights movement. Education is the single most important thing in our lives." I had to admit that it was a bit brief, if not abrupt.

As an active workshop participant, I considered their suggestions and ended up incorporating most of them in my revision process.

Hence when undergraduate students ask if they are in the "English" class and graduate students wonder if I am their "supervisor," I have responses. Instead of dwelling on their usual surprises during the first week, these students begin to imagine me as soon as I start writing with them. Within a *short* period of time, they will know me as a fellow writer who contributes frequently and conscientiously to class and whose writing is well publicized. Colleagues, likewise, have learned to greet me as a fellow writing teacher who practices writing regularly. Intentionally and practically, my writerly presence enriches the visual presence, which is professionally and pedagogically sound.

THE TEACHING LOCATION: THE ASIAN-AMERICAN WPA AS FACULTY OF COLOR AND FEMINIST

Quite inadvertently, my knowledge about WPA work began with reading the satirical, "I Want a Writing Director" by Lynn Z. Bloom. Through Elizabeth Flynn, Sue Ellen Holbrook, and Susan Miller, I have read about the field's feminization since the 1980s. As recently as 2002, Laura R. Micciche theorized the emotion-laden aspects of WPA work; in 2005, the WPA-L listserv continues to explore the WPA context, affect, and authority. Formerly mentored by Gail Hawisher and a few other national female figures, I realize that I must be shaped by their theoretical perspectives, professional roles, and work. Together, might the Asian-American WPA, the "faculty of color" (a subject location Victor Villanueva writes about), and the academic feminist march side-by-side politically and practically? Based on their arguably shared counter-hegemonic agenda and growing influences, I am quite convinced of the need of such a philosophical camaraderie and of its possibility. As a teacher coordinator, I confess an interest in this possible alignment and ponder its pedagogical implications.

In practice, Eileen Schell defines feminism as a broad label for a particular pedagogy, a research methodology, a rhetoric, and a social/political critique (97). Particularly related to this section would be feminist pedagogical methods, which Schell summarizes as an emphasis on personal voice, shared pedagogical authority, and collaboration. Fresh out of graduate school in 1992, I subscribed immediately to an eclectic pedagogy that addresses equality and equity. What I also desired was an epistemological position that could make sense of my experience as an Asian teaching English. Academic feminism seems to appeal to my need. bell hooks's theory of marginality and marginalization points to how a rhetor's location actually informs rhetoric and the types of rhetoric produced (Foss, Foss, and Trapp 283–84). At all levels, her theory explicitly takes into account race, gender, and class. For hooks, marginality becomes a "site of radical possibility, a space of resistance [. . .] a central location for the production of a counterhegemonic discourse" (qtd. in Foss, Foss, and Trapp 272). She legitimizes personal experience by asserting that in "certain circumstances, experience affords us a privileged critical location from which to speak," and rhetors, accordingly, with particular identities employ a "passion of experience" that "cannot be acquired through books or even distanced observation and study of a particular reality (qtd. in Foss, Foss, and Trapp 273)." To hooks, then, direct experience can be "the most relevant way to apprehend reality (qtd. in Foss, Foss, and Trapp 273)." Following hooks's subjectification of the black female's experience, the Asian-American WPA could further develop an epistemological standpoint by reflecting on his or her own Asian-American otherness.

Chiang argues that one should not treat the comment, "How can a Chinese teach you English?" lightly, because it reminds her, a woman of color, of other examples of marginalization like my own experience of being the "other." Although her doctorate is in rhetoric and composition, she is always perceived as an ESL teacher (requiring a different degree). Like a mystery, many have misread her professional identity without hearing from her first. At a faculty meeting in another university, her friend's colleague once argued that non-native speakers should not be awarded English degrees because they would become English teachers ("In the World of English" 27). Chiang views these phenomena collectively as a manifestation of entrenched Eurocentricity. Susan Jarratt and bell hooks, Eileen Schell posits, address such an entrenchment by "[representing] feminism as an oppositional pedagogy designed to boldly and unapologetically confront—rather than avoid—issues of gender, race, class, and sexuality" (Schell 99). Similarly, I consider direct experience a resource and the application of such as a necessary part of critical classroom discourse.

Confronting history involving non-native born English faculty of color, or the lack of such, former WPA and English department chair Villanueva makes the needed connection between tradition and change. "Hegemony exploits traditions," and he reminds us:

> The American Freireista can at least provide a way for students to discover those traditions that are in need of change. We can have students discover the traditions that form the foundations of the academy while simultaneously promoting and instigating change in the ideologies that shape the academy. Tradition and change for changes in tradition. ("Considerations" 633)

His design calls for a needed classroom space for the "dialectic between hegemony and counterhegemony, between tradition and change" to take place (qtd. in George 100). Villanueva's course has students read one canonical and one noncanonical text, discuss any relevance to their lived experiences, and then write about it. Finally, students write in a sequenced assignment about conflicts they have had to confront and to examine the sources of those conflicts. As a result, he argues that, "the dialectic might have students know the tradition critically, not only to acquire the literate, academic culture but to recognize their often antagonistic relationships to it" ("Considerations" 635). Ultimately, his belief is that "[a] dialectic between tradition and change would provide the means for access, acknowledge the political, all the while avoiding propaganda" ("Considerations" 635). In reflection, Villanueva captures a major slice of the faculty of color's growth:

> He [American mainland-born, of Puerto Rican ancestry] has gained access but not much power. He abides by rules his coworkers don't even recognize as rules, rules of a system created by, peopled by, serviced by, and changed by, members of cultures and classes and histories much different from his own; systems created and maintained by those whose memories do not include having been colonized. He is often taken aback by how his co-workers think: worldviews radically different from his own. Yet he struggles to join in the conversation with the privileged whose senses of decency compel them to seek equity for those who have been traditionally excluded from the main-

stream of society and from the academic tributary.
Sometimes he thinks he's heard. ("Considerations"
623)

This biographical portrait seems to position the faculty of color in the
postmodern twenty-first century quite strategically. Born and raised in
the former British Hong Kong, I received my graduate education in the
United States and have gone through periods of cultural clashes and
crises. Empathically, visibly, and practically, the Asian-American WPA
has close colleagues in the faculty-of-color camp supported, for example, by different diversity initiatives and caucuses at the Conference on
College Composition and Communication.

Like their feminist colleagues and fellow faculty of color who seek
to eradicate marginalization by embracing one's culture and history
as an academic vantage point or *resource,* Asian-American WPAs and
their GTAs negotiate a world of growing opportunities, sometimes,
amidst a dominant culture that has an uncomplicated understanding of identity and race. As illustrated in this section, I now offer my
stories, writing, and thinking about who I am, where I have been,
and what I am doing and thinking, to whomever is willing to listen,
see, and learn about the Asian experience. These necessary confessions
could transform themselves into pedagogy by employing personal
writing in the classroom, into professional conversation by encouraging reflection and analysis, and certainly into composition studies by
informing research methodologies and identity politics.

THE ADMINISTRATOR LOCATION: THE ASIAN-AMERICAN WPA AS A POSTMODERNIST

National graduate programs have been increasingly concerned about
the culture of the academic workplace (see MLA's *Profession* from
2000 to 2002). Recent English PhD programs' postmodern empha-
ses notwithstanding, the job candidate needs to reposition his or her
postmodern self in the modern academic setting. (In "On Syllabi,"
Villanueva calls the present time PME, the PostModernEra, in a
memorandum he wrote to his TAs.) Beset by familiar budget short-
falls, the modern institution seems more interested in industry-driven
outcomes and budget-oriented goals than soliciting different or differing dialogues or empowering students. This phenomenon, it seems,

forces the new faculty or WPA to reflect on her or his ideology of location along a spectrum of roles, ranging from the intertextual, dialogic, or even antifoundational position on one extreme and the outcomes-based, budget-driven, and uniformity-minded position on the other. Understanding "our evolving field, our priorities, and the changes in writing instruction and administration," as Bishop and Crossley remind us, is most important so that it would be possible for us to avoid "our own misunderstanding" that could perpetuate the story of victimization (78). Understanding the broader nature of university administration, and how WPA work is situated within that administration, Micciche argues, helps us deal with disappointment constructively (454).

As I moved beyond lower-division instruction in the community college, I came across the "Story of Stopping" in *WPA: Writing Program Administration* in 1996. The story captures the authors' multiple identities within the department hierarchy and among university faculty as Bishop manages to maintain personal integrity over program quality, staffing, and the value of rhetoric and composition. While Bishop keeps daily time logs and journal narratives, Crossley responds by categorizing and tabulating notable issues raised in the entries. Throughout the story, Bishop confronts clashes between a prescribed "managerial" function vs. her desired "educational" function, and between a "respected" program vs. a "quiet" program. She also realizes her odds of success, having to work with male administrators both within the department and beyond. As a female faculty administrator begging for resources, efforts of which are easily dismissed or occluded by decision makers, she is very concerned for the quality of her program and the welfare of staff members. With her colleague, she theorizes journal keeping as a systematic way to analyze narratives by writing program administrators and teachers, thus legitimizing not only storytelling but also the feministic, or simply *the personal,* as feminist scholars Flynn, Worsham, Kirsch, and Ritchie embrace.

As writing program administrator in a regional, comprehensive university, I inherited six years ago a mid-size program of one hundred and sixty sections of writing and forty staff members, including graduate teaching assistants, lecturers, and adjunct faculty. As the program had characterized uniformity, the first year my job emphasized "training" rather than "education." Bureaucratic but necessary WPA duties also included scheduling, budgeting, hiring, and staff evaluation. Apparently one of the challenges was to balance what should be done professionally and what could be done locally. While the balancing act is a common challenge for any new hire, as a new WPA I needed to go beyond connecting theory to practice in designing curriculum and conducting workshops.

I have learned, instead, to understand how modern institutions do not necessarily care about the postmodern perspectives newer PhDs sometimes bring to the job. As Bishop and Crossley indicate, institutions hire WPAs to "manage" academic programs rather than to "educate" (75). Administrators are more impressed with consistently high enrollment numbers and pass rates than, for example, critical pedagogy. Critiques of any kind are not really encouraged. Yet, we can not afford to be just "modern" managers. For instance, how might we as newer WPAs accommodate outcomes that may not be quantifiable? How might race and ethnicity, a post-process interest, influence the teaching of writing, if at all? (An anonymous survey I devised about how my ethnicity "might affect" students' "learning composition," for instance, was called into question secretly—by a department secretary responsible for copying—and finally pulled by my former chair in Colorado. The survey, originally planned as a part of end-of-term self-assessment, included questions such as: "What was your first impression of me as your instructor?" and "What kind/s of impact, if any at all, did my identity have on your writing in this course?" I was told rather directly that "surveys like that are simply asking if students are racists." In other words, it was not a matter of improving my tool for an informal study on writing pedagogy or identity politics, but rather a simple "no" from the chair to the untenured faculty in a college already obsessed with faculty assessment and management.) Where, then, do we find the space to talk about alternate questions?

A thread of discussion on the WPA-L listserv once asked if our students are "subliterate." Some list members took offense at the concept since current generations tend to e-mail, send text messages, and hyper-read in multi-mediated environments "all the time." How might the current first-year-composition curriculum consider the other modes of reading and writing, perhaps, arguably, as competing literacies? Even when postmodern angles open new and unimagined space for critical examination and discussion, do budget authorizing agents such as our deans, vice-presidents, and provosts understand such issues? How does asking or not asking alternate questions affect our career as newer

WPAs? For me personally, these questions are even more critical when junior faculty become tenured and senior. The final and real question then must remain an ethical one—the tenured WPA needs to remember all of these issues, continue with the dialogic and sometimes critical conviction, and follow up. As a teacher-coordinator or pedagogy specialist, the postmodern WPA struggles with similar challenges.

The full strengths and benefits of the postmodern, especially in composition pedagogy, are yet to be fully realized or recorded. At the heart of the challenge lies the irony of encouraging classroom dialogue and student autonomy on the one hand, while reinforcing formal academic discourse on the other. Most writing programs, for instance, endorse thesis-driven classic argumentation. As a newer WPA, I have been asked to review the program, implement the curriculum, and assume a central role in preparing new teaching assistants for the program. One significant challenge I face is to connect the new program to the old one, introducing national topics while recognizing local needs. And yet, with a graduate education from the 1990s, I had difficulty understanding the old program, which called for absolute uniformity, including a common daily agenda, an argumentative exit essay, and weekly program assignments. Before I could implement the program, some repositioning helped.

I realized that when I need to make fundamental changes, I should reconsider the phrase "practicing the writing process" based on the program's "Shared Criteria" emphasizing generalized rhetorical skills. While I situate process (and product) in the classroom as most compositionists do, I see practice as only *one* of the many needed curriculum components. (See Lindemann's "Three Views of English 101.") I also knew that my overview aligned itself more with things postmodern; for example, courses could have less emphasis on assessment and more on the dialogic or personal; discourse would include both print and nonprint media; and lecturers and graduate teaching assistants could help inform or even shape our program themselves.

Following the decentering models Jeanne Gunner and Marcia Dickson propose respectively, I have established a composition committee with graduate and undergraduate student representatives, encouraged summer instructors to adopt their desirable texts and pilot new curricular designs, and labored as a team for the design of a portfolio-based exit exam (of which the argumentative/persuasive essay is only one of the multiple entries). With graduate students I am now perfecting the language in the rubric used to assess portfolios. My future assessment report to the university's general education curriculum committee, I know, will have fewer numbers and more narratives, perhaps including concerns not easily translated into financial terms. But I think I need to continue the work that could lead to a more complex understanding of writing, a more participatory faculty, and a more diversified program.

As a teacher-model focusing on the "doing," the progressive WPA needs to imagine a dialogic approach that invites critique from student teachers and attempts to achieve equity in discourse in composition classes. From the postmodern perspective, this position statement remains tentative—as it receives responses from the community as an ongoing conversation. As a compositionist, I view research and teaching as reciprocal entities, with each interrogating and informing the other. As an administrator of a TA program, I teach others how to teach, I teach theory that illuminates practice and vice versa, and I teach both graduate and undergraduate courses. By positioning myself as a teacher-scholar-administrator, I can write professionally and take a pedagogy article in manuscript to my graduate teaching seminars. As their peer-writer, I ask students to speculate on any meaningful pedagogy based on theory and indeed value their feedback. The juxtaposition of theory and practice, of teaching and service, and of teaching and administration offers constant reflection and critique; as a result, the Asian-American professor-administrator is meaningfully progressive. At the center of this postmodern, post-process location, I hope, also lies a guarded optimism supported by a constructive understanding of the interrelationships of teaching, writing, and program administration.

MUST STORIES HAVE ENDINGS?

The three locations developed in this essay are interrelated and interdependent. The challenge, it seems, is to keep positioning oneself at a pedagogical vantage point so that, other than dispelling myths, the Asian-American WPA is teaching or administering effectively because of a meaningful incorporation of the proactive, interactive, and cultural roles that *request conversation and underscore visibility* among colleagues, students, and audiences inside and outside academia.

In 2005, my identity is still a novelty to many Americans (or Eurocentrists, as Chiang and Okihiro might qualify them within cultural or historical contexts). Although I teach more upper-division and graduate classes, I am still greeted by some students and colleagues with a similar degree of skepticism to that I received twenty years ago. The only difference between how I position myself now and how I used to function in the early anecdotes is that perhaps I have come to terms with myself with experience.

Not unlike my undergraduate composition students or graduate teaching assistants, I constantly occupy multiple roles and identities by reflecting, positioning, and repositioning. I am a faculty-administrator, an English teacher and learner, and indeed a Chinese-American teaching English. When my name is literally questioned by a store clerk, a realty agent, or even a customs officer, as it is every other day beyond campus, I offer nothing but the truth. If my legitimacy is questioned in the professional contexts, I now have location strategies which direct and redirect my thoughts, imagination, and efforts and energies to what I do best, which is to teach, write, and grow with my students. As my identity or identities continue to be questioned by some, I am also offered opportunities available to me because of my identities. As discourse, this awareness needs to be richly and complexly understood especially within the WPA context.

Interestingly, this feeling of double-consciousness, to use W. E. B. DuBois's phrase, is also manifest among my native-speaking TAs, who occupy multiple academic roles as both teachers and students, both researchers and subjects, and indeed both English language experts and learners. To many, having the experience of domination and exclusion simultaneously while teaching within a post-process culture suggests both complexity and opportunities. While post-process pedagogy exposes inequality and powers, it increasingly fosters "emancipatory imperatives of self-empowerment and social transformation" for the new "political citizenry" (George 92–93). Prendergast further reminds us of a needed critical awareness of the connection between race and pedagogy:

> [I]f we are to understand the mechanisms (like racism) that prevent some students from being heard, we need to recognize that our rhetoric is one which continually inscribes our students as foreigners. We

> might observe, for example that Asian-American students don't exist in composition studies—they are either ESL students or unnamed (white). The discrimination that Asian-Americans face (in some cases through their positioning as "model minority") is culturally unintelligible within composition's discursive space. Meanwhile our white students are not portrayed as "having race" at all. The present challenge for compositionists is to develop theorizations of race that do not reinscribe people of color as either foreign or invisible, nor leave whiteness uninvestigated; only through such work can composition begin to counteract the denial or racism that is part of the classroom, the courts, and a shared colonial inheritance. (51)

If Asian-American students are not yet included in rhetoric and composition as subjects of critical discussion, research about Asian-American teachers has just begun (Chiang, Braine). In this essay, I have attempted to locate the non-native Asian-American WPA within professional spheres of writing, teaching, and program administration. Ultimately, the Asian-American WPA must be understood beyond the arbitrary title in the dominant paradigm . Like "performative" pedagogues' refusal of identity labeling on all fronts within their context of critical queer theory (Kopelson), rhetoric and composition could endeavor to create new definitions of the Asian-American WPA independent of stable constructs of dominant ideology. I would suggest that developing a critical consciousness about the Asian-American WPA location, supported by either theory or empirical research about WPA work (archived as "research" and "needed response to NCTE policy" on the WPA-L listserv, October, 2004) is about transcending existing definitions of race labeling, stereotyping, and the simplistic understanding of American democracy. Following academic feminist research, we could also document and analyze Asian-American WPA experiences from an epistemological standpoint.

Beyond the professional spheres, it seems, Asian-American politics advances through constant struggles for inclusion within the American ideals and promises of equality and dignity. Gary Okihiro argues that, historically, "in their struggles for inclusion and equality [. . .] racial minorities [. . .] helped to preserve and advance the very privileges that were denied to them, and thereby democratized the nation for the benefit of all Americans" (151). Beyond history, Asian-Americans, as "margin," have "held the nation together with its expansive reach; [. . .] tested and ensured the guarantees of citizenship; and [have] been the true defenders of American democracy, equality, and liberty" (175). Likewise, by developing a critical consciousness of the WPA location, we can achieve a complex understanding of the forces shaping the history and contribution of the Asian-American professor of English. Critically positioning myself as a reflective and reflexive faculty of color, culture, writing, and (dialogic) program administration, I hope to transform pedagogical and disciplinary boundaries.

Works Cited

Bishop, Wendy, and Gay Lynn Crossley. "How to Tell a Story of Stopping: The Complexities of Narrating a WPA's Experience." *WPA: Writing Program Administration* 19.3 (1996): 70–79.

Bloom, Lynn Z. "I Want a Writing Director." *College Composition and Communication* 43 (1992): 176–78.

Braine, George, ed. *Non-native Educators in English Language Teaching.* Mahwah, NJ: Lawrence Erlbrum, 1999.

Burke, Kenneth. *A Rhetoric of Motives.* 1950. Berkeley: U of California P, 1969.

Chiang, Yuet-Sim D. "In the World of English Tradition, I Was Unimagined." *Illinois English Bulletin* 80.4 (1993): 22–27.

—. "Insider/Outsider/Other?: Confronting the Centeredness of Race, Class, Color and Ethnicity in Composition Research." *Under Construction: Working at the Intersections of Composition Theory, Research, and Practice.* Ed. Christine Farris and Chris M. Anson. Logan: Utah State UP, 1998. 282–91.

Dickson, Marcia. "Directing without Power: Adventures in Constructing a Model of Feminist Writing Program Administration." *Writing Ourselves into the Story: Unheard Voices from Composition Studies.* Ed. Sheryl I. Fontaine and Susan Hunter. Carbondale: Southern Illinois UP, 1993. 140–53.

Freire, Paulo. *Teachers as Cultural Workers: Letters to Those Who Dare Teach.* Boulder, CO: Westview, 1998.

Foss, Sonja, Karen Foss, and Robert Trapp, eds. *Contemporary Perspectives on Rhetoric.* Prospect Heights, IL: Waveland P, 2002.

170   Joseph Eng

George, Ann. "Critical Pedagogy: Dreaming of Democracy." *A Guide to Composition Pedagogies.* Ed. Gary Tate, Amy Rupiper, and Kurt Schick. New York: Oxford UP, 2001. 92–112.

Gunner, Jeanne. "Decentering the WPA." *WPA: Writing Program Administration* 18.1–2 (1994): 8–15.

Holbrook, Sue Ellen. "Women's Work: The Feminizing of Composition." *Rhetoric Review* 9 (1991): 201–29.

hooks, bell. *Teaching to Transgress: Education as the Practice of Freedom.* New York: Routledge, 1994.

Johnson, Cheryl L. "Participating Rhetoric and the Teacher as Racial/ Gendered Subject." *College English* 56 (1994): 409–19.

Kirsch, Gesa E., and Joy S. Ritchie. "Beyond the Personal: Theorizing a Politics of Location in Composition Research." *College Composition and Communication* 46 (1995): 7–29.

Kopelson, Karen. "Dis/Integrating the Gay/Queer Binary: 'Reconstructed Identity Politics' for a Performative Pedagogy." *College English* 65 (2002): 17–35.

Lindemann, Erika. *A Rhetoric for Writing Teachers.* New York: Oxford UP, 1995.

—. "Three Views of English 101." *College English* 57 (1995): 287–302.

Micciche, Laura R. "More than a Feeling: Disappointment and WPA Work." *College English.* 64 (2002): 432–58.

Miller, Susan. "The Feminization of Composition." *The Politics of Writing Instruction: Postsecondary.* Ed. Richard Bullock and John Trimbur. Portsmouth, NH: Boynton/Cook, 1991. 39–54.

Mura, David. *Turning Japanese: Memoirs of a Sansei.* New York: Atlantic P, 1991.

Okihiro, Gary Y. Margins and Mainstreams: Asians in American History and Culture. Seattle, WA: U of Washington P, 1994.

Prendergast, Catherine. "Race: The Absent Presence in Composition Studies." *College Composition and Communication* 50 (1998): 36–53.

Romano, Susan. "On Becoming a Woman: Pedagogies of the Self." *Passions, Pedagogy, and 21st Century Technologies.* Ed. Gail E. Hawisher and Cynthia L. Selfe. Logan: Utah State UP, 1999. 249–67.

Schell, Eileen E. "Feminism." *Keywords in Composition Studies.* Ed. Paul Heilker and Peter Vandenberg. Portsmouth, NH: Boynton/Cook, 1996. 97-101.

Sciachitano, Marian M. "Reclaiming Spaces for Our Voices, Our Histories, Our Writings, Ourselves: Women of Color in the Writing Classroom." *Illinois English Bulletin* 80.4 (1993): 28–34.

Villanueva, Victor, Jr. "Considerations for American Freireistas." *Cross-Talk in Comp Theory: A Reader.* Ed. Victor Villanueva, Jr. Urbana, IL: NCTE. 621–37.

—. "On Syllabi." *Strategies for Teaching First-Year Composition.* Ed. Duane Roen, Veronica Pantoja, Lauren Yena, Susan K. Miller, and Eric Waggoner. Urbana, IL: NCTE, 2002. 98–102.

Welch, Nancy. "Resisting the Faith: Conversion, Resistance, and the Training of Teachers." *College English* 55 (1993): 387–401.

Graduate Students Hearing Voices: (Mis)Recognition and (Re)Definition of the jWPA Identity

Brenda M. Helmbrecht with Connie Kendall

> [W]e do not simply fall into status positions that 'hail' us, nor set them aside in conscious resistance to calls from ideology. Positions in discourse are always provisional, even when they are assumed through language that is rooted in tradition and directly copied in a new circumstance.
>
> —Susan Miller

Miller's observation—though explicitly aimed at the rhetorical analysis of early American commonplace books and the ways in which ordinary acts of writing deploy already available subject positions—is all the more provocative for that which it implies: namely, the idea that discourses occasion the constitution, appropriation, and regulation of a range of meaningful, though ultimately transitory, identities. In Miller's reformulation, subject positions are stabilized strategically—provisionally—when individuals discursively take up particular identities as a means of establishing rhetorical, institutional, and/or social authority. It was with our own subject positions stable and intact within the positions that we had been hailed into that my colleague, Connie Kendall, and I instantly recognized ourselves in the call for papers that resulted in this collection.

While we knew that the "j" in jWPA stood for "junior," we assumed that the important descriptor provided by that one letter indicated that we, as graduate students, filled the subject position of a jWPA. After all, we reasoned, we both held a number of administrative positions as graduate students—or, we argued, as "junior" members of the profession. As advanced doctoral students enrolled in a rhetoric and composition program, we were regularly invited to apply for departmental administrative positions in an effort to "professionalize" our graduate education and ready us for the job market. We understood these positions to be assistantships, wherein a full-time faculty member oversees and bears the institutional responsibility for the administration of the program. We welcomed these important professionalizing opportunities and fully recognized them as evidence of a faculty committed to graduate student development and determined to maintain a departmental *esprit de corps*.

Furthermore, we were vaguely aware, though not always critical, of the material and institutional forces that hailed us, even beckoned us, into administrative positions that had been created for us to fall—or be pushed—into. It is this impulse felt by graduate students, and encouraged by graduate programs, that we will call into question in this chapter. Who or what is truly served when English departments in general, and rhetoric and composition programs in particular, create graduate writing program administrator (gWPA) positions? To that end, this chapter situates the gWPA experience squarely within the conversations shaping the definitional claims that give exigence to the issue of writing program administration in the twenty-first century, an identity that enacts Miller's notion of a more strategic subject formation, fully provisional and meaningful. What must be addressed is the willingness of both WPAs and graduate programs to reassign this work. As we see it, the issue is not just whether or not gWPAs should be accounted for and encompassed within the current definition of a WPA—clearly they need to be—but whether or not writing programs in general, and WPAs (junior or otherwise) in particular, should depend on graduate students to perform administrative duties in order for composition programs to operate effectively. In short, the entire gWPA identity needs to be reexamined.

In the summer of 2001, Connie and I began our joint administration of the university's portfolio program as graduate student assistants. Due to extraordinary and extenuating circumstances regarding faculty availability, however, we were soon called upon to oversee the program in lieu of an experienced program administrator. Given these exigencies, we understood ourselves as being asked to assume the position of a WPA (read: we believed we were being "hailed"), and we eagerly and confidently accepted the challenge (read: we "hailed" ourselves into the subject position). During the ensuing months, we each claimed our new WPA subject position as a somewhat stable identity.

Connie and I knew that our subject positions as graduate students and future faculty in rhetoric and composition relied on our ability both to assume these positions and perform successfully within them—and we knew the consequences of disregarding the call to administer (i.e., we would be less marketable, our department would have critical administrative positions unfilled, and we would have to look elsewhere for the financial support these positions provided). In other words, it was not by accident or serendipity that we found ourselves within these roles, though we were acutely aware of the fact that it felt strange being there.

Furthermore, Connie and I jointly ran a writing across the curriculum program housed in the university's school of business administration because the tenured faculty member in charge of the program was unexpectedly forced to take a leave of absence. Later, at the request of our director of composition, Connie, along with another graduate student, agreed to observe the adjunct faculty who taught the required first-year writing courses, and then composed the obligatory "letter of observation" for the director to read. Though I (Brenda) had also been offered this position, I turned it down to focus on my dissertation and prepare for the job market—a decision that was harder to make than it should have been. Even in my fifth year of doctoral work, even after writing three chapters of my dissertation, even after presenting at professional conferences and holding numerous other administrative positions in the department, a small part of me still believed that turning down administrative work that could be recorded on my CV would adversely affect me when I went on the job market, as though someone, somewhere, would know that I had turned down such an "opportunity" and would interpret that choice as my inability to work hard and contribute to a department.

Between the two of us, Connie and I served on our department's graduate committee, job search committees (for both junior and senior hires), a university curriculum council, and our department's composition curriculum committee. I also became the assistant director of composition (AD) at a time when our interim director of composition, a literary specialist, heavily relied on my training in rhetoric and composition. Due to these unique circumstances, I designed the curriculum for the required TA training course, a task not usually assigned to the AD. As I observed the new TAs in their classrooms, and again designed the curriculum for the weekly one-hour course in composition pedagogy that they took during their first two semesters, I became aware that I was doing my department a service by training, supervising, and supporting these new TAs for an entire academic year—without any additional compensation or reward. While I was financially compensated for some of my work, I was repeatedly told—and believed—that real payment came when I entered the job market with a CV full of administrative experience.[1] But now, given the current political and economic climate in which I live, I can't help but wonder: was I being professionalized, or was the work of a WPA being outsourced?

As *graduate students* invested with minimal institutional status (read: replaceable, temporary, one-size-fits-all), Connie and I were not "really" WPAs—we were not full-time faculty; we did not hold doctorates; we were not salaried like a WPA; and our positions usually lasted a few months. Rather, we were graduate students momentarily masquerading as WPAs. Why, then, did we imagine ourselves hailed into these positions? And through what mechanisms—discursive, institutional, and/or ideological—did we manage to take up the identity itself as a means of establishing rhetorical authority? In other words, had we simply been "hearing voices" and *mis*recognizing ourselves as the intended WPA subject, or does our (mis)recognition instead signal the need for a redefinition of the WPA identity?

Fortunately, by choosing to hear our voices, the editors of this collection are acknowledging the immediacy and importance of examining the consequences of asking—if not requiring—that graduate students heed the call of administration while they are still taking coursework, teaching classes, and completing dissertations and theses. No one denies the fact that graduate students are frequently recruited by their departments to assume positions that have been traditionally held by faculty responsible for administering writing programs, and current jWPAs and WPAs cite similar anecdotal evidence of the benefits of such institutional work. But because these graduate administrative positions are always already tenuous, temporary, and transitory, graduate students do not fit neatly into the institutional and professional definition of a WPA in its current conception. Therefore, any discussion of the peculiar nature of the jWPA experience, we believe, must make room for discussions of graduate students who assume that same identity.

From my present perspective as a first-year Assistant Professor directing a writing program. Undoubtedly, my subject position has been complicated in interesting ways. As was evident in my MLA interviews, my current institution and others looking to hire WPAs were attracted to my administrative experiences, and I am certain that these lines on my CV did, as had been predicted, help me find a job. Both my advising professors and composition journal editors continually told me, as Sheryl Fontaine argued in 1998, that "odds are high that individuals hired as rhetoric and composition specialists will be, at some time in their career, expected to take on administrative responsibilities in the department" (83). Such an understanding has become a given in the field. In response, rhetoric and composition programs have created more administrative positions for graduate students within their respective departments, while also designing curriculum to further train graduate students so they can qualify for administrative positions straight out of graduate school.

However, I question an institutionalized system that necessarily fragments graduate students' identities as scholars, educators, and students, such that they must determine which of those subject locations make them most marketable: Should they focus on their teaching? Their scholarship (i.e., publishing or presenting at professional conferences)? Their coursework? Or the administrative roles they hold as junior, and easily exploitable, members of the profession? Some have argued that such a fragmented view of my graduate education simply prepared me for the work I do as an assistant professor. But now, as someone who has recently become a full-fledged member of the profession, I can honestly claim that I feel less fragmented now than I did as a gWPA. I *know* that I am less stressed, experience fewer sleepless nights, have lower blood pressure, and, frankly, have a clearer sense of my role within my department. In short, I am happier. I believe much of the anxiety I felt as a graduate student resulted because the gWPA tends to reside in a subject position that is never clearly defined; whereas today, I have been able to resolve the tension that manifested when I tried to align the identities I thought I held as a graduate administrator with the one I *really* held.

In their essay, "How to be a Wishy-Washy Graduate Student WPA, or Undefined but Overdetermined," Stephen Davenport Jukuri and W. J. Williamson explore the convoluted and intangible subject position of a graduate administrator. They explain that, at any one moment, this individual is "socially and experientially" a graduate student who maintains close personal connections with other TAs (106). In the next moment they evolve into authority figures on whom the WPA relies to supervise those very same people—their friends—"to help monitor, train, and develop their teaching performance" (106). In her essay, "The Peer Who Isn't a Peer: Authority and the Graduate Student Administrator," Johanna Atwood Brown recounts the social isolation she felt during her three-year stint as a graduate WPA. She found her role constantly fluctuating between that of administrator and friend when she interacted with her peers, and never became comfortable with her dual identity. She confessed that she "never fully understood what [her] power consisted of in this position and felt profoundly uncomfortable exercising it" (124). Brown admits that she wanted it both ways: she wanted to be regarded as an authority figure at school and as a friend outside of it. She never resolved those subject positions as she filled them, and uses her reflective essay to achieve greater identity cohesion.

I confess that even as I hailed myself into a gWPA position, it never occurred to me that I would be taking on a new identity that would greatly affect my relationships with both faculty and other graduate students. I somehow had more responsibility, but did not always have the power or authority to act on it. Within this definitional vacuum, "expectations of us—from other graduate students, from administrators, even from other faculty—can range anywhere from file clerk to spy to substitute teacher to pedagogical theorist" (Jukuri and Williamson 109), and it's anyone's guess which voices will enter our heads next.

As AD, I eventually became aware of the emotional sacrifices the position required. I remember one moment in particular when I was driving home from school. Before leaving campus, I had learned that I needed to conduct fourteen classroom observations for graduate students whom I had already been teaching and mentoring and that I had three weeks to do these observations. The stress consumed me as

I tried to figure out how I would observe fourteen classes, teach my first-year composition class, and study for my comprehensive exams. I pulled my car over to the side of the road and burst into tears. While I knew balancing my time would be important for this job, I honestly had not been prepared for what I felt at that moment. Significantly, when I accepted the AD position, I did not know how many TAs I would work with. During the previous year, roughly a dozen students had been admitted; during my tenure in the position, the department gave TA positions to twenty-eight students.

In my mind, it is telling that most graduate administrators find themselves working within what Jukuri and Williamson describe as an "undefined, overlapping space" (106). That is to say, we are not vested with the institutional authority to effect change in policy, attitude, or atmosphere. In fact, most of us understand that what little power we do have has been handed to us by the WPA, and, further, we generally need permission to use it. The daily tasks completed by the WPA were easily managed: I took minutes at the composition curriculum committee meeting and distributed them to members (after the WPA signed off on them); I mentored and advised the TAs to the best of my ability; I responded to the TAs' teaching journals; I observed their classes. But when a *real* problem arose—when a TA was canceling too many classes, or refused to teach the departmental curriculum, or received bad evaluations—those situations were handled without my knowledge or input. Thus, I often heard about the *real,* thornier work of a WPA through rumor and observation.

Now, as a new WPA, I wish I could have participated in those conversations. As I make decisions about staffing courses and the first-year curriculum, and as I read student evaluations of TAs and lecturers, I don't know what to do. In other words, I was trained to do the rote work and labor of a WPA, but I was not trained to navigate the tricky political ground that a WPA treads.[2]

In their article, "Writing Program Administrative Internships"—included in the recently published, *The Writing Program Administrator's Resource,* edited by Stuart C. Brown and Theresa Enos—Daphne Desser and Darin Payne are acutely aware of this preprofessional identity tension. They argue that graduate administrative positions often lead to exploitation because "students may become overwhelmed in programmatic administration, neglecting coursework, teaching, or opportunities to develop research agendas and publishing records"

(90). As anecdotal support for this argument, I recall sitting in a graduate seminar in literature when a student who had not completed the required reading explained that when faced with grading papers or reading the assigned book, she felt like she had to choose between her students and her classes, and this time her students won. I, and many of my graduate colleagues and friends seated around the table, felt a great deal of resentment toward this person. We felt noble because we did not choose; rather, we did our best to live up to all of our obligations. We did the reading, did our best to tend to students, and maybe helped administer areas of the program in our spare time—because that's what graduate students did.

Yet, I recall that the student who had the luxury of making this choice was studying literature, not rhetoric and composition—the area of study for those of us who felt resentment. Perhaps our harsh reaction was partly due to the fact that most of our literary colleagues did not have such a fragmented view of their graduate study. We were the ones who served on committees, presented at conferences, and held the administrative positions offered by our department. We had been hailed into those positions by our mentors, by other administrators in the department, by each other, and by ourselves because making sacrifices was part of our professional training. "You won't get to choose when you are faculty," we were told.

My experience watching graduate students in rhetoric and composition assume administrative positions echoes an observation made by Louise Wetherbee Phelps in her essay, "Turtles All the Way Down: Educating Academic Leaders." She explains that while professional and administrative responsibilities are "not unique to rhetoric and composition, they are *unusually encouraged* and enabled in many of its doctoral programs" (5, emphasis added). Anecdotal evidence from my own life leads me to conclude my graduate colleagues in literature and creative writing did not feel hailed into administration in the same way as rhetoric and composition students.

Notably, my work as a graduate administrator did not "count" towards the doctoral degree I was seeking, a situation echoing that of gWPAs who find themselves in an administrative position that doesn't "count" towards tenure. I think it's essential for departments to determine how gWPA positions function within their departments. Too often, these roles are created because the already overworked and underpaid WPA ("j" or otherwise) needs an assistant to keep up with the duties her role encompasses. As a new jWPA, I confess that my mind occasionally wanders and I find myself wondering what it would be like to delegate some of *my* responsibilities to one of our graduate students. I even know which students I would entrust with *my* responsibilities and which I wouldn't. Yet, when my mind focuses again, I am compelled to admit that I would only be furthering a cycle that forces graduate students to choose between more obligations than just their work and their students.

But much of the scholarship recommends that WPAs do just that. In "The Graduate Student as Apprentice WPA: Experiencing the Future," which appeared in a 1991 issue of *WPA: Writing Program Administration*, Trudelle Thomas acknowledges the field's move to professionalize graduate students. She sees candidates in rhetoric and composition entering the job market who "quickly discover that they, more than other new instructors, must assume administrative responsibilities early in their careers" (41). Thomas concedes that in a perfect world WPA positions would be filled by tenured faculty members, but she hopes that "*in the meantime*" her article can suggest ways for WPAs to "help graduate students in gaining understanding, and, better yet, experience, in administering a writing program, even while still in graduate school" (41, emphasis added).

She articulates three qualities she believes prospective and effective WPAs must possess: they must be willing student advocates; they need creative vision; they must be adept at dealing with many kinds of people (43). While I think these qualities should be possessed by anyone working within an educational setting, Thomas argues that being able to identify these "personal traits" within graduate students will help WPAs guide students toward administrative work both within graduate school and beyond. She argues that as a WPA, you ought to

> observe your students' behaviors in various work and
> social contexts, such as graduate seminars, their own
> classrooms, conferences with writing students, and
> committee or departmental meetings. As you ob-
> serve, watch for the abilities to speak diplomatically,
> to express ideas or convictions with force, to be an
> advocate, and to cooperate with other people. Do you
> have students who display initiative in organizing
> workshops or who are leaders of graduate student or-

ganizations? Which graduate students speak up most
for their own students or for the writing program in
general? Who are your best teachers? (43)

Regarding graduate students as little WPAs-in-the-making seems
harmful to me. The qualities described above are not unique to students who would succeed at WPA work. Rather, they describe a student who is passionate about her own commitment to teaching, education, and scholarship. This passage describes a well-rounded student,
not one whose professional and personal aspirations should be further
weighed down and divided by the addition of overwhelming WPA
work. At the same time, I appreciate Thomas's drive to place talented
and creative people within WPA positions; however, I think she should
recruit from a different pool—such as tenured faculty.

Naturally, Thomas suggests that departments begin creating "apprenticeship" positions for aspiring WPAs. She firmly believes that
both the field and graduate students benefit if a "student unsuited to
administration is better off to find that out now, before moving a thousand miles for a 'permanent' position" (50). Like much of the scholarship that addresses the issue of graduate administrators, Thomas does
not step back to question the complications that arise when graduate
students hold such positions. She never wonders why the field is moving in this direction, and even seems to see the situation as temporary,
which is evidenced by her use of the phrase "in the meantime."

Since 1991—i.e., *the* meantime—the conversation revolving
around gWPAs has entered more complex realms, but still not to a satisfying degree. For instance, in a 1996 issue of *WPA*, Mark C. Long,
Jennifer Holberg, and Marcy Taylor pull from their own experiences
as graduate administrators to highlight the gaps in their own training.
Their essay aims to "transform the intellectual work of the WPA by
decentralizing and delegating day-to-day tasks of the program," tasks
which are relegated to graduate students who, they claim, will regard
them as an opportunity to "learn the practices of composition studies
by actually finding themselves in a position to shape those practices"
(67). Though the authors allow for the importance and necessity of
graduate administration, they take issue with the "apprentice model"
of TA training because "apprenticeship implies a rigid differential between master and apprentice: the apprentice serves the master, with

the payoff for his or her labor being the learning of the trade" (68), or, I would add, the line on the CV.

I agree with Long, Holdberg, and Taylor that the model, as they define it, can be conceptually and intellectually limiting for a graduate student, forcing them to identify the moments when they will become "full-fledged" members of the field. But I begin to take issue with the conception of graduate administration when they argue for a "collaborative administrative model" to frame graduate administrative experiences. Within this model, they propose three guiding principles. First, graduate students need to "become active institutional agents," a goal that is achieved by replacing the label "teaching assistant" with the more accurate title, "instructor" (72), a discursive change that I don't think will truly change the lives of either TAs or instructors.

Second, they argue for a "multi-tiered professional development program" (73) that gives graduate students more opportunities to hold administrative roles, in part, because the potential for this "under-utilized resource has only begun to be explored" (74). They further explain that the most obvious consequence of handing over administrative duties to graduate students is a reduced workload for the WPA because it "frees the WPA from many time-consuming, day-to-day responsibilities of conferencing, mentoring, doing class visits, and preparing teaching materials" (74). In effect, the WPA who is liberated from day-to-day "program operation" can become "a more dynamic force in program development" (74).

Lastly, the authors want to create a "responsive and collaborative community of teachers" (74). In this situation, more experienced graduate student instructors mentor and support newer instructors, thereby—again—freeing up more time for the WPA. They explain that when more senior graduate instructors become ADs in the composition program, they can offer closer support than the already overburdened WPA. They conclude their article by arguing that while the

> inclusion of 2nd, 3rd, 4th, or 5th year graduate students in the administrative program has eased day-to-day burdens of the WPA, participation in the multiple administrative responsibilities of the department has given graduate students real experience in not only refining the courses they are charged to teach, but

the consequences of teaching in the department and
university. (76)

I am struck by these authors' fond memories of the administrative
positions they held while completing their doctorates at the University
of Washington. Long, Holberg, and Taylor never address the long-
term institutional ramifications of regarding the gWPA as requisite to
maintaining a composition program. Nor do they explicitly address
the issue of financial compensation. And, perhaps it's the less than
nostalgic memories I have of struggling to pay my heating bills in the
winter as I administered, as I taught and trained graduate students,
but I can't help but wonder—when they did the same work as a WPA,
did they earn the requisite pay? Or, as I suspect, is pecuniary selflessness another trait that potential administrators should possess?

In my mind, Long, Holberg, and Taylor's, argument raises more
questions than it answers. What happens to the value of WPA work if
it is so easily outsourced to a second-year graduate student, someone
who has probably not finished course work, written a dissertation in
the field, published much, or presented at many conferences? Doesn't
this particular move toward professionalizing graduate students ultimately deprofessionalize the work of a WPA? Shifting responsibility
from a faculty member to a graduate student is never a "value free act"
(Fontaine 84). I can attest to the fact that when work is passed down
from someone with rank and status to someone with no institutional
authority, messages are discretely passed along because the assumption
is that "the importance of the task has diminished in the minds of
those who make the assignment" (Fontaine 84). When Connie and I
directed the portfolio program, we did so because the faculty member
who was supposed to assume the role had a publication deadline to
meet. So, yes, messages were sent: scholarship trumps administration.
When a WPA passes off a task to a graduate student, how is that task
reframed? Does it make the work of a WPA seem less like an intellectual endeavor and more like a series of jobs and tasks that have to be
completed?

Yet, many graduate students who have played the role of administrator evidently see this departmental version of outsourcing as value-
free. They don't want to admit that they are basically doing the work
the WPA doesn't *want* to do, or doesn't have *time* to do. For instance,

in her study of the "professional preparation of graduate students" (65) in rhetoric and composition that appeared in a 1999 issue of *WPA,* Sally Barr Ebest observes that new WPAs are often not adequately trained to fully perform their role. Rather than question the ethics and politics that surround the moment when an untenured ABD applies for and accepts a position as a WPA, Ebest argues that "if we want future WPAs to avoid the burdens of overwork, understaffing, and insufficient funding which so many of us have experienced, we must ensure that our graduate students learn those skills which will help them run a strong and efficient writing program" (76). In other words, the issue is not the workload, the funding, or the staffing; rather, the issue is graduate education and training—which, in my experience, do not address workload, funding, or staffing.

Ebest explains that when she was in graduate school, her mentor, Marilyn Sternglass, arranged for her to get a course release to help administer the basic writing program. Later, when Sternglass was on sabbatical, Ebest served as interim director of composition. Predictably, she found the experience to be "invaluable to [her] understanding of writing program administration and a key element in [her] marketability" (81). Ebest also seems proud to have assisted the university with its budgetary problems because her decision to assume an administrative position as a graduate student also provided for a "means of cheap labor for the university. In this era of dwindling resources and a tight job market, developing these internships benefits all" (81).

After reading scholars like Ebest discuss their work as gWPAs, I know that I am taking on a dissenting voice here. While I did a great deal of administrative work, I am not—and never really was—convinced that I *should have* held all of those positions. And I was always aware of other tasks that seemingly deserved more attention than I gave them, including my coursework, my teaching, and my dissertation. But my goal here is also one of awareness; I honestly believe that many departments have lost track of the day-to-day contributions made by gWPAs, contributions needed for composition programs to function efficiently. The sheer number of positions I have held even impressed, and seemed to surprise, my department chair, who once commented in a letter of recommendation for a teaching award that I had held more administrative positions than most tenured members of the department. Furthermore, my own faculty mentors wondered why graduate students took more than four years (the number of years that we were guaranteed funding) to complete our degrees—ostensibly unaware of the amount of time we gave in service to the department. Thus, I challenge WPAs, gWPAs, and English departments to (re)examine the institutional and professional forces that hail graduate students in rhetoric and composition into administration.

In some respects, I *am* proud of the work I did as a graduate administrator. However, I take pride in the fact that as a graduate student I was able to do the work of both junior and tenured faculty, and, as a result, felt relatively confident that I would land a job when I went on the market. But, on my first read through the MLA job list, I intentionally avoided WPA positions because I knew that taking such a position before I had tenure could overwhelm me and threaten my ability to earn tenure. At some point—perhaps while revising my CV—I realized that I had, in effect, been trained to be a WPA. Moreover, it should come as no surprise to anyone, myself included, that my first position as an assistant professor is that of a WPA. After all, my mentors and my coursework prepared me for such a position.

We can't lament the fact that nontenured faculty take WPA positions, and then turn around and train our graduate students to do that work. Right now, many institutions that grant PhDs in rhetoric and composition—my own alma mater included—offer coursework in writing program administration. The goal of such courses is to better prepare students to do WPA work—work we all know they will be doing anyway—fresh out of graduate school. This may seem like a good idea *only* if we are already resigned to the idea that ABDs and new PhDs will accept administrative work without first receiving tenure.

But we need to take a step back here. I took two years of coursework, not all of it directly related to my PhD in rhetoric and composition. As programs determine the kinds of coursework that will best introduce graduate students to the fields they will enter, should we devote these intellectual inquiries to rhetorical and composition theory, to teaching practices, to their own writing, or to preparing them to take on administrative roles where they will be overburdened? I remain unconvinced that simply designing graduate courses to help students understand the role they will likely hold as administrators truly gets at the real issues I have presented in this chapter. Perhaps certain graduate students should rightfully be hailed by their department to take on administrative responsibilities, but only under certain, clearly articulated conditions.

In their discussion of gWPA positions, Desser and Payne argue for the following guidelines:

a) internships should be appropriate to localized conditions of teaching, learning, and writing program administration;

b) internships should extend graduate students' education by enriching their course work and enabling them to apply theories to practice;

c) *internships should involve opportunities for students and faculty members to critically evaluate the political circumstances of their work;*

d) *faculty members facilitating internships and students taking them need to be compensated appropriately for their work.* (91, emphasis added)

To me, this list represents an ethical approach to training graduate students to do WPA work. Based on my own experiences, the first two items in the list seem less difficult to achieve than the last two. The sheer nature of a PhD in rhetoric and composition inherently encourages graduate students to tie their work in graduate seminars to their work in the classroom and beyond. Furthermore, the field itself seems committed to the interconnected relationship between theory and practice. The final two items, however, seem far more difficult to achieve.

At no point in my work as a graduate administrator was I ever asked to "evaluate the political circumstances" of my work. I truly believed that if I did not take on administrative responsibilities, I would be less marketable and would fare poorly on the job market. However, it hadn't yet occurred to me that my work as an administrator was never really about *me*. Instead, it was about my field's and my department's near obsessive drive to propel me into a professional position before I was ready. Before expecting graduate students to assume these same positions, I think we—both students and faculty members—need to consider the personal, professional, institutional ramifications of doing so.

NOTES

[1] Compensation often manifested in one course release as I continued to earn my regular graduate stipend, roughly $14,000 per year before taxes, of which I spent at least $600 per year on my health insurance. As is often the case with WPAs, a course release did not make up for the additional time and responsibility required of anyone in an administrative position. Furthermore, my work with the portfolio program provided me with an opportunity to earn money in the summer when the university only provided graduate students with a small stipend, currently $1,800, that did not cover my cost of living for three months. The compensation for portfolio work has since changed so that students no longer receive pay; instead, they are given a research budget, thereby preventing students from deciding for themselves what to do with their pay.

[2] The intellectual and theoretical work of a WPA, and the political overtones of such a position are seldom part of a graduate student's training. I am not suggesting that these issues are easily remedied by "more appropriate" collaboration between the WPA and graduate administrator. Nor am I convinced that such needs are fully addressed by instituting a stop-gap course on WPA work. The problem seems more insidious and complex. That is, to read my struggle in this essay as merely a personal anecdote is, in my opinion, a misreading of a system that coerces graduate students to hail themselves into these administrative positions.

WORKS CITED

Brown, Johanna Atwood. "The Peer Who Isn't a Peer: Authority and the Graduate Student Administrator." George, 120–25.

Brown, Stuart C., Theresa Enos, and Catherine Chaput, eds. *The Writing Program Administrator's Resource: A Guide to Reflective Institutional Practice.* Mahwah, NJ: Lawrence Erlbaum, 2002.

Desser, Daphne, and Darin Payne. "Writing Program Administration Internships." *The Writing Program Administrator's Resource.* Brown, Enos, and Chaput, 88-100.

Ebest, Sally Barr. "The Next Generation of WPAs: A Study of Graduate Students in Composition/Rhetoric." *WPA: Writing Program Administration* 22.3 (Spring 1999): 65–84.

Fontaine, Sheryl I. "Revising Administrative Models and Questioning the Value of Appointing Graduate Students WPAs." *Foregrounding Ethical Awareness in Composition and English Studies.* Ed. Sheryl I. Fontaine and Susan M. Hunter. Portsmouth: Boynton/Cook, 1998. 83–92.

George, Diana, ed. *Kitchen Cooks, Plate Twirlers, and Troubadors: Writing Program Administrators Tell Their Stories.* Portsmouth, NH: Heinemann, 1999.

Jakuri, Stephen Davenport and W. J. Williamson. "How to Be a Wishy-Washy Graduate Student WPA, or Undefined but Overdetermined." George, 105-19.

Long, Mark C., Jennifer H. Holberg, and Marcy M. Taylor. "Beyond Apprenticeship: Graduate Students, Professional Development Programs and the Future(s) of English Studies." *WPA: Writing Program Administration* 20.1–2 (Fall/Winter 1996): 67–78.

Miller, Susan. *Assuming the Positions: Cultural Pedagogy and the Politics of Commonplace Writing.* Pittsburgh: U of Pittsburgh P, 1998.

Miller, Thomas P. "Why Don't Our Graduate Programs Do a Better Job of Preparing Students for the Work That We Do?" *WPA: Writing Program Administration* 24.3 (Spring 2001): 41–58.

Phelps, Louise Wetherbee. "Turtles All the Way Down: Educating Academic Leaders." Brown, Enos, and Chaput, 3–39.

Thomas, Trudelle. "The Graduate Student as Apprentice WPA: Experiencing the Future." *WPA: Writing Program Administration* 14.3 (Spring 1991): 41–51.

Part IV

Rhetorical Strategies for
Mediating jWPA Locations

10 Redefining Our Rhetorical Situations: jWPAs in the Small College Context

Rebecca Taylor Fremo

About two years ago, I went to our local Panera Bread restaurant with my children.[1] Amid flying bagel parts and soup exchanges, my oldest child asked me, "Mommy, why are you a teacher?" I explained that I teach because I love to work with students, help them learn to write well, and read about their lives and ideas. I noticed the woman at the table behind me begin to pay attention; I also noticed her fuzzy-haired little boy was about my baby's age. She had two teenaged children, too. We began to make small talk about our babies, and she told me that she was a high school English teacher.

I described my position as director of writing and assistant professor of English at a small private college. I told her that I taught four courses each year, pedagogy courses for secondary teachers and composition courses, and that I offered faculty workshops for other teachers. "Amazing," she sighed. "That's my dream job." I probably gulped audibly. She proceeded to describe her own work teaching composition and her desire to pursue graduate courses. "Your job," she kept repeating. "Isn't that ideal? Teaching so few courses, doing administrative work, and having so many different things to do? The paper load of six courses was killing me once my kids were born; I had to go to part-time."

Now consider a second exchange. When I first accepted my current position, I discussed it with my dissertation advisor. I explained to her that I would direct a writing center and a WAC program. "My budget is twenty-two seventy-five."

"Not bad," she replied. "Twenty-two thousand is respectable for a small institution."

"Twenty-two HUNDRED and seventy-five," I clarified.

"Ah."

"Uh huh."

The truth is that both that high school teacher at Panera and my dissertation advisor were right about my job. It's a gift and a grind. But it's hard to think critically about either side of that coin when I read my work alongside existing scholarship about the lives and work of writing program administrators in our field. This scholarship has traditionally featured the experiences of tenured WPAs at large, state-supported institutions or the nightmare scenarios that ensue when junior faculty WPAs at large schools are not granted tenure. Neither scholarly example speaks convincingly to my own experiences as a jWPA at a small, private college.

The old real estate cliché holds true for me: location, location, location. I recognize that my ability to succeed (or not succeed) at my present location, Gustavus Adolphus College, stems directly from my own ability to manage the competing facets of own identity: my gender, my age, my "east coast" mindset and rhetorical practices, my professional reputation. And I am learning now to do more than simply acknowledge that my identity shapes my work as a jWPA. I am trying to think critically about how that works, and revise my self accordingly. In "Beyond the Personal: Theorizing a Politics of Location in Composition Research," feminist composition scholars Gesa Kirsch and Joy Ritchie urge other researchers to "theorize locations by examining [their] experiences as reflections of ideology and culture, reinterpret experiences through the eyes of others, and recognize our split selves"(8). I would argue that this act of personal theorizing suggested by Ritchie and Kirsch—a way of considering both experience and representation, ideology and culture—yields the most fruitful understanding of how jWPAs can learn to work successfully in a small college setting. This chapter documents my own process of theorizing location as a female junior faculty member leading a writing program at a small, private college.

Doctoral programs in Rhetoric and Composition try to prepare new graduates for the realities of writing program administration—despite the Council of Writing Program Administrators' recommendation that junior faculty not take on such responsibilities. The Portland

Resolution, for instance, which was adopted by the Council of Writing Program Administrators in1992 and subsequently published in the journal _WPA: Writing Program Administration (Fall/ Winter issue of 1992) states that "The WPA should be a regular, full-time, tenured faculty member or a full-time administrator with a recognizable title that delineates the scope of the position (e.g., Director of Writing, Co-ordinator of Composition, Division or Department Chair)" (Hult et al.) This statement, which falls under the "Job Security" sub-heading of the resolution, reminds us how important it is for WPAs to be able to make difficult decisions—about staffing, budgeting, and curricular planning—without fear of repercussion at tenure time.

Since a quick search of the internet reveals graduate courses in administration at well-respected universities such as Purdue (ENG 680, Writing Program Administration), Northeastern State University in Oklahoma (ENG 5223, Writing Program Administration), and Bowling Green State University (ENG 780, Special Topics: Writing Program Administration), I can only assume that these institutions want to prepare their graduate students for WPA work. While these universities clearly intend to the do the right thing by preparing future graduates for the eventual realities of this work, I wonder how much attention these programs pay to *where* junior faculty will do this administrative work. A quick canvass of my own cohort, all women who took degrees in English with a Rhetoric and Composition focus from our Research One institution between 2000 and 2002, speaks volumes.[2] Five of us now direct first-year writing programs, writing centers, or WAC programs at diverse institutions, including multiple campus locations of research universities, Jesuit comprehensive universities, and both public and private liberal arts colleges. In some cases, we direct two or three such programs at a time.

In each instance, my friends and I face a wide variety of challenges that are specific to our institutional locations. At the Jesuit institution, the WPA's authority and success depend on her ability to be a good colleague to several Jesuit priests, regardless of her own religious beliefs, and to oversee the teaching of composition courses for a group of fairly conservative Catholic students. At the public and private liberal arts colleges, WPAs must juggle administrative responsibilities, a heavy advising load, a scholarly agenda, and colleagues and students who expect night and day "service" to the institution. At the regional campuses of large research universities, my jWPA friends have learned that they are expected to produce the same quality and amount of scholarship that their colleagues do at the main campus, yet their teaching and administrative loads are heavier than those of their R1 colleagues.

In each example above, the "where" of the jWPA's work is more than geographical. Our locations as WPAs are shaped by our previous experiences and expectations as graduates of large public universities; the authority and credibility granted to us by our new colleagues; our working conditions (including course releases, teaching, advising, and research expectations); and our institutions' budgetary and cultural climates. And all of us agree: because we never discussed *where* we junior faculty WPAs would do our work after graduation, we never fully investigated how such locations might determine the range of rhetorical strategies we should employ when we get there.

In this chapter, I focus my attention on my own work as a junior faculty member with a WPA assignment at a small private liberal arts college, arguing that this work is fraught with complications surrounding the negotiation of a professional ethos, institutional authority, and collegial acceptance. This is the rhetorical situation *here*. Junior faculty members who direct writing programs at small colleges, particularly women faculty, must tailor their rhetorical strategies to acknowledge the contradictory ways that power, responsibility, institutional location, gender, and rhetorical tactics intertwine. For nearly five years now, I have survived in my current position, learning to play my multiple roles, sometimes even gracefully, but more often rather painfully, at my small liberal arts college. As a jWPA, I am still learning to negotiate the shifting demands of a new rhetorical situation, and this has meant having to literally redefine what I mean by "rhetorical situation" in the first place.

REDEFINING RHETORICAL SITUATION

According to Lloyd Bitzer, whose 1968 essay, "The Rhetorical Situation," stands as a rather definitive classic on the subject, the rhetorical situation *itself* calls rhetorical discourse into being. Bitzer seeks to refocus the more Aristotelian emphasis on rhetor and means of persuasion on the situation, arguing that a situation is not rhetorical merely because interlocutors identify an issue to be addressed and then persuade listeners. Rather, real rhetorical situations must invite rhetoric into being, demanding and necessitating response. For Bitzer, the rhetorical situation consists of three elements: exigence, which he defines as "a defect, an obstacle, something waiting to be done" (6); audience, which he names as "those persons who are capable of being influenced by discourse and of being mediators of change"(8); and constraints, the "persons, events, objects, and relations which are parts of the situation because they have the power to constrain decision and action needed to modify the exigence" (8). All three elements point to a clear focus on change—on results. By implication, then, successful rhetors are folks who can *make things happen.*

This impetus is reflected within Bitzer's definition of rhetoric as well. In the essay, he defines rhetoric this way:

> a mode of altering reality [. . .] by the creation of dis-
> course which changes reality through the mediation
> of thought and action. The rhetor alters reality by
> bringing into existence a discourse of such a char-
> acter that the audience, in thought and action, is so
> engaged that it becomes mediator of change. In this
> sense, rhetoric is always persuasive. (4)

Defined this way, rhetoric necessitates a rhetor who speaks from a position of power, a rhetor imbued with enough influence, either through an already-existing ethos or via a masterful rhetorical performance, to alter reality. This rhetor is capable of changing the thoughts and actions of others. The rhetor must impose his (most often, the rhetor is figured as male throughout Bitzer's essay) will upon others, and he succeeds only if others adopt his position.[3]

If we replace "rhetor" with "jWPA," we see how unlikely it is that rhetorical success can ever be achieved. Indeed, it becomes difficult to think of the rhetorical situations that one faces as "rhetorical situations" at all. How can a jWPA at a small college impose her will upon others, ensuring that they adopt her position, when she has no power or influence on campus? How can a jWPA in this context move an audience of colleagues to enact change if those colleagues cannot yet recognize the need for change in the first place—because of a basic lack of information about what good writing is, how good teachers help students to produce it, and how good writing programs facilitate the learning process for writers? And perhaps most importantly, how can a jWPA at a small college focus appropriate attention on audience and exigence when in this context, rhetorical constraints overshadow all the other elements of rhetorical situation that Bitzer theorizes?

First, I am constrained by my duties themselves. I advise forty or more students per semester, teach four courses per year, direct the writing center and WAC programs, and mentor, observe, and advise secondary education majors in my discipline. That's because on a small college campus, the jWPA is probably the only composition specialist and possibly the person with the most pedagogically focused graduate training. Second, I'm constrained by the fact that I'm the first person and only person on my campus to hold the PhD with a rhetoric and composition focus. Like most jWPAs on small campuses, I must represent not only the writing program but the discipline to a variety of constituencies, including an English department, the dean, the student body, the writing center staff, faculty members, even the college's board of directors or accrediting agencies. In other words, my role is to be *both* persuasive *and* informative at all times, constantly explaining and defining my job duties and the program's goals within the context of nearly every conversation. Since so few of my colleagues really understand what jWPAs do or why we do it (they used to laugh bemusedly when I told them I was a WPA—"works progress administration?"), I am the only person who realizes that a writing program exigence even exists. My audience consists of others who are less informed or uninformed about writing programs and administrative processes. It's a vicious cycle. I need to plead for funds, administrative support, or even shifts in administrative practices. But before I can begin to advocate, I must first recognize that others in the room may not fully understand what "work" the jWPA seeks to fund or revise in the first place.

By Bitzer's definition, then, most acts of persuasion in my campus community are not "rhetoric" at all. For example, when I arrived at my present institution, the WAC program had utilized the same "recommended" handbook for more than ten years; no review had been conducted since its adoption. The campus community could not understand why I insisted upon a formal review of that book, one conducted by an interdisciplinary group of faculty members. I recognized an exigence; others did not. I recognized a rhetorical situation that required response; my colleagues did not recognize the rhetorical situation as such until I devoted a great deal of time to documenting my reasons for wanting to review the book. It was difficult to gather faculty members for the reviewing committee and even more difficult to convince colleagues to adopt the new handbook once we selected it.

Perhaps the largest constraint placed upon the jWPA at a small college is the fact that we direct programs situated within unfamiliar institutional values and practices. We leave our large research university graduate programs, accept our new jobs, and face challenges that require us to interpret, represent, and advocate for policies and curricular structures that we don't necessarily agree with or even fully understand. In my case, I stepped into directing a long-established, yet stagnant, WAC program. My new position carried with it permanent *ex-officio* seats on several powerful committees; previously, I had served only as the token graduate student on a departmental committee and shadowed a tenured WPA for a day. My new job required me to direct a floundering writing center; previously I had tutored for a few semesters as a graduate student. My new job required me to prepare "new" teachers of writing intensive (WRIT) courses, most of whom were actually many years my senior, and then determine which faculty members could teach WAC courses in the first place. I had to do so without a structure for observing teachers, collecting syllabi, or ensuring curricular compliance.

Where I chafe most, though, after reflecting upon Bitzer's discussion of rhetorical situation, is when I read the word "invite" in his work. Bitzer uses the term "invite" to signal that rhetors are somehow invited to respond rhetorically to particular situations: "Rhetorical discourse is called into existence by situation; the situation which the rhetor perceives amounts to an invitation to create and present discourse" (9). jWPAs at small colleges are not always invited to speak on their campuses. In fact, when jWPAs in my context do speak, we are often *required* to do so in the *guise* of an invitation. jWPAs may be "invited" to sit on a variety of campus committees—and in my case, *ex-officio*—when other junior faculty members are often exempt from such committee work during the first year on campus. My junior colleagues spent hours on research or course development during their first year on campus, but I was "invited" to devote most of my nonteaching time to committee service. This service to the course approval committee, the curriculum committee, and the writing program advisory committee, for instance, was necessitated by my position. At the same time, I had no vote. As an untenured faculty member, I felt powerless to refuse these invitations to serve.

In short, at schools like mine, where at least one-third of the faculty members have been here twenty-five years or longer, jWPAs do not share our colleagues' values, beliefs, and educational or cultural histories. We must circumvent such boundaries in order to make connections with our more powerful, institutionally sanctioned audiences. jWPAs at small colleges must learn new strategies, new ways of conceptualizing their rhetorical situations and, as a consequence, mount more useful and appropriate responses to them.

LEARNING FROM THE RHETORICAL STRATEGIES OF MARGINALIZED RHETORS

The types of constraints faced by the jWPA at a small college are unique, especially when we consider the shortage of resources and composition-savvy colleagues. Unless we can develop strategies for success in this context, not only do we suffer, but our programs—teachers and students alike—suffer as well. For instance, WPAs at small colleges must both support the faculty who teach writing classes and ensure a certain level of instructional quality for the students who take those classes. We may find ourselves having to speak from simultaneous and opposing positions. I recognize that my colleagues are overworked and that their writing intensive courses are overenrolled, sometimes with thirty or forty students in a section; they teach seven courses per year. How can I ethically argue that they should require multiple drafts of each assignment, conference with every student twice per semester, or perform in other ways that clearly reflect best practices in our discipline? How can I respond to the complaints of students in these classes when they are not offered enough instructor feedback and opportunities for revision? What strategy can enable me to respond to both situations? Indeed, given the jWPA's complicated identities as junior faculty member, administrator, and campus committee member, what rhetorical strategies can work simultaneously to persuade multiple audiences in multiple ways?

I have turned to the rhetorical strategies of marginalized speakers and writers as I rethink my rhetorical situation and my own desire for success. I believe that the study of marginalized speakers and writers can help jWPAs, especially women, think more critically about how to tailor our rhetorical strategies. Shirley Logan and Jacqueline Jones Royster, for instance, have considered nineteenth-century African American women's rhetorical practices as examples of those who, despite a lack of invitation, continued to speak, write, and shape cultural and educational practices in both domestic and public spaces.[4] In *Traces of a Stream,* Royster analyzes a variety of such practices within the African American women's essay tradition, focusing specifically on women writers of the nineteenth century. African American literary critics, rhetoricians, and linguists, including Geneva Smitherman, Henry Louis Gates, Jr., Logan, and Keith Gilyard, have chronicled a variety of rhetorical strategies practiced within the African American community, including signifyin(g), which constitutes rhetorics of indirection. In other words, such rhetorical strategies are premised on the understanding that one message can have different meanings for insider and outsider audiences. How hearers or readers interpret messages depends upon their relationships to the rhetor and the community in which the discourse is situated.

As a white, middle class woman, I certainly cannot position myself as marginalized in the same ways that writers of color can. Still, I believe there is much to learn from the shared practices of those who have had to struggle to be heard, and develop language that can send different messages to different audiences simultaneously. I am also interested in thinking about the margins as a strategic location from which to speak, an argument made in particular by feminist writers, such as Gloria Anzaldua. In my position, I might be viewed as marginalized for a number of reasons. I am a transplanted southerner living in Minnesota; the product of large, state-funded education working at a small private school; a nonpracticing Jew navigating a Lutheran institution. And I am a woman. According to my college's most recent accreditation report, I am in good company at the assistant professor level, but I may find fewer women colleagues should I stay long enough to be promoted to full professor. In addition, I am one of only a handful of junior faculty women who have children, although a large number of my male junior colleagues have them. Many of our junior-ranked women, in contrast, have remained childless by choice or raised children prior to beginning or returning to their academic careers.[5]

Likewise, the position of WPA can be viewed as marginalized within a discipline that has valued increasingly theoretical scholarship since the 1990s. In the spring of 2003, composition theorist Lynn Worsham, editor of *JAC,* spoke to the *Chronicle of Higher Education* about the perceived split between theory and practice within the discipline. In a conversation that was published in the March 21, 2003, edition of the *Chronicle* online, Worsham told writer Scott McLemee that she was "troubled by the fact that composition studies is now making 'a fairly huge investment in the subject of writing-program administration.'" Worsham told McLemee:

> Because I'm in rhetoric and composition, people have regularly assumed that I'm a candidate for writing-program administrator [. . .]. Well, I know nothing about it. And I have no interest in knowing anything about it. For the past 30 years, people in the field have tried to define [rhetoric and composition] as an intellectual discipline, not a service component of the university. But now it seems like people are embracing it as a service component.

Ironically, her comments were offered within the context of a conversation in which she declared a "chilly climate" for composition theorists. I believe that her comment suggests that WPA work is less valued and less intellectual than other kinds of work within the discipline, a discipline that has been represented as marginalized and feminized in relation to literary studies.

Writing program administrators have responded to this marginalization by advocating a particularly proactive rhetorical stance for administrators, one that depends upon the use of explicit acts of power. Indeed, power is the word of the day for those of us who subscribe to WPA-L, where on any given morning, WPAs from all over the country offer advice about how to use their power to ensure a fair compensation package at their (usually large) universities, gain more release time from their administrators, persuade campus committees, and so on. But as Thomas Amorose points out in his essay, "WPA Work at the Small College or University: Re-Imagining Power and Making the Small School Visible," this WPA discourse community has tended to "over-valoriz[e] power as a tool for the WPA," leaving small school WPAs with an awful lot of counter-productive advice (93). Instead, Amorose argues, WPAs at small schools must learn to develop authority and use that authority to wield influence in a far more collegial way.

According to Amorose, authority and influence, not explicit demonstrations of power, can move audience members on small campuses, where the WPA position "carries with it significant moral authority" (99). Amorose explains:

> This [. . .] kind of authority gets exercised not in the hiring and training of TAs or adjuncts, the operating of an office solely dedicated to composition, or any of the other functions or arrangements that indicate hierarchical authority [. . .]. Rather, this kind of authority gets exercised at those junctures in the cultural life of the institution where issues or plans essential to how the institution defines itself are being considered. Because small schools are, well, small and therefore smaller than the program type embodied in WPA literature, the WPA can play a larger role in this cultural life; it is a matter both of mission and of scale. (99)

I agree with Amorose, and I see real connections to my earlier analysis of Bitzer. WPAs at large institutions may, in fact, be able to alter the realities of their writing programs by utilizing the power of their usually tenured positions explicitly: they can demand that TAs and adjuncts submit syllabi for review; they can singlehandedly make decisions about which handbook to adopt or whether or not to use a commonly taught syllabus for the first-year writing sequence. But jWPAs on small campuses can't. The most we can hope for is to persuade our colleagues that we mean well, that we see ourselves as aligned with them and the college's liberal arts mission. We can demonstrate an unbelievable willingness to work just as hard as they do, to attend countless meetings and teach our hearts out daily, and hope that they begin to take our advice about teaching writing.

Now, I would argue there are systematic ways to do this. Several feminist theorists and practitioners of rhetoric are particularly helpful. Remember that Bitzer posits the elements of the rhetorical situation in agonistic terms. Exigence stands opposite the rhetor, daring him to act. Audience members by definition must be changed—conquered somehow—by the rhetor. Constraints might prevent the victory and must be overcome. This model of rhetorical situation assumes a divide and conquer model of rhetorical discourse, one that leaves little room for negotiation between audience members and the rhetor. But according to feminist scholars of rhetorical theory, other models are possible.[6] Feminist rhetoricians Sonja and Karen Foss critique masculinist models of communication in *Women Speak: The Eloquence of Women's Lives*. Foss and Foss name "eight primary assumptions [that] have served as the foundation for the study of communicators and texts by scholars in the area of public address"; this list of assumptions constructs the rhetor as a lone, "noteworthy" male who speaks publicly, offering a "finished product" to his listeners (Foss and Foss 2). According to Foss and Foss, such models are dangerous because they clearly preclude women from the realm of rhetoric by defining rhetorical discourse in terms of political speechmaking, an activity from which women have been excluded historically. Furthermore, the eight assumptions have been largely responsible for "the lack of significance accorded women's communication," the forms of which often are situated within private domestic, rather than public, spaces (2). This feminist critique has implications for the junior faculty WPA at a small college, especially if she is a woman.

For instance, in *Feminist Rhetorical Theories,* Foss, Foss, and Cindy Griffin study nine feminist theorists who represent varied cultural and disciplinary backgrounds, chronicling the ways in which these women emerge as rhetorical theorists and revisionary practitioners. According to Foss, Foss, and Griffin, these nine women use rhetoric in order to "create worlds, perspectives, and identities" (7). From African American feminist theorist, bell hooks, for example, we learn to revise Bitzer's model of the rhetor, positing instead of the conquering *public speaker* a *critical thinker* whose very identity makes it possible for her to understand—and perhaps communicate—the relationship between personal experience and ideology. The rhetorical theory enacted by hooks suggests that rhetoric "involves adoption of the role of critical thinker or enlightened witness. This role constitutes a way of thinking that allows individuals to examine the harmful effects of domination in their personal lives and the public world and to discover what they can do to facilitate change" (83).

If I reconceptualize myself as a "witness" for the program, someone who comes to those in power on my campus (largely those male faculty members who are ranked at associate or full professor) and models a kind of critical thinking about the program, my job then becomes that of knowledgeable and politically savvy storyteller. I must make decisions about which narratives, or forms of witnessing, will be most powerful on a given occasion, and use those narratives to suggest the need for curricular or even cultural change on campus. The possibility for negotiation exists; the narrative form invites participation as I encourage listeners to think critically along with me as "we" work together to change the writing program in some way.

In contrast to hooks's emphasis on "witnessing," Gloria Anzaldua focuses on the necessary falsehoods that marginalized rhetors must create in order to construct an ethos for themselves. As Foss, Foss, and Griffin interpret her work, Gloria Anzaldua suggests that "marginalized rhetors can rarely speak out of their authentic experiences in the dominant culture; to be credible in that culture, they must present falsehoods and "make faces" that are appropriate for and adjusted to those in control" (122). Here, then, Anzaldua helps me to understand the need to pull back from certain acts of truth telling on campus and to remake myself in the image of my colleagues. For instance, when I offer faculty development workshops for teachers of writing intensive courses, I rarely am able to truly communicate to my colleagues what it means to teach writing in responsible, theoretically sophisticated ways. I cannot simply stand up during a workshop on revision, for example, and tell colleagues the truth: Yes, it takes longer to be a good teacher of writing. Yes, we should respond to several drafts of an assignment if we want our students to really learn what revision means. Yes, students only learn to revise well when something real is at stake, and it's our job to help them come to articulate what that "real thing" is. Yes, it's important to show students our own work if we want to construct a kind of integrity for ourselves as working writers.

As any WPA knows, the typical afternoon faculty development workshop doesn't really allow us to fully address such topics. Participants may want to straddle the uneasy line between a therapy session and a ritualistic griping ceremony. For instance, one colleague may enter an afternoon WAC workshop on teaching revision with the *need* to feel better about her practice of not allowing students to submit rough drafts for her commentary. Despite her understanding that a teacher's time is better spent responding to rough, rather than final, drafts, she may not be able to handle the paper load each term—the load can be prohibitive for faculty who teach six or seven courses each year. Another colleague may come to the workshop looking for like-minded peers who will agree with his particularly harsh sentence-level error policy. He may even want to challenge "the program" for its lax attitude on the subject.

If I approach such a situation with the desire to utterly *change* my colleagues' approaches, let alone their minds, I am bound to fail. My discipline is relatively unknown to them, and thus unauthoritative (so trotting out the experts won't help). I am a younger and less experienced teacher than anyone else in the room, so I don't automatically earn credibility. But if I approach the workshop with a willingness to "make faces" like my colleagues, I may be able to join with them in solidarity for a few minutes. I can stretch the truth as I work to construct a sense of our shared enterprise. I may even need to bite my tongue and validate their frustrations about the paper load and the "gross negligence" of student writers. This way, I construct myself as a sympathetic member of their community, and position myself as a person who might be able to influence them and their teaching practices.

THE SITUATIONS WE LEAVE AND THE SITUATIONS WE ENTER

One of my favorite Seinfeld episodes includes a subnarrative where Elaine Bennis finds a new group of friends to hang out with: Kevin is the anti-Jerry. He is polite, considerate, giving. His friends, a short, stocky bald guy named Gene and a tall, wacky guy named Feldman—who eerily resemble George and Kramer, respectively—are equally charming. Elaine, of course, recognizes the irony. She sees that she has entered a world that closely resembles the other. She sees that she has entered a world that closely resembles the one she left, at least structurally. But still, she sees what a difference those attitudes make. She dubs her new digs at Kevin's apartment "Bizarro World."

In some respects, I shared Elaine's experience when I came to interview at my small, private institution in January of 1999. The job the department chair described to me *seemed* like the WPA job I knew and loved as a grad student at Ohio State: writing intensive courses to administer, handbooks to review, faculty development workshops to plan. As the department chair discussed the WAC program and writing center duties, though, I clearly imagined directing both in a collaborative way, drawing upon the expertise of colleagues, the support of a secretary, perhaps even rotating the administrative work with another compositionist on campus. It didn't occur to me that I would be expected to go it alone. Such an administrative model was beyond the scope of my Big Ten imagination. Certainly I didn't think to ask about secretarial support. Who ever heard of a writing program without a secretary?

When new PhDs in rhetoric and composition leave the suite of WPA offices at a large public institution, our R1 expectations may get the better of us. And then we enter Bizarro World, where we direct multiple programs alone (sometimes the English department will loan us a work study student for an hour or two, though) while teaching four, five, or—as is the case for one of my colleagues in Georgia—six courses per year. We may be disoriented by the scope of our positions at small colleges. Consider the many hats suggested by the following advertisement for my current position, which was featured in the MLA *Job Information List* in 1999. The position was assistant professor of English and director of writing at a private liberal arts school of approximately 2,400 students:

> Seeking a tenure-track assistant professor, beginning Fall, 2000, to direct, promote, and advocate for the existing college-wide writing across the curriculum program; to teach a variety of writing classes in the English department (Research and Writing, Intermediate Composition, Reading and Writing Essays, etc.); and to teach courses in English teaching methods and adolescent literature. Requirements: PhD in hand (dissertation in composition/rhetoric preferred, but other fields with extensive, focused experience in composition/rhetoric considered); teaching certification in English or Language Arts (any state); and college teaching experience. Experience in a writing across the curriculum program highly desirable. (*JIL* 1999)

The advertisement is fairly typical within the world of liberal arts colleges. Such schools must cobble together what we at my institution affectionately term "Frankenstein positions" for obvious reasons. When resources are scarce and faculty members must work as generalists within their fields of study, the composition scholar must simply become "the writing person," which means that she is the "composition teacher," the "pedagogy person," the "writing center person" *and* the "WAC person."

Initially, I imagined myself well prepared to direct a writing program at this Lutheran liberal arts college in southern Minnesota. After all, during my five years as a PhD student at Ohio State University, I spent one third of my time on fellowship, one third in the classroom teaching composition, and one third doing administrative work. I was a graduate student WPA for first-year writing, as well as a graduate administrator for the Writing Workshop, a basic writing program. I learned a great deal about the nature of WPA work within large public institutions. I needed to *unlearn* an awful lot, though, if I was to earn tenure in Bizarro World. I began a rather Socratic dialogue with myself.

1. What, exactly, is a writing program? How can I tell if I'm actually directing one?

At large institutions, WPAs know that they direct programs. After all, a good writing program probably features one tenured WPA, as well as an assistant director—a faculty member, professional administrator, or graduate student—as well as an administrative assistant. These writing programs may also employ graduate student WPAs and undergraduate work-study students. They offer faculty development opportunities, hire teachers and schedule their courses, and conduct regular methods of assessment to ensure that students learn to write well. But at small institutions like mine, writing programs are hard to define. First and foremost, most small schools hire nontenured people to direct their programs. They can't afford not to. Second, most small school WPAs work alone; we rarely have collaborators or support staff. Some small colleges have actual first-year composition requirements; others, like mine, have writing across the curriculum initiatives augmented by thematically organized first-year seminars for entering students. While a small college with a strong endowment and/or a particularly strong commitment to writing instruction may create an elaborate writing program, many small colleges manage to teach students to write simply because the faculty are committed to one-on-one conferencing. You might hear small college faculty members scoff at the "need" for a writing program altogether: "Students write plenty. It's a liberal arts college, after all!" In this climate, how can jWPAs be recognized as necessary experts?

2. How will my colleagues view my expertise as a composition specialist?

At most large institutions, program directors, assistant directors, and graduate student WPAs study composition theory, pedagogy, and history. These experts are respected, necessary members of campus culture. They sit on important campus committees and help others understand the value and importance of writing instruction. These WPAs oversee a fairly novice staff of writing teachers, particularly graduate teaching assistants; they may also supervise more experienced part-timers or adjunct faculty. But at smaller colleges, the teachers are not novices. A jWPA—who may or may not be a composition expert—must "mentor" teachers who have been working at the institution for decades. Indeed, full-fledged faculty members most likely teach the majority of a small college's composition or writing intensive courses. Here, the jWPA finds herself at a particular disadvantage on a small college campus. Other faculty have far more teaching experience than she does—though not necessarily more experience teaching *writing*. While all WPAs find themselves having to fight for authority and credibility to a certain extent, jWPAs on small campuses must wage this battle in a particularly grueling way until they achieve tenure.

3. If there's not really a "program," and I'm not always recognized as an "expert," then why do these colleges need a jWPA in the first place?

This is the question that keeps me up nights. The nearly universally required, first-year composition course at most large universities virtually ensures the continuing presence (even if not always a healthy presence) of the writing programs and WPAs who administer them. When writing courses are graduation requirements, writing programs can depend upon a certain level of budgetary and staffing support. The composition experts may write a common syllabus or other shared curricular materials, and the fairly novice teaching staff may appreciate the help—more evidence for the continuing need to budget the program. At my own institution, however, every course is viewed as equally necessary for the curriculum, and each element of the curriculum may be perceived as "owned by the faculty" as a whole. All faculty develop their own courses, usually in conjunction with their departments. New courses are approved by the whole faculty. There are no programs created by "experts" and then passed on to a group of teachers who are hired to teach for/in the program. Certainly faculty members are not eager to have an untenured (and hence unproven) colleague write their curricular materials for them. My "real" expertise as a WPA is thus automatically rendered unnecessary. What I know best is curriculum development and assessment; what I feel least empowered to offer are curricular or assessment directives.

4. Okay. Then who—or what—authorizes a jWPA?

WPAs at large institutions are infamous for sending countless memos, missives, reminders, and flyers to teachers and students alike. Writing programs create handbooks and catalogs, policy manuals, and curricular guidelines. Some offer a common core syllabus or sequence of writing assignments, helping to ensure that courses taught by inexperienced teachers have strong theoretical and pedagogical scaffolding. As WPAs, I would argue that we are what we write; the documents communicate power to others. Small college faculty hate nothing more than programmatic documents, policies, and other unifying measures. Small college faculty may resist standardization of any kind, balking at anything that might erode their academic freedom or pedagogical decision-making. At my institution, we offer few guidelines to help faculty plan their WAC courses (i.e., students need to produce at least twelve pages of prose per semester), and most faculty are not at all interested in uniform assignments. My most experienced colleagues send a strong message: Trust us to design our own courses, please. We don't need a "composition expert"—especially a junior faculty member who doesn't really know our institution yet—to design writing assignments for us, and those assignments needn't all look alike. This *is* a liberal arts college, is it not?

5. How can jWPAs at small schools ever know if students are learning to write well?

At large institutions, where the WPA is most likely a tenured faculty member, she can ask for syllabi to review, visit classrooms, and demand some kind of accountability. Assessment strategies are often multilayered. WPAs and their assistants may observe and evaluate teachers, survey students, read student portfolios, and conduct focus groups with students and/or staff members. Mentoring systems for new teachers can also facilitate assessment. Faculty at small colleges prefer individual methods of assessment. Small college teachers like to develop their own methods of assessment, which may or may not be augmented by formal methods conducted through the dean's office or personnel committee at tenure or at promotion time. At my college, we can administer standard evaluation of teaching forms in all of our courses, but it is not mandatory to do so. But this approach to assessment on campus means that programs such as WAC find it difficult to conduct assessment projects on a large scale. If I have a good relationship with the teachers in my program, I may be invited to observe classes or survey students. If I am perceived as "overseeing" in any way, I will not be invited in. jWPAs at the small college may have little more than anecdotal data and a strong hunch to back them up when they argue that things are (or aren't) going well in the classroom.

6. This job is complicated! How am I going to do it and produce enough new scholarship in my field to achieve tenure?

WPAs are scholars and researchers, and writing program administration is intellectual work. Tenured WPAs often teach a 1–1 or 1–2 load, including the composition theory and practice course for teaching assistants; this enables them to further their research agendas, which are often tied to the programs they direct. According to the position statement published by the Council of Writing Program Administrators, "Evaluating the Intellectual Work of Writing Administration," administering a writing program "may be considered intellectual work when it meets two tests. First, it needs to advance knowledge: its production, clarification, connection, reinterpretation, or application. Second, it results in products or activities that can be evaluated by others."[7] The document, revised in 1998, emphasizes external evaluation, suggesting that expertise shared with outsiders is most valuable. At my college, however, faculty produce new knowledge for both internal and external audiences. My college encourages scholarship from faculty, delineating "an emerging pattern" of scholarly development as the second most important criterion for tenure. But the realities of life at a small college—teaching loads of three to four undergraduate courses each semester, twenty to eighty student advisees per semester, and committee work—leave jWPAs with less time to devote to scholarship. When

I was hired, I planned to conduct ongoing research as WAC director and writing center director and finish my book project. Happily,
research leading directly to curricular or pedagogical innovation on
campus is highly valued. Unhappily, my colleagues don't always recognize that such research comes at the expense of my other scholarship.
I'm a feminist scholar in composition theory. My book project, which
has remained incomplete for the last five years, draws upon that part
of my intellectual life. I face a constant choice as a pretenure faculty
member: Do I try to finish my book and get tenure, perhaps at the
expense of the program, or do I teach myself to conduct the programmatic research, perhaps to the detriment of my own career path?

Theory into Practice: Learning to Succeed in Bizarro World

Socratic dialogues, of course, are supposed to enable us to reach definitive answers to our questions. My questions seem to spiral out of control, so I guess that wasn't really Socratic dialogue. Still, the questions
and answers that play in my head rather constantly do help me to go
about my work on a daily basis. I recognize that mine is an institution
that means well, that it's an institution with a rich WAC history and
a commitment—at least in the abstract—to writing instruction for all
students and support for writing teachers.

In 1986, William Zinsser published an article entitled "A Bolder
Way to Teach Writing" in the *New York Times*. His essay reflects upon
the WAC movement in general and focuses on his visit to what is now
my own institution. When Zinsser visited us, we were experiencing the
heyday of the WAC revolution. The professors interviewed by Zinsser
spoke enthusiastically of their participation in writing across the curriculum efforts; a quotation from the article continues to appear on
a brochure for the WAC program that we use to recruit students and
new faculty members alike.

A WAC school for more than two decades, our college now offers
a fairly typical approach to writing across the curriculum. There is no
first-year composition sequence. Instead, we offer a writing-intensive
first term seminar to all entering first-year students, as well as selected
transfer students at mid-year. Then, all students must take two additional "W" courses, one of which must be "writing intensive" and
one of which must be "writing in the disciplines." We have no teach-

ing assistants (save those few international students who work for the department of modern foreign languages). Our WAC program simply seeks to ensure that all 2,400 students take at least three writing intensive courses from visiting, tenured, or tenure-track professors before they graduate. I feel relieved to have no adjuncts to oversee.

When I arrived, the system for proposing writing intensive courses had been in place for twenty years; the criteria had remained largely unchanged since the program's inception. I revised a bit of the language when I first arrived to allow specific disciplines a bit more leeway in determining what constituted "formal" writing (unit plans in education courses, lab reports in biology courses, and so on), but despite frequent complaints from faculty about having to teaching writing intensive courses, there was little interest in discussing our reasons for doing what we do. There was also no real enthusiasm for changing it.

It was a tough rhetorical situation. I knew the criteria needed to be changed. I knew that our faculty were overworked and exhausted, unable to do the work of teaching writing intensive courses with such high enrollments, sometimes as many as forty students in a class. But I knew I had not been "invited" to persuade my colleagues to change the system, and I knew that I was not in a position to win any battles that might ensue. I had to rethink.

Like hooks suggests, I had to convince my new colleagues that I was, in fact, a critical thinker who could communicate that relationship between the college's current WAC ideology and my personal intellectual experience as a composition theorist, which clearly challenged that ideology. During my first year on campus, recognizing the cultural dissonance that I experienced coming from a large, state supported first-year composition program, I studied our college's institutional history to learn more about the ways that the WAC program did—and did not—reflect the values of the college. My analysis of documents, such as the mission statement and curriculum committee records, as well as my interviews with experienced faculty who had participated in our WAC program, was instructive.

I learned, for instance, that one of the faculty's primary values is collegial trust. Thus, programs like mine have traditionally operated under the assumption that colleagues should trust one another to teach courses well, imposing few, if any, measures for ensuring the quality of writing instruction. Program directors do not make it a habit to collect syllabi or require classroom visits. Some programs, such as the first term seminar, do provide evaluative instruments for their courses, but do not enforce data collection. Here I could not depend upon reams of documents to declare my authority, nor did I have a team of collaborators to back me up. Instead, I learned quickly that my best chance to learn more about how W classes were taught would have to come from conversations—not programmatic requests. That means, of course, that I am always on duty as a WPA. Lunches are actually fact-finding missions. Coffee breaks are opportunities to check in with the program's teachers. Committee meetings are opportunities to advocate for the program and its needs.

And in every instance described above, I was constructing myself more and more as an insider, first "witnessing"—again, as hooks suggests—to my colleagues about my experiences on this campus and then modeling a way of thinking critically about our situation. By the end of my second year, I was able to share a written document with the curriculum committee, one of our campus's most powerful and influential committees, and one upon which I sat *ex-officio*. This document described our existing approach to WAC, discussed the ways in which that approach actually conflated two contradictory models of composition theory, and advocated for another model of teaching writing intensive courses on campus. While the document in no way was meant to persuade my colleagues on the committee to change their minds immediately, it certainly planted a seed that I could cultivate in future years.

Next, I chronicled great resistance to what some faculty termed a rush for new professors to "over-professionalize." New faculty were publishing too much too soon. They felt pressured in ways that more experienced faculty could not understand. This was a tricky finding to negotiatebecause here the faculty exhibited a generational split. Faculty members hired in the last decade clearly valued scholarly work and continued to produce a great deal of it; faculty members hired in the previous decades enacted their commitment to the ideals of a traditional liberal arts college by emphasizing teaching and service. While all colleagues value one another's work, and while I know that all are committed to teaching excellence, I sensed clear resistance from many experienced faculty toward workshops and other forms of professional development "unrelated" to their academic fields. Newer faculty, however, seemed hungry for such opportunities for a variety of reasons.

The workshops constituted chances to get to know colleagues outside the home department. Some summer faculty development opportunities even carried stipends—helpful for new faculty trying to pay off their student loans. These new teachers had grown accustomed to such workshop opportunities when they were teaching assistants at large research universities.

Thus I began to "make faces," per Gloria Anzaldua's suggestion, to my older colleagues, agreeing with them that they clearly didn't need my workshopsto succeed in the writing classroom. I'd gladly use this position in order to construct a kind of ethos that suggested I recognized I had much to learn from these, my more experienced colleagues, and I'd use more informal opportunities to share my knowledge about teaching writing with them: at lunch, after chapel, during other kinds of meetings. At the same time, I began to focus my attention on the newer faculty, teachers who actually made it much easier to offer the kinds of workshops I intended. These new faculty members had often been teaching assistants during their graduate school years; many had taken composition theory and pedagogy courses, and all were amenable to many of the ideas I presented to them: peer response, process-oriented assignments, experimentation with genre.

Finally, and perhaps most importantly, my study of the college's documents and culture revealed a strong institutional commitment to apprenticeship or mentorship models of education. For many faculty on campus, the most fulfilling educational experiences seemed to be those where novice students became increasingly expert through close contact with professors. This was true for faculty regardless of the number of years on the job. Thus I recognized a way to respond to both constituencies: my senior colleagues would serve on the personnel committee and decide my tenure case without ever attending one of my workshops; my junior colleagues needed help and valued my knowledge. I knew already that this would not be a campus that would respond well to external authority (i.e., the outside reviewers or visiting scholars), and most faculty had little time to devote to my workshops.

In the end, I decided to focus my work as a WPA on the writing center, revising the WAC program within that context. Our writing center, which I direct, is staffed entirely by undergraduate tutors from across the disciplines. The center is funded primarily by campus employment programs and work-study dollars. In my first year, for instance, I piloted a new program, WAC-UP (Writing Across the Curriculum Undergraduate Partnerships), which put undergraduate student tutors in charge of outreach and information gathering. My intention was to foster relationships with both older and younger faculty, capitalizing on the faculty's desire to help students who themselves were learning valuable skills: writing, reading, thinking, listening, and talking. The program fizzled, however, as busy teachers claimed that they were simply unable to stop long enough to meet with the tutors to discuss disciplinary conventions. But I see now that I had misread a crucial part of our institutional culture: the faculty's desire to foster the distinction between *mentoring* and *collaborating* with students.

My colleagues were not yet ready to label undergraduate students "WAC consultants," and resisted meeting with those consultants to share assignment prompts or resources. Indeed, I learned that our faculty requires and respects a fundamental distinction between "student" and "teacher" while simultaneously valuing student-centered, exploratory experiences in the classroom. In my second and third years, then, I continued to focus on undergraduate tutors at the writing center, but linked them with interested teachers of W courses across the curriculum in a mentoring model that we call the Designated Tutor program. I paired faculty members with tutors who were particularly interested in their disciplines and/or teaching styles. In turn, many of these faculty members developed strong mentoring relationships with the tutors, which translated into good will toward the writing center and the program. Then these faculty participated in a series that we called "WAC Nights at the Center," opportunities for interdisciplinary panel discussions about reading, responding to, and evaluating student writing across the campus. In short, the work of faculty development got done, but not when it was labeled "faculty development."

In each instance described above, I worked hard to foster a sense of institutional identity for the WAC program as well as an identity for myself as a member of the College community; I did so in ways that insisted that the program exists and that I am an "insider" as its director. I also suggested a kind of common faculty ownership. In order for the program—not just the requirement—to live, faculty members could not think of the writing program as "Taylor's program." Even now, when I write memos or promotional documents, I refer to the program as "we," when, in fact, I'm the only faculty member assigned to the work. Thus "we" at the writing program sponsor workshops, "we" invite teachers to submit writing assignments and sample syllabi, "we" request that they order the recommended handbook (never, ever a requirement), and "we" thank the faculty for their support of the writing center each year. But that "we" is very different from the one I helped to construct as a graduate student WPA. While that former "we" was an attempt to forge connections with a fairly disempowered group of teaching assistants, this new "we" is an effort to construct a program where only a requirement exists. The "we" does more than contribute to the construction of my authority as a jWPA; it literally constitutes the program that authorizes me.

A Cautiona(rily Optimistic) Tale

It is disconcerting to step for the first time into a role as jWPA at a small liberal arts college. The sudden responsibility for such a fundamental part of the curriculum can be overwhelming. But it can also be liberating. Junior faculty status has certainly undermined my authority, but it has also afforded me the opportunity to play what I call the inexperience and enthusiasm card. The window of opportunity was narrow: I could only ask innocent, enthusiastic, strategic questions of new colleagues for about a year. Example: "So let me understand what I'm seeing in the catalog. All 2,400 of our students need to take three writing intensive courses to graduate. But faculty members are not required to train or prepare to teach those courses. Did anyone ever try to make such workshops mandatory? Oh, I see. After the grant ran out, there was no money for those workshops. So what kind of faculty development opportunities exist now?" After that first year, unfortunately, colleagues no longer considered me new; our colleagues simply expect us to try to solve the same problems that predecessors, folks who directed writing programs for twenty or thirty years, long ago abandoned. All jWPAs need rhetorical strategies to help us face those problems with new energy and commitment.

But we also need to keep our eyes on the institutional problems that stem from lingering gender inequities on our campuses. I need to be wary of the fact that five of the seven interdisciplinary programs on my campus are directed by women, and only one has tenure. I need to be more vocal about my concerns as my WAC directorship becomes increasingly clerical. And I need to call upon my tenured colleagues to be more actively engaged with the making of policies that affect women faculty, staff, and students most directly. Then the real work of the jWPA on a small campus can begin: helping colleagues to fill the gap between "best practices out there" and "real practices" on our campus. Once we are willing to acknowledge that this rhetorical situation is unlike any other we may have experienced, jWPAs at small colleges can begin to study our institutions' culture(s) and rhetorical practices. Then, we can make more appropriate choices as we perform, daily. our precarious relationship to the writing program, the institution, our colleagues, and students.

NOTES

[1] Substantial portions of this essay appeared in "Preparing WPAs for the Small College Context," published in *Composition Studies* 32.2 (Fall 2004). See pages 53–73. I am grateful to *Composition Studies* for permission to reprint this material.

[2] It seems important to note that my closest male friend completed his PhD but walked away from the profession in disgust after a half-hearted attempt at the job market did not yield the kind of offer that he hoped for. He, I believe, couldn't begin to imagine himself one of the composition "bosses" described in Joseph Harris's essay, "Meet the New Boss, Same as the Old Boss: Class Consciousness in Composition." See *College Composition and Communication*, 52.1, 2000.

[3] Bitzer's piece appeared in the first edition of Philosophy and Rhetoric in 1968. By 1973, the same journal featured Richard E. Vatz's essay, "The Myth of the Rhetorical Situation," which critiqued Bitzer's "realist" philosophical stance, claiming that such a stance had "unfortunate implications for rhetoric" (226). Vatz argued against Bitzer's assumption that actual situations or exigencies exist in a sort of Platonic reality. Vatz argued instead that we should pay attention to rhetors themselves as creators of rhetorical situations because they, in fact, make choices to respond to particular situations in particular ways. People create rhetoric through language; pre-existing rhetorical situations do not merely create rhetors and rhetoric.

[4] Here I recognize the tension inherent in aligning myself, a white, middle-class, twenty-first century professional, with the rhetorical practices and subject position of "disempowered" rhetors such as the African American women studied by Royster and Logan. Rather than trying to co-opt terms here, I'm forging connections by recognizing that my location as a minority person on my campus is a discursive product of my institutional culture.

[5] At most small colleges, where faculty members teach three or four classes per semester, the important and labor-intensive work of committees takes place early in the morning or early in the evening, and working parents

must choose on a regular basis between attending meetings and preparing and sharing meals with their families.

⁶ Here I draw largely from Foss, Foss, and Griffin's important book *Feminist Rhetorical Theories* (1999) because I find it the most comprehensive, accessible resource to date. Its focus on the relationship between rhetorical theory and practice is refreshing and clear. It is important to note, however, that a number of feminist scholars in the history of rhetoric and composition have done important work that is more focused on feminist historiography, including Susan Jarratt, Cheryl Glenn, Andrea Lunsford, Shirley Wilson Logan, and Jacqueline Jones Royster.

⁷ (http://wpacouncil.org/positions/intellectualwork.html).

WORKS CITED

Amorose, Thomas. "WPA Work at the Small College or University: Re-Imagining Power and Making the Small School Visible." *The Allyn and Bacon Sourcebook for Writing Program Administrators.* Ed. Irene Ward and William J. Carpenter. New York: Longman, 2002. 91–105.

Bitzer, Lloyd. "The Rhetorical Situation." *Philosophy and Rhetoric* 1 (1968): 1–14.

Foss, Karen A., Sonja K. Foss, and Cindy L. Griffin. *Feminist Rhetorical Theories.* Thousand Oaks, CA: Sage, 1999.

Foss, Karen A., and Sonja Foss, eds. *Women Speak: The Eloquence of Women's Lives.* Prospect Heights, IL: Waveland P, 1991.

Hult, Christine, and the Portland Resolution Committee: David Joliffe, Kathleen Kelly,

Dana Mead, and Charles Schuster. *WPA: Writing Program Administration* 16.1/2 (Fall/Winter 1992): 88-94. http://www.wpacouncil.org/positions/portlandres.html

Kirsch, Gesa, and Joy Ritchie. "Beyond the Personal: Theorizing a Politics of Location in Composition Research." *College Composition and Communication* 46.1 (1995): 7–29.

McLemee, Scott. "Deconstructing Composition: The 'New Theory Wars' Break Out in an Unlikely Discipline." *Chronicle of Higher Education.* 49.28 (2003). 7 April 2007 <http://chronicle.com/weekly/v49/i28/28a01601.htm>.

Mortimer, Victor Ronald. *Composing Ourselves: Ethos and the Negotiation of Teacher Identity.* Diss. Ohio State University, 2000.

Royster, Jacqueline Jones. *Traces of a Stream: Literacy and Social Change Among African American Women.* Pittsburgh: U of Pittsburgh P, 2000.

Vatz, Richard E. "The Myth of the Rhetorical Situation." *Philosophy and Rhetoric* (Summer 1973). Reprinted in *Contemporary Rhetorical Theory:*

A Reader. Eds. John Louis Lucaites, Celeste Michelle Condit, and Sally Caudill. New York: The Guilford Press, 1999. 226-231.

Zinsser, William. "A Bolder Way to Teach Writing." *New York Times*. 13 April, 1986: Education Life 58–63.

11 Administering Writing Programs in the "Betweens": A jWPA Narrative

Sandee K. McGlaun

> I was within and without—simultaneously enchant-
> ed and repelled by the inexhaustible variety of life.
>
> —F. Scott Fitzgerald

As I sit down to write this text, I am acutely conscious of my immediate context: I sit in the long, narrow office I share with a department colleague, an adjunct professor who teaches the only three German courses offered at our small state university. I sit in the back part of our cement-block walled office, closest to the window; as a fourth-year, tenure-track assistant professor of English, I "outrank" my part-time colleague and therefore occupy the choicer half of our space. I sit with my back to the office door whenever I work at my computer, as I am doing now, and I confess that I am mildly unnerved by this position. As absurd as it may sound, thoughts of Billy the Kid enter my head. Certainly, the ideas I present in my designated roles as director of composition and director of the writing center have sometimes been treated as suspect, but I hardly expect to be shot in the back. Still, what might my colleagues say, were they to peer over my shoulder and read a narrative in which I declare that, since taking on my director of composition and writing center mantles just eleven months after joining this institution, I often feel, in a Billy the Kid kind of way, WANTED?

At times, of course, I feel genuinely "wanted," even needed: I am a rhetoric and composition specialist who was brought in to share ex-

pertise and guide a growing writing program. But at other times, I feel
WANTED: I am an outlaw, a troublemaker, and (I fear) a prospective bearer of blame. I sometimes have to suppress the urge to petition
the Law of Those Who Came Before Me for pardon. But more often
than not, I work in a space located somewhere between these two extremes. As a jWPA, I work in what rhetoric and composition theorist
Nedra Reynolds calls the "betweens" (333). Reynolds describes the
"betweens" in her 1993 essay, "*Ethos* as Location," drawing on Karen
Burke LeFevre's suggestion that ethos is constructed "'in the point of
intersection between speaker and writer and listener or reader'" and on
Kate Ronald's proposal that ethos is created "'in the spaces between
personal and public life'" (qtd. in Reynolds 333). Located neither at
the center nor on the margins; the "betweens" are spaces of negotiation, sites for the construction of *ethos* that "highlight the multiple negotiations" inherent in the process of that construction (332). Though
Reynolds's work focuses specifically on how *ethos* is constructed by
writers in written texts, I wish to argue that the metaphor of the "betweens" can help jWPAs describe and reflect upon the multiple negotiations we must make as we construct our professional *ethos* within
our positions, our institutions, and our discipline.

jWPAs are typically located in the "betweens" not by choice but by
default, a result of institutional context and circumstance. A teacher-
scholar assuming a jWPA role is likely to find herself located between
the promise of a position and its implied power and the reality of a
title that does not appear in any official administrative organizational
chart or job description—the betweens of task and position,[1] faculty
member and administrator. Or a jWPA may be asked to administer
a "program" that carries the title but none of the coherence the name
implies, or carry the workload of program administration without the
recognition or resources that might accompany an established "program," locating the jWPA between what David Schwalm calls program*ming* and program. And often, a jWPA will be hired under the
auspices of a particular department to direct a program (or manage
programming)—such as first-year writing or a writing center—that
directly serves the whole institution, thus situating the jWPA between
department and university in terms of loyalty and accountability. Located in the midst of all these betweens, jWPAs must also negotiate
the competing demands on our time and energy of teaching, administration, research, service, and life outside the academy, and, further-

more, cope with the fact that while we are often hired into an institution because its members have recognized and even expressed a need for change and guidance, we are likely to experience stark resistance to actually urging that change. Thus we become both wanted and WANTED.

Given the professional reality that jWPAs more often than not work by default in one or more (if not all) of these betweens, it behooves us to cultivate an awareness of this positioning and to learn how to make strategic use of it. I propose that jWPAs reclaim this liminal, shifting space as one of creative negotiation. By using our location—and, in some cases, choosing to locate ourselves—in the "betweens," we can reinvent that location as a space of personal agency and programmatic growth. To do so, I suggest that we follow Reynolds's recommendations for writers, replacing that term where it appears in her text with "jWPAs" in my restatement of it, here: "How might this idea of 'the betweens' work in practice? I think it means attending to the rhetorical strategies [jWPAs] use to locate themselves, their texts, and the particular discursive communities they are mediating within and between" (333). We must first acknowledge the politically charged location that the "J" perforce assigns us to; then, we must examine how the betweens position *us,* and, finally, reclaim them and use them strategically to our advantage. Specifically, I wish to argue that by using (and sometimes choosing) their location in the betweens to cultivate fluidity, the ability to inhabit a sort of multiple ethos, jWPAs may claim authority and enact policy while still attending to the political challenges attached to their junior status.

The Betweens: An Idiomatic Interlude

Between a rock and a hard place. Between the devil and the deep blue sea. The idiomatic expressions that traditionally locate one in the "betweens" are far from comforting. To be in either of the aforementioned locations is, according to the *American Idioms Dictionary,* to be in a "very difficult position," or "facing a hard decision" (Spears 35). To choose between the lesser of two evils is to have no real choice at all. And to be betwixt and between is to be undecided, even befuddled. Between you, me, and the fencepost (or lamppost, depending on one's regional orientation), this catalog of "between" expressions is getting downright depressing.

In all seriousness: it is no secret that being a jWPA often means being in a difficult position, one marked by hard decisions, one that may even leave its occupier, on occasion, befuddled. Indeed, what most of us no doubt long for is the "twin" implied by "between's" second syllable, which etymologically descends from "two" and "twin." I know I have often wished for a doppelganger who could divide my tasks "by two each" (Ayto 61) and so double my accomplishments—without doubling my workload.

To revise the metaphor in the sense that Reynolds uses it, to reclaim the betweens as a location of agency, then, is no small challenge. Yet, several of the idiomatic expressions above suggest, even depend upon, an either-or fallacy: if the choice is between the devil and the deep blue sea, then there is no third, or fourth, or sixteenth option. The origin of the word "between" itself implies this most limited set of choices, as does its traditional usage. The current edition of *The St. Martin's Handbook* reminds us: "In referring to two things or people, use *between*. In referring to three or more, use *among*" (Lunsford 983). But as good rhetoricians, we know that there are always more than two options. Thus, the first move toward (re)location I wish to suggest is that we focus attention not on the choices presented on either side of the between, but on that space in the middle. This is the space where one is located prior to making a decision or claim; it is the space of possibility, the space in and from which we may cultivate fluidity.

When I first began my work as a jWPA, I felt that most choices were either-or: either I could choose to maintain the status quo, or I could choose to forward and enact dramatic change. We often think of making strong choices as action, and action as the locus of agency. But most of the time neither of these strong choices was palatable, for the first often set me at odds with myself and my disciplinary knowledge, while the other was likely to set me at odds with my colleagues. I needed a different way of thinking about my WPA work; I wanted to be wanted without being WANTED. Since I am already located in the betweens by virtue of being a jWPA, I have found that working with and within them, in that space of possibility, has in many cases provided me with a more flexible, tractable agency, better suited to my multiple and multilayered location(s), than positioning myself outside or against them did. In the narrative that follows, I outline the ways in which jWPAs are situated in the betweens by default, detail some of the accompanying hazards and the specific challenges I have encountered as a jWPA working in these "betweens," and suggest some specific strategies for re-imagining this location as a space of creative negotiation. Enacting these strategies may, for others, as for me, open up the "subversive, transgressive potential" (Gunner 17) of the jWPA as an agent of change and renewal.

BEGINNINGS, OR HOW I CAME TO BE AN OUTLAW

Hired by my current institution fresh out of graduate school, I entered the department of language and literature in the fall of 2000 as an assistant professor of English; this is the formal title of the official position I hold. It was understood that within a few years of my arrival I would assume several additional administrative responsibilities, including the chairship of the department's composition committee, the governing body of our two-semester first-year composition sequence, and direction of the university's writing center. Upon joining the faculty I immediately became a member of the composition committee, served for one year as a member, and was appointed chair in the fall of 2001. At that same time, I took over direction of the writing center, a small but successful enterprise that had followed the now-familiar developmental path of many such centers: opened in 1994 as a remedial skills-based "writing lab" housed and financed within the language and literature department, it was renamed "The Writing Center" in 1996 to reflect a new commitment to helping writers at all levels of proficiency. Two years later it was moved out of the department and assigned its own budget and physical space, largely to emphasize its usefulness as a resource for cross-curricular and advanced writers' needs. Three years after that, in 2001, I took it over.

My assumption of these administrative responsibilities less than one full year after my arrival at the university brought with it two new titles: "Director of the Writing Center" and "Director of Composition," though the latter is used (by both me and my colleagues) interchangeably with "Composition Committee Chair," a strategic rhetorical choice I will address in more detail later in this essay. In December of 2002, I was assigned yet another title: chair of the soon-to-be-revitalized university writing across the curriculum committee. At this point I was shouldering a four-four teaching load (the replacement of the regular three-credit-hour course with a one-hour tutor training course each semester relieved me of four credit hours per year; it was

assumed to be ample release time, though I still had four course preps
each semester), direction of first-year composition, and direction of the
writing center, as well as coordination of WAC.

Before proceeding further, I wish to insert a caveat: I do not in any
way advocate that others seek or accept a position such as mine, which,
in essence, is the equivalent of three full-time jobs. The reasons for my
having taken this job—and staying in it for the years I have—are multiple and complex, and include personal reasons, such as the fact that
my parents, in good health but growing older, live twenty-five minutes
away from the university town, as well as the fact that I did not know,
when I was hired, that I would be asked to take on the two directorships at the same time and so early in my tenure at the institution. I
have made personal and professional sacrifices in this position, and I
do believe that were I married or had I a family, I simply would not
have been able to manage the workload without damaging those relationships. Now that I am looking to establish those kinds of relationships, I am convinced that something must change if I am to succeed
in that area of my life.

Thus mine may be read, in part, as a cautionary tale. Despite the
challenges I have encountered, however, I have managed to accomplish a great deal at my university, including developing a successful
writing concentration in the English major (graduating our first cohort last year), revising the outcomes for our first-year writing courses
to incorporate process pedagogy and rhetorical theory, and increasing
the writing center's usage rates, over two years, by seventy percent. So
while I cannot in good conscience recommend a position that places
so many demands on its occupier, I believe that the coping strategies
I have developed may well serve those in other, less burdensome but
still challenging jWPA positions—other jWPAs who, like me, work in
the betweens.

I like to think that, had I been less naïve, I would have said "no" to
something when the titles (and their accompanying workload) started
piling up, despite my eagerness to be involved and improve the program. But the truth is that I really did not believe I had a choice,
caught as I was in the too-familiar bind of the junior faculty member
who feels she cannot refuse senior faculty members' requests without
risking her professional progress. I was specifically told (warned?) that
the four credit hours of annual release time[2] that accompanied the two
directorships had only been approved several years before because one

faculty member, my predecessor, had agreed to hold both positions simultaneously. She, unsurprisingly, was also untenured at the time. I will discuss my colleagues' resistance to release time in more detail later in the essay, but suffice it to say that the precedent had been set, and it was clear that change would come slowly, if at all. I could either look for another job immediately, or I could find a way to negotiate these challenges. In more ways than one, my work was cut out for me. But that had been clear from my very first faculty meeting.

ON BREAKING AND ENTERING: BETWEEN TASK AND POSITION

It was the second week of August, and I was looking forward to my first semester as a full-time faculty member. During pre-semester planning week, I became acquainted with another of my junior colleagues, a young woman in comparative literature who had been hired one year prior to my arrival, and who was also on the composition committee I had been asked to join. During one of our informal mentoring conversations that week, she told me that she had chosen not to speak at the first English faculty meeting she attended as a new hire, nor had she elected to speak at the next four or five meetings. Instead, she had preferred to observe her new colleagues and their interactions carefully and enter the departmental discourse slowly and deliberately. I could see the wisdom in her choice, and I have since watched several new hires who succeeded me enact a similar pattern.

But I, like so many other jWPAs, was not to have the same luxury. The first English faculty meeting I attended was focused on discussing the formal requirements of and designing a plan of study for the new writing concentration in the English major, as well as its corollary in literature (the latter being quite similar to the single-track English major that had preceded the split). Though I was not yet formally in charge of the writing program, my role and the position(s) I would someday inherit had been laid out for me from the initial job interview forward. Hiring their first full-time, tenure-track rhetoric and composition hire (me) was the first step in bringing the new major to fruition, and now its proponents in the department were ready to take the next step. I knew, then, that I would at some point be leading this program, and that I would be charged with developing and teaching most of the new upper-level writing courses during its early years. And I suspected that I would be held partly if not largely accountable for its success or lack thereof when in four years we would graduate our first writing concentration majors—and I, coincidentally, would be coming up for tenure. Remaining quiet at a meeting in which I had so much at stake was not an option.

And yet speaking up was not easy. Within half an hour, I found myself going head to head with a senior faculty member who wanted at least four of the twelve required major classes in the writing concentration to be upper-level literature courses. I argued that only two upper-level courses should be in literature studies, given that it was a writing degree, after all, and that we were requiring only two upper-level writing courses from literature concentration majors. After several minutes of wrangling, I became aware of the raised eyebrows my apparently bold assertions were eliciting. I decided to suggest a compromise: three literature courses. My suggestion, to my great relief, was immediately accepted.

Although not yet officially a WPA at the time of this incident, I was already anticipating and fulfilling the administrative role that was to be assigned to me. While I have since been awarded the rather weighty list of professional appellations enumerated above in addition to my assistant professorship, the reality is that I have no more officially sanctioned power today than I did at that first frightening and exhilarating faculty meeting. At my institution, none of these titles other than my professorship denote actual positions; none appears on my contract. They are merely descriptors for tasks I must complete.

This distinction between tasks and positions is made by David Schwalm, one of the 2001 WPA Summer Workshop leaders;[3] in an article included in the workshop materials entitled "The Writing Program (Administrator) in Context: Where am I, and Can I Still Behave Like a Faculty Member?" Schwalm notes that a faculty member housed in a smaller institution who assumes the duties of a WPA is less likely to occupy a formal position than to fulfill a task—"something that needs to be done around the campus, but [that] includes no positional standing in the administrative hierarchy and often is quite open-ended or ill-defined in terms of responsibilities, expectations, and rewards" (2).[4] While such a WPA may have one or more powerful-sounding titles, her "position" is often not officially recognized as such within the departmental or institutional hierarchy; as Schwalm notes, "the position exists only as a line on your door sign and business card" (2).

In this context, the jWPA finds herself positioned neither at the center nor on the margins (Reynolds), located not as faculty colleague nor recognized administrator. Instead, she functions simultaneously inside and outside both of those roles; she is located *between* administering and administration. She is indeed an outlaw, a "person deprived of the benefit of the law" of the institutional hierarchy, one who necessarily defies that law by definition of her location. Functioning in this space between institutional disempowerment and programmatic authority can be extremely difficult, for not only is the jWPA's role unprotected by the law of the institutional hierarchy, but in fulfilling that role, she must also habitually break what are often understood as the "laws" of seniority.

I challenged both the law of institutional hierarchy and the law of seniority—albeit somewhat unwittingly—at that first faculty meeting. Negotiating these politics of location is a tricky business but inescapable in the world of the jWPA. Like many jWPAs, I am charged with guiding a first-year composition program in which several of my senior colleagues have been teaching longer than I have held the degree that authorizes my work. Such jWPAs may find that their suggestions for program change are read by senior colleagues as direct challenges to the latter's pedagogical expertise. Though one might argue that this conundrum is easily solved by WPAs adopting a transactional leadership style in which the WPA "maintain[s] the status quo and keep[s] workers happy by managing well and convincing workers that [she] understand[s] the organization," the not-yet tenured WPA is more often than not expected to be more of a transformational leader, one who "defin[es] a new vision" and "seek[s] consensus around common goals" (Mirtz and Cullen 95). For not to advocate curricular revision or reform may result in the equally damning perception that the jWPA is not an effective or active contributor to the department or university community, a dangerous place to be when annual and tenure evaluations loom large.

Although I did not, at the time, consciously choose to strategically make use of my default location in the "between" of task and position, I see now that I began to learn how to negotiate my ethos in that very first faculty meeting. My dilemma that morning, one frequently encountered by jWPAs, is neatly summarized by Rita Malencyzk in "Administration of Emergence": "Generally we want things to work out and for people to just get along, *and* we don't like to give up" (82, emphasis added). I wanted the writing concentration to have what I considered an appropriate balance of literature courses, largely because I sensed that the desire to weight it more heavily with literature cours-es signaled a lack of confidence in its "seriousness" as a major.[5] *And I needed* to cultivate positive relationships with my new colleagues, who would largely determine the success of any future writing pro-gram initiatives with their support or lack thereof—and who one day would also be voting on my tenure candidacy. I was being confronted with what Jim Corder terms "genuinely contending narratives" (qtd.. in Malenczyk 81). In this case, there were two sets of contending nar-ratives: first, authority accorded by discipline and degree versus the authority conferred by seniority and experience; and second, my need to influence the design of a program I would ultimately be respon-sible for versus my desire to be accepted by my new colleagues. When confronted thusly, jWPAs must be willing to step out of the either-or scripts those narratives have created for us and move into a new place, a "between"—what in this case we might call a space of "both/and."

In the simplest terms, the strategy I chose that day was a compro-mise. Certainly most jWPAs have made their fair share of compro-mises and are well aware of the benefits and sacrifices that accompany doing so. But locating oneself in the betweens does not necessarily (or merely) equate to compromising on an outcome. Even more important than my efforts to negotiate the (temporary) design of the major was my negotiation of an ethos that was neither (junior) faculty member nor (future) administrator, but some place between. In compromis-ing, I was able *both* to lay claim to some much needed authority *and* still reassure my senior colleagues that I recognized their expertise and experience and would honor it as well. Had I elected stubbornly to assert the absolute authority of my disciplinary knowledge, I might have gotten the course list I felt best served students in place imme-diately, but winning the gunfight would have made me a WANTED woman. On the other hand, had I simply given over that authority to the laws of departmental hierarchy and seniority, I would have been neither WANTED, nor wanted—because I would not have contrib-uted anything of use to the departmental discourse in my role as resi-dent writing expert. By locating myself between those two extremes I managed to remain wanted without becoming (overly) WANTED; I demonstrated good will toward, and thus elicited it from, my col-leagues, which, in the long run, has been of far greater benefit to me and our writing students than insisting on immediate change would have been. In identifying and recognizing the contending narratives we are likely to face, and situating ourselves in their betweens, jWPAs can subvert these antagonistic narratives that too often position us at odds with our (senior) colleagues. Though the comparison may risk mixing the metaphor, I think of the laws of physics: for every action, there is an equal and opposite reaction. By constructing a flexible and tractable ethos, I create the possibility of a like response from my colleagues in the future. In this way, the betweens benefit me and the program I direct: I may not achieve immediate change, but I create a space in which *lasting* change can be made.

WORKING THE I'M OKAY, YOU'RE OKAY CORRAL: FACULTY MEMBER OR ADMINISTRATOR?

Tim Peeples notes that "[t]o remake writing space, we must acknowledge and understand the spaces of which we are writing subjects" (125). Peeples's choice of the word "subjects" here is most evocative. In a sentence, the subject is often the actor, the agent of action, the one who makes things happen. But "subject" may also refer to one who is ruled over. Certainly there is no other word so apt to describe the jWPA, who must be an agent of action in her role as administrator, but who may, as a (junior) faculty member, feel subject to the demands of others. Given the fact that the spaces in which we carry out these roles are politically charged, both needful of change and simultaneously resistant to it, it becomes even more necessary to find strategies to cultivate an ethos of fluidity and flexibility.

Peeples offers us such a strategy in the metaphor of traveling, described in his theory of writing spaces based on the work of planning theorist David Perry. Peeples describes how the metaphor of traveling is realized in the work of the WPA:

> For instance, if we are planning a Writing Fellows program, we might travel between what the WPA literature tells us about building such programs, the data we have found during our local research into cross-disciplinary writing instruction and needs, program budgets, similar Fellows programs that might already be on our campuses, the classrooms of our

> students and participating professors, a campus writ-
> ing center, and actual writing assignments students
> are doing in first-year writing and subsequent writing
> courses, among other places. (125)

Peeples focuses largely on the physical (writing centers, classrooms)
and philosophical (WPA literature, local research data) spaces that
WPAs travel among and between. I wish to suggest that traveling between the roles we play at our institutions may prove equally fruitful as
a strategy for jWPAs negotiating the highly politically charged spaces
of which we are subjects. Neither quiet junior faculty member nor
powerful senior administrator, we find ourselves neither at the center
nor on the margins, but in a less-definable elsewhere; in some cases,
that elsewhere may be precisely where we want to be.

For example, I strategically locate myself "between" two of my titles, "Director of Composition" and "Composition Committee Chair."
The composition committee, a departmental body composed of four
to five English professors who organize quarterly teaching circles and
make curricular recommendations for new textbooks and common
course outcomes, oversees the two-course first-year composition sequence taught on the English side of the language and literature department. The current configuration of the composition committee
had only been in place for a little over a year when I arrived at the university; prior to that time, there had been two course subcommittees,
one each for English 1101 and English 1102. In an effort to support
more coherence across the first-year writing sequence, the composition
director's "position" was created and the two committees consolidated
into one.

The role, or task, that each of the titles describes is essentially the
same: the faculty member who chairs the composition committee is
the *de facto* director of composition. And yet—I realized, soon after
taking over direction of the program—the connotative powers of each
title are quite different. Our department, like any other, is served at
any given time by several standing committees (like the composition
committee) as well as a number of ad hoc committees; each of these
committees has a chair. One of the expected duties of every member
of the faculty is service on committees, so most every faculty member has at one time or another been a committee chair. Thus, to send
out a memo in which I referred to myself as "Composition Commit-

tee Chair" was to locate myself in the space of the faculty member completing necessary service. I claimed what (limited) authority was lent to me, but my rhetorical choice allowed me to enact still another ethos-negotiating strategy that I have found useful as a jWPA: feminist writer and philosopher Starhawk's power-with, which Foss and Griffin define as "the influence wielded among equals in order to empower them" (334). By situating myself as one committee chair among many, I positioned my colleagues as equals even as I wielded my influence, so to speak, on matters of concern to the writing program. Power-with, and the "Composition Committee Chair" title, located me (and my colleagues, ultimately) in the space of "both/and." While it is necessary for a jWPA to take a stand, I have to be careful not to take a stand *against*. This choice enacted a classic Rogerian rhetorical strategy: by recognizing the need my colleagues had to be seen as equal contributors to the writing program, I again elicited good will and moved us toward positive change.

Had I, on the other hand, referred to myself as "Director of Composition" each time I wrote or emailed my colleagues about writing program business, I would have risked reinforcing my outlaw status, casting myself as an "other"; at the same time, I would likely be viewed as (unnecessarily) pulling rank. Using that far more authoritative title positions me as an administrator, one with a dominant place in the hierarchy, one with "power-over" (Starhawk qtd. in Foss and Griffin 336). The second appellation does have its uses, but I am judicious in selecting it. Its use is limited to those times when a stronger stance is needed, such as when I had to instruct my reluctant colleagues that everyone in the department would be required to shift to the new edition of our common textbook *en masse* in order to prevent student confusion and bookstore chaos. I also use "Director of Composition" when corresponding with those above me in the university's hierarchy, as in those instances when it enhances my ethos as an administrative equal; in such situations, it is the formal title that shifts me into the role of power-with.

The choice, ultimately, is one of emphasis. While not all jWPAs have two titles they may strategically employ, the strategy of traveling is available to any WPA. Strategic language choices extend beyond titles. We are almost always both faculty members and administrators, but we can decide which role to emphasize in any given conversation, text, or presentation. Sometimes it behooves me (and the programs

I serve) to cast my ethos as a faculty member who "must" act in an administrative capacity, while at other times I am an administrator who is also a colleague on the faculty. Rather than adopting one or the other of these titles, I have chosen to place myself neither at the center nor "so clearly 'outside' as the margins" (Reynolds 332–33), but instead to travel, to move strategically between.

Plan? What Plan?: When "Program" Is an Alias

In June 2001, the summer prior to my second year, I felt overwhelmed at the prospect of taking on the direction of both the first-year writing program and the writing center in the coming fall, and I requested that the department provide funding for me to attend the WPA summer workshop in Arizona in July. It was at the workshop that I first became acquainted with what I have come to call the between of programming and program. Like the title "Writing Program Administrator," the phrase "Writing Program" may have many different meanings; it often implies programmatic coherence and official recognition where in fact there is little or none. David Schwalm notes that there are varying degrees of "program-ness" in individual programs (3); in many cases, what is termed a "program" may simply be "programming," a set of isolated or loosely related courses that emerged over time and only later were collected into a semicoherent sequence. Jeanne Gunner attributes this "foregrounding of course over program" to the "history of composition instruction" (7), which is generally accepted to have originated with Harvard's "Subject A" course in 1870, initially developed in response to growing numbers of academically under-prepared students enrolling at the university. As the courses proliferated, the need for course coordinators emerged; coordinators formalized the course sequences into programs. Individual writing programs, as Gunner points out, have tended to mimic this disciplinary development pattern, beginning with isolated writing courses (often, that originate out of a deficiency model), which develop into a sort of sequence that then requires someone to administer it. This pattern of development, however, does not often lead to theoretically sound, coherent writing programs.

I immediately saw ways I could bring this theory to bear on practice at my university, for I recognized at once that my current institution had followed this model of development. Our first-year composition courses are the oldest part of our writing program; the writing center, initially conceived as the writing lab in the early 1990s, came some years later, envisioned as a crisis intervention resource for students struggling in English composition courses. Then, coincidental with the restructuring of the composition committee that took place about a year prior to my arrival, were some heated debates about the possibility of creating a writing track in the English major and the need for bringing in a rhetoric and composition specialist. As this hire, I came in 2000, followed by the proposal and subsequent approval of the writing concentration in the English major, described above. This new major-track necessitated the addition of several upper-level writing courses to the curriculum. By 2001 our departmental "writing program," not yet formally recognized as such, consisted of the first-year writing sequence and the emerging writing concentration courses. My institution also has an across-the-curriculum writing intensive policy, overseen at one time by a WAC committee whose first incarnation had dissolved sometime before I arrived. Of all these elements, the only one to be formally recognized and described in the *Undergraduate Bulletin* was the writing intensive policy. We had programming, but we did not yet have a program.

I was energized by this revelation, but dismayed at another the workshop brought: it confirmed my suspicions that the load I was being asked to shoulder—full-time teaching *and* administration of two programs—was unreasonably demanding for most anyone, much less a junior faculty member in only her second year of full-time employment. Still, eager to make use of my newfound knowledge—and hoping to address the workload issues up-front—I decided, once back at home, to develop a proposal to share with my department chair and the other members of the composition committee upon our return to school in the fall.

In the proposal I first described the history and elements of our writing program and how its development mirrored the conventional developmental history outlined by Gunner; then, drawing upon the recommendations for "thinking programmatically" that had been delineated at the workshop, I proposed that our composition committee implement a five-year plan for improving program coherence—in other words, to turn our programming into a program. Specifically, I suggested that we do the following: articulate the writing and pedagogical theories that our courses were based upon; develop a program description that distinguished the different components of the program and described the relationships between them; write mission statements for the overall program and its various components; compose job descriptions for one or more WPAs who would manage the different components; develop outcomes statements for our courses that were in line with national writing program standards; and implement the changes suggested by these documents and plan for an official assessment of their effectiveness in the future.

I presented a draft of the proposal to two of the three other members of the composition committee at a lunch meeting held at a local restaurant early in the fall semester. I can still clearly picture the stony expressions on the faces of my colleagues: Linda, a non-tenure-track assistant professor with an interdisciplinary degree in rhetoric and composition and higher education administration, who was also my good friend; and Donna, a Milton scholar with graduate training in rhetoric and composition who was both my mentor and forerunner—she had directed both composition and the writing center before I was hired. We had had many great conversations about where to take the writing program, and though I would have expected resistance from almost any of my other colleagues, I did not expect it from them. I can still remember the awkwardness of the long silence that followed my cheery "Well, what do you think?" as Linda pursed her lips and stared hard at the proposal. Donna shook her head, almost imperceptibly. The silence was only emphasized by the noisy background clatter of dishes in the restaurant kitchen and the murmur of conversations around us.

I was genuinely surprised at the cool reception. Perhaps I was a little overeager, I thought, but it was a carefully developed plan, theoretically and historically contextualized. I had included a suggested timeline for the implementation of the various points of the plan, and had proposed a step-by-step process. What had gone wrong?

The reluctant response of my colleagues highlights the difficulties in negotiating the between of programming and program. The first-year writing "programs" we sometimes are asked to direct are simply sequences of two or three courses; in the case of small teaching-oriented institutions such as my own, these courses have often been taught by other, more senior faculty for years. The same may be true of writing majors or concentrations, which are typically cobbled together initially out of existing courses supplemented by a few new additions, and writing-across-the-curriculum or writing-in-the-disciplines programs, which may similarly originate in existing courses that are then revised to include additional writing assignments and a modicum of writing instruction.

This programming-masquerading-as-program is often marked by two features: first, a lack of the coherence one would typically accord to a program that was envisioned as such and then realized; and second, a resistance to change. In my case, I had identified the lack of coherence in our program(ming) while teaching advanced composition during the spring semester of my first year at the university. Though the course was listed at the 3000-level, I found myself having to backtrack and teach the students basic rhetorical concepts such as ethos, pathos, and logos, which only a few had been exposed to in their 1000-level writing courses; most of their first-year courses had focused on practice, with much of the theory underpinning that practice left unarticulated. And since there was, at the time, no 2000-level intermediate course in composition, they—and I—struggled with the transition to an upper-level course where an understanding of the theory behind the practice was crucial to their success.

The others on the composition committee, including Donna, the committee's former chair, had made it known they were aware of the coherence problem, so I thought that a proposal directed toward addressing those issues would be welcomed. But this is where the resistance to change surfaced. My committee colleagues were concerned, first, about audience. To whom was I planning to show the proposal? Several of our senior faculty were highly protective of their classroom autonomy, and committee members expressed concern that suggesting so many changes would create resistance in other English faculty toward our committee's work. (It was not lost on me that fear of others' resistance to change was manifesting as resistance to change.) Second, and most surprising to me, was the idea that I was rushing things, trying to change too much too quickly. Rushing things? In a five-year plan? I left the meeting a little stunned and deeply disappointed.

In this instance, I found myself painfully lodged between my desire for a more formalized, coherent program with clearly delineated relationships between materials, courses, and their support systems, and the current programming, which, while it had its flaws, had been serviceable up to this point—and with which, more importantly, everyone else was already comfortable. Although I had not done so intentionally, in making the proposal, I had located myself at the pole of dramatic change, what in this case I might call the marginal position. When my proposal was met with such strong resistance, I traveled all the way to the other pole, the status quo, so often located at the center: I put the proposal away and simply sat on it for several months. Neither of these extreme locations was tenable, however, in terms of getting the work done. To remain intractable myself was to prevent change and growth, because it was clear to me that, in its current form, my five-year plan was unacceptable. But, as the primary teacher of the upper-level writing courses as well as the lone and therefore overburdened jWPA, I was not willing to continue watching under-prepared students struggle while I valiantly tried to fill in the gaps for them, nor was I willing to make (at least not for more than a year or two) the personal sacrifices that balancing my two administrative positions and a full-time teaching load was going to require. I knew I could not lead nor grow any of the programs to my satisfaction with my energies spread so thin. Located by default in the betweens, yet again, I knew I had to do something to turn my position(ing) into something workable.

While my specific experience may not translate directly to the experiences of other jWPAs, I would suggest that the central issue here was, indeed, rhetorical awareness—or rather, my lack thereof. Although I thought I had gathered and painted an accurate portrait of my department's and university's history in my proposal, I quickly discovered that I simply did not have enough knowledge of context. Through several ensuing conversations with my department chair and composition committee colleagues, it became apparent that there was support for a number of the individual steps proposed in the plan; it was, ultimately, its "plan-ness" that provoked resistance, particularly the piece regarding formalizing the WPA position(s). Although I had not specifically suggested that the person or persons serving in administrative capacities receive additional course releases (a more accurate term would be "re-assigned time"), I had requested that we compose formal job descriptions for "one or more WPA positions" and "[b]ased on the program description, mission statements, and preliminary outcomes statements—which together will demonstrate the value and complexity of our program—establish the need for the more formalized WPA positions [. . .] and petition for supporting changes in the structure of these positions."

I had not yet learned how sensitive my overworked colleagues—who do not have the opportunity for sabbatical—were to others being compensated with any form of release time. A former department chair and dean who had repeatedly crowed over getting as much work out of his faculty members as possible had created deep resentments that were still manifesting themselves. It became apparent that faculty members had comforted themselves for years with the idea that at least everyone else was working as hard as they were; it simply was not acceptable (or bearable?) to imply that any one person deserved a release (literal and metaphorical) more than another. This history is of course complicated by the additional fact that writing program administration is, generally, misunderstood by the majority of my senior colleagues, only a handful of whom have any training in rhetoric and composition. They simply cannot fathom what I (or anyone else serving as jWPA) need the time for. I was, in fact, once advised by my mentor that I would have to "do the work first" (i.e., prove myself, and then I might be able to get release time as a sort of reward).

And though five years seemed a long time to me, apparently the struggle that had ensued before I came to win acceptance of the current program*ming* (i.e., the current configuration of the composition committee and the addition of a writing concentration in the major) had taken such a toll that others were wary of suggesting more change. Thus, while more coherent programming was indeed desirable, the idea of a formalized program—and a clearly defined director or directors of that program—invoked paralyzing fear.

Awareness of context was the first step. Then, the strategy seemed simple enough, if overtly subversive—without my identifying the plan as a plan, I would lead the committee and department in implementing each step, one at time. Essentially, I would work toward program while sustaining the perception, one might even say the ethos, of programming. In the meantime, I reclaimed my position as one between "wanted" and WANTED (for the first few weeks after submitting the proposal, I had wondered if my face was going to start appearing on posters). But, located outside of the laws of the margins or the center, I was able to turn the lawlessness of the betweens toward advancing the rhetorical education of our students as well as enhancing the teaching experience of our faculty. Ironically, it was the very perception of lawlessness that has allowed us to begin developing a more formalized and centralized program. However cynical it may sound, the lesson I learned from negotiating this particular between was this: have a plan, have a vision—but be cautious about forwarding it as such. My hope was, and is, that by leading the department through the transition from programming to program by focusing on one isolated change at a time, we will eventually arrive at a place where the need for a more formalized directorship (and the resources to support it) will emerge organically[6]—or at least *appear* to have emerged organically.

I will recount just the first few steps we have taken so far. First we defined the program and its components. The "Writing Program Mission Statement," drafted by the composition committee and voted into formal policy by the English faculty, is now published in the university's *Undergraduate Bulletin* under "Academic Regulations," immediately preceding the description of the written and oral communications competencies. The mission statement identifies the writing program as a subset of the department of language and literature and notes that it includes "the First-year Writing sequence and the Writing Concentration in the English major. It supports and works in tandem with the University's Writing Across the Curriculum Program" (70). One would, in fact, be hard pressed to call the current writing across the curriculum program a program, either—it consists primarily of a set of published policies that describe and govern all writing intensive courses—but in naming it and the departmental program as such in an official, public document that is distributed to both students and faculty, we have begun to build the formal structure and campus-wide recognition we need to support future requests for additional faculty lines and other resources. Since adopting the mission statement, the composition committee has also administered two departmental surveys, one on each of the two first-year composition courses, and implemented several changes arising from the survey results—one of which was the addition of basic knowledge of ethos, pathos and logos as a common outcome in English 1101.

Devising a formal plan was threatening to my colleagues' sense of autonomy; the plan positioned me, in my colleagues' eyes, as one desiring power-over. When I "traveled" back to the between and relocated myself in the both/and space of faculty member/administrator, I was able to enact Starhawk's power-with—exercising influence among equals as a means of empowering not merely oneself, but all—as a strategy for maintaining the collegial support I need to cultivate and maintain, while still moving toward change. And while change has been slower than I might have initially desired, it has been steady, and it has had the added advantage of being supported by most everyone in the department.

There are additional, more personal, advantages to working in the between of programming and program at this stage of our development. While I continue to believe that a formal WPA job description would necessarily move the department and university in the direction of a more reasonable workload, it would also limit the flexibility I currently have as faculty member and jWPA. My work as director of composition and director of the writing center has been, for the purposes of annual and tenure evaluations, classified primarily as "service." I have my disagreements with this categorization, which tends to diminish the intellectual and pedagogical value of writing program administration work. But I am also aware that the demands of my WPA work have been acknowledged, and its influence lauded, as more than satisfactorily fulfilling my service obligations to the university. I recognize that I might well undermine my own career progress were I to insist on its being formally redefined or categorized differently.

Here again, awareness of one's institutional context is key. My university's guidelines for tenure and promotion to associate professor clearly state that a candidate must distinguish herself in teaching and *either* service *or* professional development (i.e., research and publication). Formalizing my jWPA position would have risked moving my WPA work not into the latter recognizable (and rewardable) category, but into the more nebulous (and even less understood) category of "administration." Since I have been able to devote very little time to publishing given my teaching and WPA load, I would have placed my tenure and promotion candidacy at much greater risk had I insisted on formalizing my position. Locating myself in this between has had tangible rewards: my tenure and promotion were recently granted, on schedule.[7]

Therefore, while I cannot recommend that all jWPAs should choose to retain the flexibility of a less formalized position if they have other, viable options, I propose that for those who do find themselves located in this between by context and circumstance, there are ways to make it work. Working strategically within the between of programming and program, especially in those writing spaces where there is extreme resistance to change, can actually enable change more easily, and help ensure that it lasts. After all, it is largely my ability to move

strategically *between* my roles as faculty member and administrator
that has allowed me to access power-with, a necessary tool for making connections with colleagues and ensuring my own staying power,
while simultaneously creating positive change within my own program—and/or program*ming*.

Loyalty Oaths: Between Department and University

jWPAs find themselves located between faculty member and administrator; as administrators, they are often between role and position,
as well as programming and program. For many jWPAs, especially
those who direct writing centers, there is yet another between: that of
department and university-at-large. This between may simultaneously
be the one most productive of change—and the one most difficult to
negotiate.

In my position of assistant professor of English, I am located firmly
within the bounds of the department of language and literature, which
is part of the college of arts and letters. In my role as writing center director, however, I officially report not to my department head,
nor to the arts and letters dean (whose office is located directly across
the hall from the center itself, a physical location that creates its own
complexities amongst all these betweens). Instead, I report directly to
the vice-president for academic affairs, the second-in-command at our
university; the writing center budget is also allocated through the vice
president's office. I also report to the vice-president for academic affairs in my role as chair of the newly re-constituted writing across the
curriculum committee, albeit less formally, since there is no budget
attached to that office. Because I make presentations to new and existing faculty on behalf of the writing center and WAC, my name and
face are associated strongly with these entities across campus. Many
faculty assume that since I direct the writing center, it must be a part
of the department in which I teach, a perception further supported by
the fact that the tutor training course is listed as an upper-level English
course, and my performance in teaching that course is evaluated by
the language and literature department chair.

It is no wonder that the between of department and university gives
rise to issues with program identity, with accompanying repercussions
for funding and program resources. When writing center usage increases or we receive a grant, the department likes to claim it in their

annual "brag memo," but they are reluctant to allocate funding to pay me a stipend for keeping the center open in the summer when I am not under contract. After all, the writing center is not funded by the department—even though my faculty salary is. Still, the department does currently pay for the writing center phone, because the past and present department chairs recognize how necessary having a phone in the center is—and academic affairs has steadfastly refused to accommodate the annual $360 increase in our budget a phone would require.[8] The phone number for the writing center is still not listed separately in the offices and resources section of the campus directory, however, despite multiple requests to include it.

And there's more: it took two years of requests to convince the office of business and finance—who have consistently sent me monthly budget reports—to also send me the annual deadlines for budget proposals, so that I could actually request additional monies on schedule with all other departments; they seemed to think the writing center was under the auspices of the college of arts and letters. And after being passed over for computer lab updates several years in a row—the center is a public lab, if a small one, open to any student who wishes to come in and write or conduct research—I discovered that the office of institutional and instructional technology also thought we were housed within language and literature; therefore they had not put us on their rotation. That also explained why they had linked our fledgling web page off of the language and literature department page. To get a link from the library or campus resources page, we have to petition the Web advisory council for special permission, even though we are a campus-wide service.

And then, there is the pedagogical—or perhaps more accurately, the promotional—angle: though the writing center is an independent unit within academic affairs, I had to make a special request of the vice-president for academic affairs to be included in the academic units who give brief reports at the annual faculty meeting. Being publicly recognized as an independent unit was a crucial step in reminding the faculty that the writing center serves all students in all disciplines, not just those enrolled in English courses. And yet no matter how often we emphasize our cross-disciplinary services, we continue to have trouble convincing others: not long ago I pulled up to a stop sign where a colleague from the department of political science was waiting to cross the street. I rolled down my window to say hello, and he quickly congratulated me on how great of an idea it was to offer the "new" APA formatting workshops—workshops we have been offering in one form or another for at least two years.

Perhaps a few of these scenarios sound familiar; each coincides with the WPA's being located, by default, between department and university. Issues of budget and identity may be further complicated for jWPAs because they are still learning how to negotiate the hierarchy of their particular institution. As relatively new members of the institution, jWPAs may not know whom to ask, what to ask for—or how to ask for it. After two years of meetings with various members of academic affairs and the development office, the director of development informed me (at last) that the writing center had no foundation funding. Since that was the most likely possibility for additional monies, he suggested I put in a request. He gave me a form for doing so—a form I had never seen up until that point. In this situation I felt my lofty list of titles served me only too well—it was assumed I *already* possessed knowledge and power that I, in fact, neither had nor knew how to access expediently.

So how can jWPAs turn this confusing and often frustrating location between department and university to their advantage? As with the previous examples, fluidity, the ability to inhabit a sort of multiple ethos, simultaneously both and neither department representative and university servant, has proven to be the most successful means of cultivating authority and getting work done. To get my name, as writing center director, on the list for the annual budget memo sent to unit budgetary supervisors, I asked not academic affairs but my language and literature department secretary to make the request for me. Like magic, it appeared in my mailbox during the next budget request cycle. To get new computers for the writing center, I followed the example of the department-housed language lab and requested a student technology fees grant; however, within the grant, I emphasized that the writing center was an independent unit so as to avoid reluctance on the part of the selection committee to award a grant to the "same" department two years in a row. We received the grant, and are now in the process of updating our center's technology. Though I remain frustrated at my higher administration's lack of understanding of what the writing center needs to best serve students, demonstrated by their refusal to fund a communication device as fundamental as a phone, I have learned to be content that the department recognizes the need and fills it—and I am already planning to visit the new vice-president for academic affairs we will be hiring next year. I keep seeking out new ways to publicize our cross-curricular services to faculty and students in other disciplines. And while I provide the department chair with a copy of my writing center annual report that she may quote from in her department brag memo, I send the original annual report directly to the vice-president for academic affairs.

I fear that that these choices may seem opportunistic or even manipulative, but in each case, my strategy was based on a simple rhetorical concept, one taught in most every composition classroom: know your audience. For the jWPA between department and university, that means recognizing that there are multiple audiences for the work she completes and the texts she produces, and that different audiences have different expectations. To return to the above example: after two years it finally occurred to me that perhaps the business and finance office simply did not know how to "read" a request from an individual, non-tenured faculty member for a copy of a department-directed memo. I knew, however, that that office is used to receiving requests from department secretaries on behalf of department chairs and program directors (most of whom *are* housed within departments or hold official positions). Once I understood my audience, I was able to "travel" between university writing center director and department member. Working from the location of both/and instead of either/or, I was able to use all of my resources to complete the task.

Most WPAs, junior and senior, serve both department and university. Sometimes we serve the university through our service to an individual department, but often, as in the case of a cross-curricular writing center or a writing across the curriculum program, our work serves the university community directly. Here again we work most effectively neither at the margins nor the center, fully within an individual department or fully allied with the university administration, but in that elsewhere, between. There we may draw upon the greater understanding, and, often, greater support that those within our own or closely related disciplines have for our work, while at the same time moving beyond the boundaries of our discipline, stretching those boundaries, perhaps, with us. If ethos is location (Reynolds), then we may remake writing spaces simply by virtue of inhabiting new ones. And if we inhabit the betweens, we make those boundaries ever more permeable; perhaps we may even dream of dissolving them.

Outlaws, Scofflaws, and jWPAs: A
Few Last Lessons from Billy

As the "Idiomatic Interlude" suggests, "between" often implies a choice, a choosing of one role or duty over the other. Perhaps one of the most difficult decisions for jWPAs to make is where to devote their time and energy. Many of us, especially at small colleges, are only part-time WPAs, even if we are fortunate enough to hold an official position rather than simply fulfill a task. In addition to administering one (or more) writing programs, we still teach classes, often several.

It would be easy to place these two demands in conflict, and sometimes we are asked to. One last, brief anecdote. Last spring, as my application for tenure loomed, I was advised by my department chair to focus on teaching "instead of" devoting so much of my energy to the growth of the writing center. Scheduled to teach the new senior seminar in writing that semester, I sensed that there was a lot at stake for me in making the course a success. Somewhat reluctantly, I turned the bulk of my attention to that course and another upper-level writing course, advanced composition. The classes went very well, if student evaluations are any indication, but the writing center's usage rates dropped—largely, I felt, because I had not promoted it as consistently and fervently as I had in previous semesters.

The mistake made by both my department chair and by me was to see teaching as being other than, in competition with, my WPA work. Such thinking demonstrates a fundamental misunderstanding of the instructional nature of WPA work, however. There is an irony inherent in the fact that by devoting my energy to, for example, improving the first-year writing program as a program, I am perceived—or may perceive myself as—shortchanging the students in my own writing classes, or vice-versa. And yet the reality is that while the "variety of our lives" as WPAs is "inexhaustible," we, as human beings, are not. Some days I think I simply cannot read one more paper. I cannot take another initiative. I find myself forgetting meetings, birthdays—important things I would not have forgotten in the past—because there is just no room in my head for another thought. And devoting energy in one direction or the other sometimes seems the only way to manage the heavy load.

How might we negotiate this most fundamental of betweens—not simply that of program and classroom, but that between our service to others and our care for ourselves? For these two betweens are closely related: if our administrators and colleagues can be brought to understand that the work of the writing program administrator is the work of the teacher, that they are, fundamentally, the same endeavor, then we can effect change, however slowly, in our working conditions. If we locate ourselves between what is possible and what is desirable, then, perhaps, we can learn how to do the work without doing ourselves, or our students, harm. Though located last in this discussion, learning to negotiate this between must come first in our professional lives.

Historians tell us that the famous WANTED poster featuring Billy the Kid that most of us have seen never actually existed—it was created some time later, as a kind of souvenir. The closest to a WANTED poster ever issued in relation to Billy the Kid was a "reward notice the governor [placed] in the *Las Vegas Gazette*," the same Governor Wallace who had promised Billy a pardon in exchange for information (Brothers). So it turns out that Billy was, indeed, just as much wanted—for knowledge and information, expertise that only he could provide—as WANTED. And it seems that this may be the case for the jWPA as well. As a jWPA, I necessarily work in the space between wanted and WANTED. I am positioned in the betweens by default, by institutional context, professional circumstance. But I can also *choose*, when expedient, to *use* that location. In the betweens, I can claim authority while effectively negotiating the political challenges of my junior status. I can use my knowledge as a rhetorician—my knowledge of context, of audience, of the strategic choices that shape ethos—to locate myself in the space between the desire to be recognized for my expertise and the desire not to seem too "different" from my mostly literature-focused colleagues, so that I might foster collegiality alongside authority. I can travel between the desire to take credit for initiating the positive changes being made in our first-year writing sequence and the desire (and need) to deflect credit onto—and engender a sense of ownership of those changes in—others, so that we grow, as a faculty, with (and not against) the changes in our writing program. And in choosing to reclaim and negotiate the fluid, ever-shifting "betweens," jWPAs may transmute the often less-than-ideal conditions of our professional lives into transforming and transformational spaces of administrative agency.

Recently, I moved to a new office, one with space enough to arrange my furniture so that I do not have my back to the door when I sit

at my desk or computer. In this office I sit instead between a window
and a door, the former admitting a late afternoon view of the campus
and the low surrounding mountains, the latter admitting students and
colleagues with questions, conversation. Each brings its own kind of
light. I wait there, between.

NOTES

[1] The distinction between "task" and "position," as well as the distinction between "programming" and "program" is David Schwalm's; I discuss
his terminology and work in greater depth later in the essay.

[2] During my second year as writing center director, I proposed a change
in the tutor training course structure. Now the course meets only in the fall
semester for two hours. The amount of release time has stayed the same (four
credit hours), but I now have a four-three teaching load, teaching fourteen
hours in the fall and twelve in the spring. It has made some difference, but
I remain frustrated at what I am unable to accomplish, given how scattered
my energies are.

[3] As a side note: I highly recommend participation in the WPA summer
workshop to any new writing program administrators, especially jWPAs.
The information was invaluable.

[4] This essay has since been published in *The Allyn and Bacon Sourcebook
for Writing Program Administrators*, edited by Irene Ward and William J.
Carpenter. New York: Longman, 2002. 9–22.

[5] My location as jWPA further complicated this issue. As Keith Rhodes
notes in "Mothers, Tell Your Children Not to Do What I Have Done," jW-
PAs risk reinforcing senior faculty members' beliefs that "[w]riting [can] not
be the more serious discipline [we are] trying to make it if [we are] in charge
of it," given that our junior status suggests that "after all, a mere rookie [can]
run the thing" (89).

[6] We have made some progress towards dividing the responsibilities for
writing program administration between two faculty members. The position
of English coordinator was created in the department in 2003 to relieve the
chair from some of the burdens of scheduling and faculty observation. At
my suggestion, the coordinator position—which is compensated by a small
stipend—was to be made coincidental with the director of composition position, which would be assumed by someone other than me. This change
would have enabled us to separate the two director positions and compensate
one with a stipend and one with release time. There have been some challenges in this process. I continued as director of composition during a period
of transition, and stepped down only a few months ago so that the coordinator could take over; I continue to direct the writing center. However, plans

are in the works for another junior faculty member—who is not the current English coordinator—to take over as director of composition next year; the reasoning is that the scheduling is too great a burden for one person to manage it and the composition program while teaching a full load. Release time is still very hard to come by.

   [7] I must confess that now that that hurdle appears to be out of the way, I have paid visits to the dean and wice-president of academic affairs, requesting that I be granted a two-two teaching load on a one-year trial basis to demonstrate what I could accomplish in the writing center if I had more time to devote to its growth. There is precedent on our campus for this structure, as the language lab director only teaches a two-two load each year. The dean is supportive of the idea but does not know whether he can finance the change at this time.

   [8] For purposes of clarity, I wish to note that the position of the vice-president for academic affairs is in transition at this time, and that all references in this section refer to the former VPAA rather than the current (interim) holder of that office. I will, of course, make another request for a phone once a new permanent hire is made.

WORKS CITED

Ayto, John. *Dictionary of Word Origins.* New York: Arcade, 1990.

Brothers, Marcelle. *About Billy the Kid.* Billy the Kid Historic Preservation Society. 10 Nov. 2004. 12 Oct. 2004 <http://www.aboutbillythekid. com/>.

Corder, Jim W. "Argument as Emergence, Rhetoric as Love." *Rhetoric Review* 4.1 (1985): 16–32.

Foss, Sonja K., and Cindy L. Griffin. "A Feminist Perspective on Rhetorical Theory: Toward a Clarification of Boundaries." *Western Journal of Communication* 56 (Fall 1992): 330–49.

Gunner, Jeanne. "Ideology, Theory, and the Genre of Writing Programs." Rose and Weiser, 7–18.

Lunsford, Andrea A. *The St. Martin's Handbook.* 5th ed. New York: Bedford/ St. Martin's, 2003.

Malenczyk, Rita. "Administration of Emergence: Toward a Rhetorical Theory of Writing Program Administration." Rose and Weiser, 79–89.

McGlaun, Sandee. "The Writing Program of the Department of Language and Literature: Historicization, Preliminary Analysis, and a Proposal." Proposal to Composition Committee, North Georgia College and State University. August 2001.

Mirtz, Ruth M., and Roxanne M. Cullen. "Beyond Postmodernism: Leadership Theories and Writing Program Administration." Rose and Weiser, 90–102.

"Outlaw." *The New International Webster's Comprehensive Dictionary.* Deluxe
Encyclopedic ed. 1996.

Peeples, Tim. "Program Administrators and/as Postmodern Planners: Frame-
works for Making Tomorrow's Writing Space." Rose and Weiser, 116–
28.

Reynolds, Nedra. "Ethos as Location: New Sites for Understanding Discursive Authority." *Rhetoric Review* 11.2 (1993): 325–38.

Rhodes, Keith. "Mothers, Tell Your Children Not to Do What I Have Done:
The Sin and Misery of Entering the Profession as a Composition Coordi-
nator." *Kitchen Cooks, Plate Twirlers, and Troubadours: Writing Program
Administrators Tell Their Stories.* Ed. Diana George. Portsmouth, NH:
Boynton/Cook, 1999. 86–94.

Rose, Shirley K. and Irwin Weiser, eds. *The Writing Program Administrator
as Theorist: Making Knowledge Work.* Portsmouth, NH: Boynton/Cook,
2002.

Spears, Richard A. *American Idioms Dictionary* 2nd ed. Chicago: NTC Publishing Group, 1994.

12 Fitness for the Occasion: How Context Matters for jWPAs

Paul Ranieri and Jackie Grutsch McKinney

Paul Ranieri: In 1988, at the age of thirty-five, I said "yes" to my department chair's offer to become associate director of the writing program, to be followed by a regular three-year term as director. Now at the age of 54, having completed those terms as well as serving as associate chairperson and then chairperson of the department, a year as interim associate dean, and with eleven years in the last seventeen as an administrator in a doctorate-granting department, what generalizations might be beneficial for others faced with similar decisions to serve? Should I have said "yes" in 1988, my fifth year at my institution? What consequences have these decisions had for me professionally?

Jackie Grutsch McKinney: I started my job search in the fall of 2002 as I finished my dissertation and thus my PhD in rhetoric and composition. In the first academic year post-9/11, forecasts for job prospects were dismal. Budgets were already cut and searches suspended. So when the MLA list appeared online, I was pleasantly surprised to see many jobs available in my area. What was not a surprise was that many of the positions, even those clearly for beginning assistant professors, were administrative in nature. Of course, I was warned against becoming an administrator immediately. One member of my dissertation committee thought I would never publish if I were to do so, that such a move is simply antithetical to being a scholar.

In the field of rhetoric and composition, disciplinary "lore" asserts that taking a junior faculty WPA position is career suicide. One who does so, we are told, will be overworked but under-supported, will make enemies out of colleagues, will sacrifice all scholastic endeavors only to find that she or he is denied tenure. This narrative of untimely jWPA demise spans the decades. Both of us, though we entered the profession twenty years apart, were quite familiar with this cautionary tale when seeking our first jobs. Nonetheless, we both decided, based on the overlapping contexts of the changing field, the institution, and the particular position's requirements to take administrative assignments as junior faculty. We offer our stories here as an alternative to the cautionary tale that dominates our field; we believe those considering taking jWPA positions ought to hear a wider range of experiences, including stories from those who do not feel they have committed career suicide by becoming untenured administrators.[1]

Understanding context is important for deciding whether to assume an administrative position, and even more critical for succeeding in a position. With that in mind, we explore the context of our own two situations, twenty years apart in an institution, a field, and positions that are, as the classical philosopher Heraclitus would surely note, both the same and not the same across that two decade divide. Many remember Heraclitus as advocate for continual change. Yet, his quote, "In the same river, we both step and do not step, we are and we are not" (Freeman 28), demands we both study what changes and what stays the same in any rhetorical situation. Understanding similarities and differences in our own context will shed further light on those rhetorical principles and guidelines that might be useful to others.

Surely, the work of a WPA is rhetorical. Ascertaining contexts and deliberating how best to make decisions and communicate within those contexts is at the heart of our work. As members of a rhetorical discipline, we should be trained and prepared for just those challenges.

Before we relate "rhetorical context" specifically to our work as former, current, or potential WPAs, working within specific institutions, within specific programs, and with specific position descriptions, "context" deserves its own context, within an ancient, honored view of liberal education and specifically within rhetorical studies.

In most rhetoric classes, students learn about "context." "Context," we are taught, is *a*, if not *the*, determining factor in public discourse.

Discourse that takes a stand must answer to the context in which that stand is taken; discourse that calls for action must understand the demands for and consequences required by the context of that action. For the classical rhetorician and educator Isocrates, in particular, context is of utmost importance; general rhetorical principles fail because they "screen out the particulars of a given situation, which must be taken into account in all truly good moral and rhetorical decisions" (Bizzell and Herzberg 44). As Isocrates himself warns in "Against the Sophists," rhetors should not confuse an "art" with "hard and fast rules [with] such a creative process," as oratory. Oratory, for Isocrates, is "good only if it has the qualities of *fitness for the occasion,* propriety of style, and originality of treatment" (171, emphasis added).

Whether our professional starting points within a department of English are as specialists in rhetoric and composition, English education, or literary studies, our common center of gravity lies in the nature of language. Yet, as a rule, our approach to language in post-secondary education is one based more on confrontational rhetoric than on a rhetorical sense of logos. We often fail to practice what we assume to be true in theory.

Henri Marrou, Werner Jaeger, James Kinneavy, and Bruce Kimball all note the *rhetorical* basis for liberal education, either as "the" source for the concept itself or as a shared source with what we have come to see as Platonic philosophy. Our center in "language" has been called the "scribe" root by Marrou, the "rhetorical" root or "manger" by Kimball, and Kinneavy (20) respectively, while Marrou simply notes that the philosopher, rhetorician, and educator Isocrates is known by many to be the "father of 'humanistic culture'" (46) a reference that Marrou, Kinneavy, and Kimball either implicitly or explicitly support as well.

What are the main features of that Isocratean or rhetorical basis for the humanities?

- that a life and education centered on *logos* (thought/language) distinguishes humans from other living organisms; in turn, clear thought, clear language leads to clear action;
- that language is used with other humans as the means by which we define ourselves and share our identity with them, and they with us;
- that through language humans work to solve both the personal and social problems of the polis, or society, in which we live;

- that through language adults measure the skill by which children can be marked as adults, ready to take their place in the public discussion about issues that concern the whole; and
- that language is especially sensitive to the context and time bound problems within which questions arise and within which solutions to those questions reside.

We need, then, to return to our historical roots—or risk allowing our current twenty-first century context, which is not rhetoric sensitive, to determine our values, ideals, and goals. In contrast to the current clash of the ideal and the real, the pseudo-rhetoric of the debate between what is "true" and what is "fact," we need to regain our rhetorical sensitivity to context or our current context will continue to define us, digging us deeper, as Henry David Thoreau might say, into the confrontational "rut" where we are currently mired. How deep, says Thoreau, are "the ruts of tradition and conformity" (270). How deep are the epistemological ruts of Western thought that have dictated our sense of language over the last eight centuries or so?

What aspects, then, of a *logos* view of language and education can we productively carry with us to our own work in our own institutions and administrative positions, within a field evolving over the last twenty to twenty-five years? What lessons have we learned and are learning that might be useful for others?

THE FIELD

Paul Ranieri: I agonized over my decision to become associate director of the writing program in 1988. I felt relieved that I had selected the full-time teaching position offered to me, rather than the position teaching only one class per quarter in addition to administering the writing program. I did consider the director's position. Maybe ego prompted me to consider it, but I remembered one of the few real "truths" my undergraduate training in education had taught me—"take three to four years to become comfortable in a position before judging how one best fits in that position." In rhetorical terms, I recognized that I needed three to four years to develop my ethos on campus, ethos being, for Aristotle, "almost [. . .] the controlling factor in persuasion" (38).

For five years then, I took the chance to pursue my longitudinal research on writing and cognition, but I also opted to develop my own sense of institutional ethos by becoming involved with the university's core curriculum, the newest version of which was in the final process of being approved the year I arrived. "Gen. Ed." reform was again on the national agenda (Harvard would phase in their new general education program from 1979 to 1983, thus marking an "official" national effort to do so). Also, just appearing on college campuses was the "competency skills" movement, and a desire by administrators to "standardize" curriculum so that competency exams might measure the "value-added" portion of learning at the post-secondary level.

I entered the job market late, in January of 1983. I had already agreed to follow my colleague Cindy Selfe as assistant director of the writing program at the University of Texas-Austin, assisting John Ruszkiewicz, but the chance to return to the Midwest was worth the effort to compile my application materials. Many family members and friends worried that I would not find a position. Later research on the MLA *Job Information List*, however, would show that though the number of openings was nearing the end of a decade-long plateau, positions in rhetoric and composition were more available than those in literature ("Career"57).

As graduate students we were offered no training in administrative work. What we *were* offered, however, I would find very valuable—models of senior faculty, with their own traditions of liberal education, exercising their rhetorical voices both on campus and off, faculty such as Kinneavy and Ruszkiewicz in the department of English, and Edmund Farrell and Julie Jensen in the department of English education, faculty who practiced what they taught. Combined with my four years teaching secondary school in which I early witnessed the intersection between teaching and administration, I felt as ready as any young faculty member to join the professoriate.

Jackie Grutsch McKinney: During my years in graduate school, I watched closely as colleagues went on the job market. I saw many before me taking positions that had reduced course-loads for administrative duties such as writing program administrator, writing center director, director of English education, or state writing project coordinator. Therefore, when I started applying for jobs, I did not shy away from jobs with administrative components. Naïve or not, I wasn't nervous about taking that sort of position. By the time I was finishing my degree, the squeaky tight job market was a reality, and my attitude about taking an administrative position was certainly affected by that. Those of us going on the market had the same desperate mantra: "I just want a job, any job." But it wasn't only desperation that led me to consider administrative positions.

In fact, I had quite a bit of experience with administrative work, and I liked it. In graduate school, I had coordinated a first-year writing contest, served as both assistant writing center director and assistant WPA, and helped coordinate a community and university joint venture—a workshop for high school girls and their parents. In addition to this on-the-spot training, I had graduate coursework in writing center theory and administration. Having this degree of administrative experience was not entirely unique at the University of North Carolina at Greensboro where I received my PhD or, I would venture to guess, at many other rhetoric and composition programs. (Of course, when having experience before graduating is no longer unique, it becomes expected.)

Furthermore, throughout graduate school I worked with a number of great faculty mentors—Rebecca Jackson and Stuart Brown at New Mexico State and Elizabeth Chiseri-Strater, Hephzibah Roskelly, and Nancy Myers at Greensboro—all who served as administrators. From seeing their work, I understood how administrative positions allow one to work as public intellectuals, working within the university and the community to foster change. Sure, I understood that to do the work of the public intellectual the administrator had to wade through seas of bureaucracy and political tides. Even so, it was more appealing to me than the utter isolation of not being a part of something larger.

Without doubt the field of rhetoric and composition has changed in the last twenty years and will continue to change. Currently, nearly seventy universities belong to the Doctoral Consortium in Rhetoric and Composition, all of which offer PhDs in rhetoric and composition. In 2004, CCCC celebrated its fifty-fifth annual meeting. In turn, the nature of being a WPA has also evolved. The Council of Writing Program Administrators passed The Portland Resolution, which outlined fair practice for WPAs, in 1992. Graduate students now are able to specialize in rhetoric and composition and, at some schools, take courses in administration.

A look at Linda Peterson's 1985 survey of WPAs provides a glimpse of other changes in the field. The majority of respondents to her survey (all WPAs or former WPAs) were male, tenured, faculty members in English who specialized in English or American literature. Most felt that they carried heavier workloads than their colleagues—especially since for many, publications in rhetoric and composition were not respected, sometimes not even counted toward tenure or promotion (13–14). Accordingly, Peterson urges others to learn from this and "to publish in both composition and literature" (15).

If this study were to be replicated today, surely different trends would emerge, as well as different advice. For one, the field now has many more women than men. Most new hires have degrees and training in the field and are required to publish in this area of expertise. This drastic change in demographics and ideologies in just the past two decades is surprising given the usual slow nature of change in the academy. Still, despite changes in the field and the professionalization of writing program administration, attitudes have not caught up. Maybe we need to resist perceiving administrative work as Peterson describes it twenty years ago, as something forced upon someone, outside of one's expertise, without adequate compensation, which inhibits one's scholarship. Maybe individual campuses are out of tune as well with a current sense of writing program administration—and that fact needs to be considered when a position is offered.

In addition, junior faculty working as WPAs must be well-versed today not only in how the larger field of higher education embraces rhetoric and composition and the work of a WPA, but also in those broader areas that affect their administrative positions once they become linked with a particular institution. In 1983, the year of *A Nation at Risk,* those forces included general education reform, competency skills, and high stakes testing (National Commission). In 2004, general education reform is once again on the horizon, but with it a desire by many administrators to reduce first-year writing courses for theoretical as well as financial considerations. Also, on the WPA's agenda are topics such as testing, living-learning communities, the nature of the millennial generation, distance education, and technology-enhanced classrooms and teaching.

jWPAs should read widely both within their field and within the broader literature focused on postsecondary education. Today, list-servs for both the Council of Writing Program Administrators and the International Writing Center Association help administrators in writing programs identify current issues and their effects on writing programs. Broad-based publications, such as *The Chronicle of Higher Education, Change, Liberal Education,* and *Peer Review,* will help the young administrator assess if a particular position at a particular time is doomed for failure.

All that considered, however, such a grasp of contextual features relating to specialty, discipline, and higher education in general is only part of the challenge. Such features are static characteristics about which we are able to read or study. The dynamic part of the challenge to young administrators especially is how to maneuver among such variables.

Many classical rhetoricians, including Isocrates, Aristotle, Cicero, Quintilian, and Augustine debated, and disagreed, about the relationship among talent, training, and practice in the development of one's rhetorical powers. Surely talent plays a role in one's ability to administer a writing program within any twenty-first century American post-secondary institution; however, with a combination of observing models and specific training, jWPAs can further develop that critical element required for successful administrative work, that element Isocrates called *phronesis,* or practical wisdom.

A logos-based philosophy of administration, one based on the five principles noted earlier, acknowledges that at some point, successful young administrators must make the transition—by a combination of training and practice—between acquiring conceptual knowledge ("the what") and the use of that knowledge to negotiate successfully within specific, defined contexts. It is one thing to *know that* language is sensitive to context and time-bound problems; it is quite another thing to have the practical wisdom to, not know, but *use* knowledge relevant for a specific situation, not to mention *say* what needs to be said at what time to which audience (a "dynamic" sense included in the ancient notion of *kairos*).

Gerard Hauser notes that this "practical reasoning in rhetoric involves making choices about the *preferable* and the *good* specific to our rhetorical situation that will lead to *public happiness*. There is no god's-eye view that offers a single account of what [such happiness] may be. We locate this through deliberation tempered by the fortunes of our particular way of life" (151). For Hauser, "phronesis" centers rhetoric as "a civic art we practice to create and maintain community" (149). A logos-based view of administration would thus presuppose decision-makers who are sensitive to the collaborative power of language, able to define a current question, to speculate about possible solutions, to seek solutions suited to a time and place, and then to communicate the solution and monitor both its implementation and its need for future attention.

For Hauser, exhibiting phronesis leads not only to successful decision making, but also to its etymological cousin *phronemos* or "prudence": "As we observe the public behavior of those with *phronesis,* we see their habits of prudence revealed in the choices they make. From discerning their habits, we draw inferences about their character, or ethos" (152). Exhibiting *phronesis* leads to increased *ethos,* which in turn provides the WPA with increased rhetorical power in the future. One cannot only *be* ready; one has to *act* ready, which belies those who feel that somehow there is a magic point at which one is ready to administer. One has to act. In a sense, any administrative act is a step out on the limb, a gamble, a career risk. The reward is heightened *ethos* and a healthier civic atmosphere.

In other words, though training can precede practice, training is incomplete without practice, and practice provides its own unique type of training. We must acknowledge that someone with talent and some training may be ready in the right context to begin acting—and learning—within a specific institutional administrative role. When is that "leap" appropriate? What type of support might be needed early in an administrative career? Does that support exist? Would it be appropriate for someone to gain a few more years of experience in a specific institution before "leaping" into an administrative position, or can another person "leap" right into it? Again, no "hard and fast rules" exist for such decisions anymore than ancient rhetoricians felt that one could compose "hard and fast rules" for writing for all situations. On the one hand, decisions have to be made, and mistakes will be made. On the other hand, as rhetoricians we should be able to share our experiences with each other, learn from them, and use the lessons learned to help determine what decisions for our current position need to be made.

Within complex institutional situations, we need to set our sights on both local and global factors that affect us. We need also to realize that successful administrators need both what experience brings (i.e., knowledge of the context, successes and failures resulting from working within the complex rhetorical situations that are universities), and what youth typically brings as well (i.e., new knowledge, new analyses, fresh energy, lives lived within current cultural tensions). What we cannot assume is that successful administration lies solely on either end of this artificial continuum. Any WPA new to the position will eventually have to account for what s/he does *not* bring to the position on that first day on the job. *That* is what gives "practice" its real power as a tool for learning.

The Institution and the Positions

Paul Ranieri—In 1983, the Department of English at Ball State University hired its first two rhetoric and composition scholars fully trained in that field. The department was at that time almost fully tenured (36 of 40) and suffering from an already ossifying atmosphere of having hired nineteen assistant professors in 1967 and 1968 but only two in the fifteen years since. This "new" field called rhetoric and composition was looked upon with suspicion by my colleagues; however, both the department chairperson and the leading voice on composition issues in the department knew that the future of our department depended partly on developing trained expertise in this ancient but quickly renewing field.

When I was offered my position, I was told that I could select either of the two open positions—the "research position" or the "administrative position." The latter would have made me the first faculty member trained in rhetoric and composition to direct our writing program. A few senior department faculty suggested that I not take the administrative position, that I settle in first in a department that may have forgotten how to treat new assistant professors. Their advice fit my sense of my own ethos. Besides, I had a specific research agenda and thought I would carry that out for a few years. The young faculty member who chose the administrative position had a very difficult next couple of years, working to administer and change a program whose faculty were extremely resistant not only to change but to the value of this new perspective in the department (70 percent of tenure-line faculty specialized in literature, 12.5 percent each in linguistics and English education, and 5 percent—the two newest—in rhetoric and composition). I remember leaving one department meeting during my first two years and an adjunct colleague saying that he would not attend any more meetings because senior colleagues were "just plain mean."

As noted earlier, I opted to develop relationships outside the department, specifically within the university's core curriculum program, where writing courses played a key role. My training in liberal education helped me to appreciate and be appreciated at the college and university level where fruitful discussion relied on seeing broader contexts for issues and broader implications for possible solutions. In addition, my philosophy of the relationship between language and liberal education was compatible with the views of our new dean, in contrast to the previous dean and provost who did not understand nor appreciate our resistance to their new writing competency exam, a high stakes, one-shot essay required for graduation that demanded a standard five-paragraph theme. As my experience at the university level increased, I came to find particularly "enticing" the potential for the role of the WPA on my campus: the potential for bringing new, tested ideas to a traditional, tired program, the chance to extend the role of writing in the core curriculum program, the chance to put into practice Aristotle's view that rhetoric knows few disciplinary bounds, and the chance to bring to life a philosophy that saw education, as James Kinneavy said, born in a "rhetorical manger." Though I would have to be wary of "radical" changes to the program, the atmosphere had changed enough to make possible effective administration *within* the program at first, and maybe more extensive departmental-level changes by the end of a three-year term.

In the spring of 1988, as I pondered the offer to become associate director of the writing program, with the understanding that I would follow that year with a three-year term as director, I could not help but consider the earlier rocky years for my colleague, so rocky that a senior literature professor was assigned after three years to bring, in the eyes of our tenured colleagues, respectability to the program again. Though my rhetoric and composition colleague would leave the university in 1996 for a position in the business world, and do so tenured and fully promoted, in 1988, the critical question remained, was the department ready so soon for another rhetoric and composition director? By that year, the department had two additional rhetoric and composition faculty, but more importantly seven literature faculty members had retired, many of whom had helped to make my colleague's administrative life so uncomfortable. I determined that I would not allow myself to engage needlessly the confrontational rhetoric many senior faculty members relished, partly because I did not believe in it, and partly because they were so successful at it.

Within the department itself, rhetoric and composition had become an administrative area along with British and world literature, American literature, language and linguistics, and English education. We had added a doctoral program in composition; it was growing. With five faculty members in our area, rhetoric and composition comprised 12 percent of the voting tenure-line faculty, with literature making up 65 percent, linguistics 5 percent and English education 9 percent: still unbalanced, but continuing to readjust. Though no member of the rhetoric and composition area had yet reached the critical sixth-year tenure review, the level of published activity currently exhibited seemed sufficient, particularly since all four continued to receive yearly reviews of "satisfactory progress toward tenure."

The department had also hired from the outside a new department chairperson, one who was not so sure about my administering a program so large (enrolling each year over 8,000 students in over 400 sections taught by more than 75 full and part-time faculty) while yet untenured. Though I felt he did not understand the broader possibilities for the program within university goals, I did feel his caution needed to be considered. Taking advantage of my contacts outside the department, I arranged a meeting with the dean with whom I had worked closely on a college symposium and within a liberal arts think tank. Though she would not tell me directly to take the position, nor would I have expected her to do so, when I asked if she would strongly consider it if she were in my shoes, she smiled and said "yes." So I did.

Jackie Grutsch McKinney—When offered the position at Ball State in 2003, the department of English had five faculty members in rhetoric and composition teaching graduate students in the MA and PhD programs, as well as undergraduates in the new rhetoric and composition major. The overall student enrollment hovered around 18,000 students. The English department was and is the largest on campus due to the writing program and required FYC.

I was asked to be the director of the writing center, a position previously assigned to graduate students, for a term of no more than five years. By this time, the department had an unwritten policy about not giving untenured faculty administrative positions, but no one really saw assigning me as director of the writing center to be a violation of that understanding. I would receive a one-course reduction for directing the Center each semester, so I would have a 2/2 teaching load comprised of both undergraduate and graduate courses. I would be expected to publish—though the hiring committee and the faculty I met during my site visit were clear that I would not need to publish a book to receive tenure.

In deciding whether or not to take the position, it was very influential to see that Ball State had an established rhetoric and composition area with mostly tenured faculty members and a graduate program in rhetoric and composition; I knew I did not want to be the only rhetoric and composition person on a faculty, and having a graduate program showed there was respect within the department for rhetoric and composition as a scholarly peer to literature. The writing program, too, was impressive. Nearly all the teachers in the program were full-time contract faculty with decent benefits and retirement accounts; several had been on staff for over twenty years. These things helped me gauge the climate during my brief site visit.

I wasn't able to tell much about the writing center. Although the center had been around since 1967, they had never seen the need or been able to make a persuasive case for a faculty director. I was nervous that the department at large did not value the writing center and how that might make my position difficult. At the same time, I wasn't taking over the position from a long-time faculty member or beloved director, so I wouldn't be rocking the boat if I wanted to make any changes.

Obviously, I took the job weighing offers and options, benefits, and drawbacks. My reading of the departmental context two years ago has mostly been confirmed. I am a part of a rhetoric and composition area that has drive and clout. My entry into my position as director of the writing center was difficult within the center (since the former director became my assistant director), but I didn't ruffle any feathers in the department at large mainly because the writing center had and continues to have a visibility problem in the department and university. I've had to become my own advocate, explaining to colleagues what it is I do.

In many ways, our field acknowledges that "context matters." In research methodology, for instance, we no longer feel the need to argue the value of "nonempirical" research. We acknowledge the need for and value of "thick description" to understand why research subjects make the decisions they do. The parallels are obvious. Considering whether one's talents suit a particular position demands as much "thick description" as any case study in order to understand the context in which one is being called to act.

When a jWPA considers either taking a position with an administrative assignment included, or assuming an administrative post while serving in a pretenure capacity, she must consider the context within which decisions will be made: university strategic plans, department atmosphere, expectations from rhetoric and composition colleagues themselves. None of us is an amateur at such an analysis process—most adults and certainly most academics are in constant analysis mode; however, young faculty may need to be reminded of all the factors that play a part in any administrative position.

Questions of context for potential administrators would include the following:

- Does the university, college, or department have a strategic plan and what role is asked of the writing program in that plan?
- How would one describe the role of the writing program in the university's core curriculum or general education program?
- How would one describe the department's reputation in the university as a whole? With the dean? What is the dean's sense of the strengths and weaknesses of the department? If relevant, what would the dean like to see accomplished by a new faculty member in this position? Is the dean comfortable with such an appointment?
- How would one describe the attitude of the department toward the writing program? Is it considered, and treated as, a vital part of the department, or is it viewed simply as a "credit hour generating" program that benefits other major and graduate programs?
- Given research showing "that women at doctorate-granting universities advance more slowly on the tenure track than men do, are paid less than their male counterparts, and are more apt to be dissatisfied with their jobs" (Wilson A8), what has been the record of this university, this department with the hiring, tenuring, and promoting of women colleagues?
- How many rhetoric and composition faculty currently work in the department, what has been their level of success during tenure and promotion review, and what has been their level of success with peer-reviewed scholarship and grants?
- What rhetoric and composition programs are offered by the department? How well enrolled are they? What might graduates of those programs tell you about how students perceive faculty and the programs themselves?
- Have any rhetoric and composition faculty left the institution in the recent past? What were their reasons for leaving? Were any of those reasons related to promotion and tenure review?

- How did the current open position come about? Is it a new position? If not, who held it before, and what were the reasons for that person's leaving? If it is a new position, who wrote the position description, if there is one?
- Do colleagues work well together, present papers together, co-author articles?

For those interviewing from the outside, many answers to these questions may be hard to ascertain. Still, some can serve as useful discussion points during any interview process. Answers to them by a dean, a department chair, potential colleagues, graduate students, and undergraduates can be compared for consistency and, if possible, accuracy.

Obviously at some point the offer for a WPA position must be accepted or rejected, or to place the decision in rhetorical terms—is accepting or declining such an offer the "timely" decision to make? Again, few decisions come without alternatives; almost all involve risk. All certainly involve consequences that must be rhetorically analyzed and confronted.

USING CONTEXT TO NAVIGATE THE JOB

Paul Ranieri: Maybe the most important decision I made in my four years in the writing Program office was not to tackle any problems that required department approval (e.g., master syllabi). Though by this time I might have won any votes I had initiated, I did not relish the thought of enhancing further any split in the department between more traditional faculty and that growing number ready to update our writing pedagogy. My focus remained *within* the program. With the assistance of the department's graduate director, we restructured the graduate training program, enabling new graduate assistants to spend an entire semester observing, being mentored, and practice teaching before being assigned a classroom of their own (subsequent complaints about those classrooms all but disappeared).We redesigned the "remedial" entry-level class into a true developmental course that gave those students what they needed to succeed—smaller classes (a limit of eighteen students) and more time (a full year) to develop the skills needed to move to the second writing class required of all students. We nurtured carefully the emerging role of the program in distance education, teaching both required classes for the first time on the state's one-way video, two-way audio system, while promoting for the first time computer-enhanced classrooms available for all writing program courses. We continued to place the writing program at the center of the university's core curriculum program, even taking a leadership role in the first university-wide assessment of core education. Finally, in what would bode well for the university's nationally recognized efforts with first-year programs, we continued to nurture the writing program's presence on university committees dealing with first-year students, as well as on committees dealing with excellence in teaching, honors in writing, and accreditation.

To illustrate how rhetorical principles played their part, I clearly remember our challenge to redesign our "remedial" writing course, ENG 099. In an attempt to improve the university's image, the provost decided that the three "099" "remedial" courses in reading, mathematics, and English would be eliminated. To my knowledge, no attempt was made to keep the other two in any form. Our course, however, had existed for years and had served a vital role in bringing 750 weaker students per year to a level where they could succeed in the typical first semester writing course. I asked a number of experienced ENG 099 faculty to join me in discussing options that would satisfy the parameters established by our dean whom I had approached about reorganizing and preserving the course in some form. For a couple of months, we struggled to design a course that would be truly developmental but still fit the dean's parameters. Looking back I realize that those months were a good exercise in collaboration, in listening and creative thinking, but the breakthrough came in an article on general education I happened to be reading from an online discussion board. That timely piece of information—having to do with course structure—provided us the solution to our problem. One could call us "lucky," but if we had not successfully completed our collaborative work first, listened to the dean who listened to our arguments based on what our experience said students needed, we would not have solved this problem successfully. Preparation, communication, collaboration, and timeliness—all served "practical wisdom" in this case and others during my multiple administrative careers.

By the end of my three-year term as director of the writing program, we were assured of those votes that affected long-range policy, and major changes to department syllabi, for instance, were passed, with little rancor. In 1992 the program was turned over fully to the rhetoric and composition faculty in the department, with the virtual blessings of the rest of the faculty.

Jackie Grutsch McKinney: The first year on the job, I spent much of my time figuring out how the writing center had functioned in the past, what of that was good, and what else was needed. Each week my first semester, I was alerted by someone on the writing center staff that we typically do "x" this month, or people will expect "y" to happen before midterms. The constant question being posed to me was: "How do you want to do it?" Since I was just figuring out the context in which I was to make these decisions, this haunted me. I didn't always have an answer; as a result, I left many things intact my first year, relying on past wisdom or tradition because I didn't know enough about the specific context to risk the consequences of making changes.

However, during my second year, we gained a new department chair who in turn appointed a new WPA. Since I had a year to assess what we needed at the writing center and since this new guard would not rely on what had been done in the past (necessarily) to make decisions, I took this opportunity to ask for new computers, new software, supplies, and a budget. I believe I was awarded these things during this year, despite being turned down in the past, because of the dire need, my ability to articulate this need, and my timing.

Recently, the department has reconsidered its policy of having department chairs hold office for only a three-year term. Those who have served in this capacity and outside consultants have described an administrative learning curve which takes two good years to puzzle through. I worried my first year that I didn't know enough about Ball State to make intelligent decisions. Yet hearing this discussion on department chairs has reassured me a bit. If we are acknowledging that department chairs—who are typically the most senior and/or most actively involved members of the department—need two years to really understand their positions, then I ought to give myself the same latitude to figure out my job.

Walker Gibson, in his 1993 *College English* essay, "In Praise of the Sophists," shows how ancient rhetorical sensibilities based on *logos* can help us understand and change our public rhetoric, enabling us to evolve closer to a rhetorically based decision-making process. Gibson, after reviewing both ancient and contemporary understandings of the gulf between language and reality, notes that such knowledge can lead to "cynicism and indifference" or a realization that "if language is what there mostly *is* [. . .], then it behooves [us] to watch [our] words, for [we] have to live with them. The consequences of this conviction can be a spirit of caution and modesty" (286). Gibson adds, "It's precisely because rhetoric makes us sensitive to the *limits of our powers* that it should play a major role in any curriculum" (287). As users of language, we know the wide gap between what we say and what we want to say, and thus we want our listeners to give us a little leeway, not to hold us exactly to what they perceive we said. In turn, if we want such leeway for ourselves, we need to be willing to grant it to others—not an easy attitude to develop in this era of "gotcha" journalism, media, and debate. Gibson argues for a greater respect for language that in the end leads to attitudes of caution, modesty, even humor by those who strive to use language well. For Gibson, "if *we* are the originators of the world as we make it, then we'd better watch our step and speak softly" (289).

Assuming that untenured faculty members are able to develop such a rhetorically based administrative style, would they be able to utilize it within the political structures that characterize today's universities? Some critics, such as Roxanne Mountford, argue that graduate training in rhetoric and composition is important, but it does not prepare students for messy politics. She argues that even students who learn to administer through an apprenticeship, such as a term as an assistant WPA, are guarded from the real experience by their mentors (49). While it is probably true that some graduate assistant WPAs are protected by their mentors (and others are probably left to hang themselves), the reason jWPAs are not *immediately* ready for the politics of a new job is because they have yet to develop either a sense of the context in which they have to make decisions, or the *ethos* and *phronesis* necessary for their positions.

Graduate students rarely earn a doctorate without knowing quite intimately that universities are political places; they are not naïve enough to believe that universities exist in a world outside of grudges, power plays, bureaucracy, and/or inane traditions. So, it is not that new faculty members confront politics *per se* for the first time at their new jobs, just new political contexts. New faculty have to navigate complex histories and hierarchies that might not be immediately apparent. Because of this, some believe that a few years on the job might be helpful before one takes on an administrative role. While this may be helpful, the context would still change immediately when one has to make decisions. Friendly colleagues might turn unfriendly if one's decisions affect other programs or courses in the department. Thus, at any point that a faculty member becomes an administrator, she or he will have to reassess the political terrain and make rhetorically sound decisions based on what she or he understands of the context.

WPAs have a long history of using rhetoric to navigate their positions, yet often do not describe what they do in terms of rhetoric. Barry Maid in "How WPAs Can Learn to Use Power to Their Own Advantage" and Edward White in "Use It or Lose It: Power and WPA," for instance, talk about their decisions and their "power" as WPAs. Both describe problem situations at their institutions and how they affected change. In essence, both describe the contexts, which once understood, allow them to make rhetorically sound decisions. In each case, they found ways to address both the problem and the context, keeping themselves in favor with others at the institution (for the most part). In the same vein, Melissa Ianetta writes explicitly about how having multiple classical rhetoric approaches in one's bag of tricks can help one administer more effectively. In "If Aristotle Ran the Writing Center," she states that "being conscious of the options various rhetorical postures can offer may strengthen [the WPA's] resistance to both unsavory options and provide instead a variety of strategies for the administrator-rhetor" (57).

Is there, then, a means for providing a willing, young faculty member, one with the talent and the training, the means for developing real "practical wisdom" within the context of a new position? Maybe at this point such responsibility lies with the department and the institution to define assistant or associate director positions in which untenured faculty are able to practice their decision-making powers where real consequences exist. Clearly, departments and institutions have a large stake in a young faculty member's success. Providing an environment in which such critical experience can take place without sheltering that novice administrator from real decisions and consequences would allow the institution to fulfill its responsibility to the full development of a valued member of its learning community.

Without a doubt, "power" follows along with rhetoric. Both need to be treated with the fragility we know characterizes them. "Power" and "language" are often associated in our society with metaphors of war, battle, and conflict. Maybe they are both better associated with metaphors of crafting, designing, or sculpting, more quiet, reflective skills that enable us to build but also to observe, listen, and discern direction. In such an environment we might better come to understand that educational and administrative world in which we operate, so that we are able to "nudge" our way into the power structures in which we operate, and in the process come to recognize better its ancient *kairos* (timeliness), harness its power, and in the end determine both our "fitness" for a position, as well as the "fittingness" of any decision we contemplate.

WHERE ARE WE NOW?

Paul Ranieri: The writing program is now with its fourth director after I left the post in 1992, all drawn from the rhetoric and composition faculty. In 1998, one director proposed fully converting all first semester courses (about 100 sections) to technology-enhanced classrooms, thus building on many of our earlier successes while taking advantage of a unique local situation whereby administrators were looking for a program willing to take risks, program-wide, with new approaches to teaching and learning. The first two years of my three-year term as department chairperson were consumed with overseeing the remodeling of eight classrooms, and assisting the writing program director with gradually shifting staff and pedagogy to these environments. On the other hand, the program has become somewhat insulated, separate from the fortunes of the university core curriculum. Where once writing program courses were seen as the center of our Freshman Connections program, writing faculty did not fully embrace that role, and Freshman Connections, part of a nationally award-winning and nationally recognized living-learning program has redefined its center away from writing courses. At the risk of stating the obvious, context changes, never standing still for any one faculty member, or any one program.

It is worth noting, that decisions to administer as an untenured faculty member are not irrevocable "life sentences." Shortly after I became chairperson, I did not ask two untenured colleagues to continue in their administrative posts, one of whom served in my previous position as director of the writing program. In both cases, these colleagues were at crucial points in the promotion and tenure process. In both cases, I turned to senior colleagues to fill those posts at a time in which the department was retiring two to three senior colleagues a year and hiring assistant professors to take their places. In fact, by 2004, only five tenure-track colleagues remained from the forty I began with twenty-one years earlier. Still, we were able to fill the administrative gap for a couple of years in one case and three years in the other before both young colleagues returned to their previous posts, though now tenured and promoted to the associate level.

Jackie Grutsch McKinney: What's funny is that the context has changed pretty quickly. When I arrived, no one was surprised or appalled that I, as junior faculty, would be writing center director. Since the position had been held by graduate students, it wasn't perceived as involving much work, finesse, or intelligence. However, now in my second year, colleagues in literature have voiced concern to me about my position. More than one has advised me to get out sooner rather than later. I believe that seeing a faculty member holding the position has changed their perception of the job quickly. Although they may have seen memos and initiatives come from the writing center in the past, they see them with my name on them now. They understand that in addition to the teaching, research, and service that we all do, I also have another whole aspect to my job.

Some of my colleagues, I believe, see administrative work as a sentence, completely detached from their intellectual endeavors. They know that administrative work can suck the life-force out of other endeavors. Yet, for me, my administrative work helps me accomplish more than my teaching or research does on its own, and it feeds into my scholarly work. Nearly all of the presentations and articles I have worked on since taking this job have benefited from my experience as writing center director. I have just received my second favorable review towards tenure with positive feedback on my teaching, scholarly works, and my administrative work in the writing center.

Decades ago—and we still deal with this false perception—people thought that anyone could teach writing. Now those in departments of English, and maybe in the discipline, feel that anyone can administer. It is safe to say that our discipline could very easily have well-regarded theoreticians and researchers who do not belong in an administrative office. As our discipline matures, we need to recognize Ernest Boyer's point that departments, and rhetoric and composition areas need to be made up of a "mosaic of talent" (58): faculty who might be excellent researchers, others who are excellent theoreticians, others excellent teachers, and others excellent administrators. In reality, especially in small departments, these descriptions might not apply to individual personalities. Though all would exhibit their scholarship in formats appropriate for their own institutions, individual colleagues would exhibit unique but complementary levels of skill in basic research, theory, teaching, and administration. As a revived, late-twentieth-century discipline, rhetoric and composition must resist the temptation to contribute to the academic Tower of Babel in which a certain type of work attains the highest respect and all other efforts merely serve that interest.

SUMMARY: TALENT, TRAINING, AND PRACTICE

In the end, we hope we have shed some light on our experiences, determined in one sense by context, but in another sense, determined by us, using our sense of the power, timeliness, and fittingness of our own words. As we each assay our own context, our own talent, our own training, and our own ability to practice our skills for "practical wisdom," we need to determine if *this* administrative position is right for "me" in *this* time and *this* place. In graduate classes on classical rhetoric, students ask whether they can make *kairos* (timeliness) possible, or whether they can only train themselves to watch for it and capitalize on it. The answer, of course, is both. What does that mean—in direct terms?

- New WPAs should exhibit a true rhetorical temperament, one that respects a *logos*-based view of language, developing as Gibson argues, related attitudes of caution, modesty, and even a sense of humor. These skills build on a wealth of other abilities and bodies of information, including excellent teaching skills, case study training in the challenges of daily administration, basic understanding of the cognitive and social demands of learning, and a working knowledge of the key issues being faced by institutions as a whole (currently, recruitment, retention, technology, and assessment).

- New WPAs should exhibit a true rhetorical sense of *phronesis* and *kairos,* if only at a nascent stage. Future administrators, as well as their mentors, need to be honest with themselves about their abilities to make decisions that best suit the problem at hand, decisions often borne out of collaborative problem finding and solving processes.

- WPAs should resist seeing their work as "service" in a "service" program, but rather as program building directly relevant to an institution's goals for learning, teaching, recruitment, retention, and technology. WPAs should not shy away from placing their programs in the context of broader university strategic goals.

- Our training in doctoral programs does not stress larger trends in American education, trends to which WPAs must respond. Our training in doctoral programs generally has not prepared us to move from a teaching-centered philosophy to a learning-centered philosophy. Virtually no one, for instance, discusses developmental issues anymore. On our campus, for instance, those graduate students and staff who know the most about millennial students and their intellectual and social developments are young residence hall directors. How did that happen as institutions have attempted to move from a teaching to a learning culture?

- The scholarship efforts of the WPA do not have to collapse in the face of the administrative pressures of the position. Besides taking regular time for reading and writing, WPAs should seek to combine aspects of "office" and "publishing." In our department that means an emphasis on securing grants, on presentations at national and regional institutions that evolve into written texts, and on collaborative work, especially in the area of what Ernest Boyer calls the scholarship of teaching.

- Young faculty and their institutions need to understand the strengths younger colleagues do bring to appropriate administrative positions: up-to-date training, experience in learning closer to that of our undergraduates, and deep pools of dedication and energy, a desire to try what others of us have written off as unsuccessful for our students. As one of our associate provosts recently stated, "try to find all of that in a senior faculty member"!

- Institutions and departments must provide close mentoring for young administrators, and even positions (e.g., assistant or associate directors) in which those young administrators are able to make real decisions with real consequences within the political contexts which they must come to know and serve. "Practice" provides a unique kind of training. If jWPAs want to succeed, and institutions want them to succeed, various types of mentoring are essential.

- Finally, we assume too often that both personal and personnel decisions should be "risk-neutral" when no decision has such a characteristic. Isocrates judged his students ready for the public forum when they exhibited *phronesis,* the skills to make, through language, the best decision for the moment. A jWPA is ready for an administrative position when that objective is reached as well. Antonius in Cicero's *De Oratore* says that from the school of Isocrates, "as from the Horse of Troy, none but leaders emerged" (269). *Phronesis* was the measuring stick then; it should be now.

In his essay "Confessions of an Associate Dean," Charles Schuster makes many of the same points about our role as WPAs in a larger university, though his discussion of the role of an associate dean paints a picture of an embattled, faceless, "entombed" administrator facing collective forces against which one must struggle merely for periodic, empty victories. Administrative work seems drearily confrontational and oppositional in nature. As experts in rhetoric, we must think deeply about how what we *know* about language actually informs what we say and do, while undercutting potentially disruptive philosophies of language based more on conflict and confrontation. Our role as WPAs, especially young WPAs, is defined, as Walker Gibson argues, by *logos*, that is, the use of language and thought to address daily problems, an activity that defines our human identity. We need to analyze that role more deeply from a rhetorical perspective and then become determined to act according to those rhetorical principles, some if which we have illustrated and presented in this discussion.

One final caution: a well-developed sense of *logos*, or more dangerously, a personal tendency to share deeply such confidence in the power of language, might nudge the prospective jWPA into a decision for which she is not ready. A *logos*-based personal philosophy, as well as a *logos*-based professional philosophy might give a person permission to seek out situations in which language is used for the benefit of students we are meant to serve. In other words, given our belief in the power of language, we might naturally seek involvement in situations in which language can have results. Why are so many rhetoric and composition, as well as department of English colleagues in administrative positions, in contrast to our colleagues in the sciences? Given the rhetorical powers most WPAs have developed, is it any wonder they seek out venues for such a use of their powers? Given such an innate tendency to serve, maybe we ought to be even more careful about context, choosing to serve only at the *right* time and place.

REGRETS/FUTURE DECISIONS

Paul Ranieri: Professionally I have few regrets, though I have not been promoted in twelve years. My career trajectory arched away from research as I successively became assistant chairperson, chairperson, and then interim associate dean. In the last two years, I have returned to my full-time teaching role and am trying to resuscitate my research in cognition and pedagogy so that I might be promoted to full professor in the near future. However, my broader work in the core curriculum has more fully developed my parallel interest in rhetoric, liberal education, and the scholarship of teach-

ing. I used my administrative and rhetorical skills to help build a
program for first-year students that has been recognized nationally twice in the last two years for its excellence. As for salary, what
people often worry about for me, my administrative stipends have
guaranteed that my current salary is the same, if not slightly more
than that of the other young faculty who arrived with me on campus in 1983, all of whom have since been promoted to professor. If
I wanted to move from Ball State, I might find my mobility limited. Institutions have approached me to gauge my interest in se-
nior-level positions, but almost all of those positions would require
that I first be fully promoted. Thus, I recognize some professional
cost, but given the rhetorical nature of my career, I find that not
to be such a long-term nuisance.

Our university has just hired a new president, one not familiar
with this institution's past respect for the "teacher-scholar." How
might the context completely change in the next couple of years?
In a few years, should I suggest an untenured colleague not assume an administrative position? Maybe, maybe not. Much would
be based on the character (*ethos*) and skills (*phronesis*) of that
young colleague. Part of my advice would also be based on what
I see from others in our current administration (where ironically
the new dean seems to want to deepen our sense of Ernest Boyer's
sense of scholarship and the "teacher-scholar"). Another part of
my advice would depend on the nature of the department, and
a final part on the ability of my colleagues in rhetoric and composition to nurture and mentor such a young professional. It just
depends.

Jackie Grutsch McKinney: It's really too early to tell if I made the
right choice; I'm only in my second year in the job. I imagine that
my term of "no more than five years" could be extended. I also
suspect that I may be asked to be WPA shortly after achieving tenure, if I stay, or frankly, if I go elsewhere. In my experience, most
rhetoric and composition faculty serve at one time or another in
an administrative capacity. For many of us trained in this discipline, it is not a surprise, nor is it a chore as outsiders may see it.

I do not regret my choice to take an administrative position my first year on the job, but I will not say it is always a good idea. It depends. It depends on the position—not all writing center positions are the same, not all WPA positions are the same. I have several colleagues from graduate school who are also administrators. Some are clearly in untenable positions, and thus, are back on the job market. Some, like me, are pretty satisfied. One, in her third year on the job, received a new title, a sizable raise, and a larger office. Had she not taken this particular position, she would not have met with such early career success. Other colleagues who are not administrators seem to have about the same likelihood of finding satisfaction (or gaining tenure) in any particular position, which reminds me that being a junior faculty member in general can be tough.

NOTE

[1] Throughout this article, we have used the term of jWPA to cover a range of administrative positions held by junior faculty since there are countless variations to these positions with overlapping responsibilities. Although some perceive the position of writing program director as necessarily the most challenging of these, that is not always the case. At some institutions, the course load and expectations of a WPA may be clearly and fairly developed, but a writing center director or a coordinator of basic writing may flounder, struggling to stay afloat in a position that is deemed "easier" and thus is given less than adequate support or course release time.

WORKS CITED

Aristotle. *On Rhetoric: A Theory of Civic Discourse.* Trans. George A. Kennedy. New York: Oxford UP, 1991.

Augustine. *On Christian Doctrine.* Trans. D.W. Robertson, Jr. New York: Macmillan, 1958. 119-120.

Bizzell, Patricia, and Bruce Herzberg, eds. *The Rhetorical Tradition: Readings from the Classical Times to the Present.* 2nd ed. Boston: Bedford/St. Martin's, 2001.

Boyer, Ernest L. *Scholarship Reconsidered: Priorities of the Professoriate.* Princeton, NJ: Carnegie Foundation, 1990.

"Career Information for Graduate Students and Junior Faculty Members." *ADE Bulletin* 132 (Fall 2002): 56–59.

Cicero, Marcus Tullius. *De Oratore*. Vol. 1. Trans. E. W. Sutton. Cambridge, MA: Harvard UP, 1959.

Freeman, Kathleen, trans. *Ancilla to the Pre-Socratic Philosophers*. Cambridge: Oxford UP, 1983.

Gibson, Walker. "In Praise of the Sophists." *College English* 55.3 (1993): 284–90.

Hauser, Gerard A. *Introduction to Rhetorical Theory*. 2nd ed. Prospect Heights, IL:Waveland, 2002.

Ianetta, Melissa. "If Aristotle Ran the Writing Center: Classical Rhetoric and Writing Center Administration." *Writing Center Journal* 24.2 (2004): 37–59.

Isocrates. *Isocrates, II*. Trans. George Norlin. 3 vols. Cambridge, MA: Harvard UP, 1968.

Jaeger, Werner. *Paideia: The Ideals of Greek Culture*. Vol. 3. Trans. Gilbert Highet. New York: Oxford UP, 1944.

Kimball, Bruce. *Orators and Philosophers: A History of the Idea of Liberal Education*. New York: Columbia, 1986.

Kinneavy, James. "Restoring the Humanities: The Return of Rhetoric from Exile." *The Rhetorical Tradition and Modern Writing*. Ed. James J. Murphy. New York: MLA, 1982. 19–28.

Maid, Barry. "How WPAs Can Learn to Use Power to Their Own Advantage." *Administrative Problem-Solving for Writing Programs and Writing Centers*. Ed. Linda Myers-Breslin. Urbana, IL: NCTE, 1999. 199–211.

Mountford, Roxanne. "From Labor to Middle Management: Graduate Students in Writing Program Administration." *Rhetoric Review* 21.1 (2002): 41–53.

Marrou, H. I. *Education in Antiquity*. Trans. George Lamb. Madison, WI: U of Wisconsin P, 1982.

National Commision on Excellence in Education. *A Nation at Risk*. Washington DC: U.S. Department of Education, 1983. Available http://www.ed.gov/pubs/NatAtRisk/index.html

Peterson, Linda. "The WPA's Progress: A Survey, Story, and Commentary on the Career Paths of Writing Program Administrators." *WPA: Writing Program Administration* 10.3 (1987): 11–18.

"The Portland Resolution: Guidelines for Writing Program Administrator Positions." *WPA: Writing Program Administration* 16.1/2 (1992): 88–94.

Quintilian, Marcus Fabius. *Quintilian: On the Teaching of Speaking and Writing*. Ed./Trans. James J. Murphy. Landmarks in Rhetoric and Public Address. Carbondale: Southern Illinois UP, 1987. 116-118.

Schuster, Charles. "Confessions of an Associate Dean." *WPA: Writing Program Administration* 24.3 (Spring 2001): 83–98.

Thoreau, Henry David. *Walden; Or, Life in the Woods*. New York: Holt, 1948.

White, Edward. "Use It or Lose It: Power and the WPA." *WPA: Writing Program Administration* 15.1–2 (1991): 3–12.

Wilson, Robin. "Where the Elite Teach, It's Still a Man's World." *The Chronicle of Higher Education* 3 Dec. 2004: A8-A14.

Conclusion

Ethical Options for Disciplinary Progress on the Issue of jWPA Appointments

Debra Frank Dew

Good writing avoids the cliché, and junior faculty should never begin their careers as WPAs. Still, the train is out of the station—the junior faculty WPA line is quite firmly established as a professional category for newly minted PhDs in rhetoric and composition. These positions are annually advertised in the MLA *Job Information List,* and we know full well that graduates will apply for them and their mentors will support such applications. The full force of any putative WPA initiative to abolish these lines is unlikely to succeed, and such a disciplinary about face would not stop the proliferation of WPA assistantships or internships and graduate WPA seminars within our programs. True—the growth of our discipline has enabled some institutions to hire WPAs at the associate level, but this is yet a rare occurrence. Most recently, our field response includes critically reconstituting WPA training, perhaps as Theresa Enos describes her graduate program's innovative approach to "disciplining" graduate students in writing program administration.[1]

What we presently do to prepare students for the academic market tells us exactly what the discipline defines as legitimate work for our junior faculty. If we truly opposed junior faculty accepting WPA appointments, would we launch administrative training so early and hand administrative responsibilities over so readily to gWPAs enrolled in our graduate programs (Helmbrecht)? Would we also establish and

279

hence promote our new WPA seminars (Fremo)? Market demand compels programs to supply jWPAs, and our field's increased understanding of WPA work through research and scholarship and enhanced professional status compels us to educate our graduates for administrative careers. Thus, we might concede that market forces and the ideological and material currents which fuel them are stronger than any professional desire that these hires or positions were "otherwise."[2] Sometimes repetition enhances awareness and further motivates a concerted professional response. The train is out of the station—jWPA tenure-track positions abound, and newly minted PhDs in rhetoric and composition habitually desire such administrative work.

If we surveyed the rhetoric and composition positions as advertised, say, in the past ten years, what categories of work would appear as viable options for our graduates? Research-intensive institutions may hire a rare historian of rhetoric and composition, a high-ended theorist or a specialist in ethnic minority rhetoric, but such lines are scarce, thus competitive, and often earned by experienced faculty across time. A new recruit, even a graduate from a premiere program, competes rigorously for such lines given that few institutions can yet afford such specialized lines at the graduate level.

Teaching-intensive lines often appear, but they appeal less because everyone knows that research is revered more than teaching. If we weigh the 4/4 load against a 2/2 plus WPA work on a workload scale, applicants may conclude that the 4/4 is more arduous, especially if research and service expectations remain in place for the 4/4 position. However, the 2/2 load may be deceptively more appealing when we consider the administrative workloads described by jWPAs in this collection or as delineated in our own professional documents, where the scope of a healthy writing enterprise is quite fully mapped. In some contexts, then, a 4/4 teaching line with its work limits sharply defined may, in fact, be a healthier position for junior faculty.

Besides the rare and highly competitive historical and theoretical lines, and the common teaching-intensive lines, institutions need WPAs no matter their local understanding of administrative work, no matter the current state of their writing program, or their program-*ming* (Schwalm, qtd. in McGlaun), or their material ability to hire responsibly. jWPA lines are advertised regularly, so new PhDs first negotiate their appeal by appreciating their sheer number of positions advertised annually. Many of the tenure-track lines posted every year

include administrative duties, either to begin immediately, or to be assumed at a later date, often within a year. Lines with deferred administrative expectations promise new hires a bit of time to get their bear-
ings, but it is often true that WPA work beckons, and the new hires
are hailed early and invited to review policies and practices for the
program's future. jWPA lines are plentiful. They appeal if we imagine
that a course release exchanged for WPA work is a *better* workload,
and, most definitely—they appeal for all the ideological reasons we
have already discussed within this book.

   If we grant that PhD programs aim to educate professionals for
positions as they appear in the academic arena (market place demand)
and to succeed in their chosen discipline (as our professional accrediting bodies ask of us), we would do well to ask several questions about
the current state of our graduate programs. To what extent do we now
or should we explicitly design graduate curricula to prepare students
for administrative work given that the market clearly defines the need?
If graduate programs deliberately choose their areas of professional
emphasis, and secure graduate faculty with these specialties or areas
in mind, we may then consider the instructional needs and ethical liabilities "to do no harm" (Horning), which, in this specific case, are
integral to the education of rhetoric and composition professionals for
junior appointments in program administration. *If we agree* that the
train is already gone, and thus our programs do consciously choose
to educate and train jWPAs—again, given that the WPA jobs exist
and we want our graduates to succeed—how might we (all stakeholders included) thoughtfully discuss the educational needs and further
negotiate the professional concerns raised here for disciplinary consideration?

A Stakeholder Roundtable as an Imagined Beginning

Our Disciplinary Interest in jWPA Success

Who are the stakeholders with professional and personal interest in
mapping this issue in all of its problematic dimensions, and proposing
viable strategies for moving ahead in our common pursuit of "good
work?" As a senior scholar, a rhetoric and composition professional
with extensive administrative experience, Richard Gebhardt offers
compelling claims for jWPA appointments, adding some very clear

qualifications. Without jWPAs producing intellectual work—administrative scholarship—we perpetuate our field's sub-disciplinary status, or at least, we do not advance the profession in the context of these WPA appointments. Given the proliferation of jWPA lines, the promise of such disciplinary advancement on a large scale supports his claim. The jWPA line is arguably our institutional point of disciplinary entry, and rhetoric and composition's advancement is surely for the greater good. jWPA tenure cases as test cases may serve our field's aim of reconstituting the academic "tape of value" (Royster, qtd. in Gebhardt) as linked to academic production. In Gebhardt's terms, *strong* jWPAs in the *right* institutions may fulfill our professional desire for enhanced disciplinarity.

Understanding the ethical liability of asking *some* junior faculty to launch our discipline in remote locations and work as WPA test cases, Gebhardt charges their mentors and senior WPA professionals with establishing and sustaining responsible oversight (proverbial lifelines) while the jWPA progresses toward tenure. His vision might be cast as the preparation of our very own jWPA Special (administrative) Forces for the risky mission of discipline building. Hence, our senior WPA mentors must provide ongoing support for junior faculty who secure positions, especially when they are the very first of their rhetoric and composition kind to join a more traditional English department.

If our graduate programs choose to produce jWPAs, will faculty further commit to sustaining professional relations after their graduates leave home? Is this a fair request if we embrace an ethical standard of doing no harm? Is such work likely or possible given the demands of mentoring other students who are yet enrolled? Without sustained mentoring, harm is the more probable outcome.

To be sure, the call for more professional oversight and sustained mentoring may meet with some resistance. Perhaps a professional with a PhD in hand should not be infantilized or otherwise diminished as incapable of choosing wisely or as one who sorely needs a paternal presence (Duffey). Still, let us honestly admit that the demands of a jWPA appointment justify continued mentoring, and it is for this reason that our WPA guidelines ("Portland") advise against the jWPA line, and Gebhardt forcefully qualifies his support for them. Graduate faculty, those whose administrative expertise informed the jWPAs preparation, need to be accessible and invested in sustaining junior faculty as they work toward tenure. Even as graduate mentors surely do not know the jWPA's institutional context well enough to mediate local politics, they may counsel and reaffirm, and in some cases, their very best advice may simply be that the jWPA should go back on the market and secure a healthier position.

Our mentors' interest in sustaining these professional relationships includes an earned reputation for producing successful rhetoric and composition professionals, and the ethical satisfaction of doing "no harm," first by addressing the challenges inherent in administrative work as part of their program's graduate education, and then by supporting their graduates upon placement as jWPAs. As stakeholders, senior faculty earn their disciplinary reputation not only for the placement of their graduates, but for their graduates' professional advancement as well. Consider the assessment standards articulated by our accrediting bodies, which include requests for external data gathering. The graduate alumni survey, for example, is often recommended as an effective instrument for qualitatively assessing the educational effectiveness of our graduate programs. How might such data help senior faculty assess the efficacy of graduate curricula relative to the administrative success of the rhetoric and composition faculty, specifically the jWPAs they produce?

Gebhardt also locates agency in the jWPA's responsibility for choosing one's position wisely. He imagines some junior faculty who are so "drawn," and so "committed" that choosing administrative work is perhaps a good thing. Still, we might remember the something or someone whose work draws them or hails them into the work, and critically question whether the jWPA can be responsibly committed without an informed understanding of the work itself. Consider most immediately the number of jWPAs in our collection who committed as gWPAs or jWPAs first and discovered later (Fremo, Helmbrecht, Dew, McGlaun) or are yet "figuring out" the full scope of their jobs (Grutsch McKinney).

We may reasonably grant that no graduate program deliberately withholds the "truth" about jWPA appointments, but neither is it the case that we are purposefully forthright about the rhetorical demands and political risks of advancing rhetoric and composition as a discipline from the jWPA location. We are still mapping the dimensions of administrative work; many WPAs are discovering, problem solving, theorizing and publishing as fast as they can because of the urgent need to help WPAs succeed. This analysis is less about educational

neglect than about future directions and urgent needs from the junior perspective at this historical moment. Now is the time to move
beyond our broad-stroke theoretical training by fully addressing both
the politics and professional demands of writing program administration within our graduate curricula. Graduate faculty must strive to
define WPA work with its complex and conflicted dimensions, so that
making an informed professional choice is not just a possible outcome,
but an integral part of one's graduate education in rhetoric and composition.

The Table Turns: What Say the Hiring Institutions?

So how do we understand the hiring institution's interest in the jWPA
appointment? Hiring a junior faculty member may be read as evidence
of the department's sincere interest in advancing our discipline in institutions where the jWPA is the very first tenure-track hire in rhetoric
and composition. Such departments may claim they "do no harm"; in
fact, a tenure-track line signifies their respect for the work as worthy of
a PhD hire. Hiring departments and their institutions thus aim to do
"good work" when they build WPA tenure-track lines. Furthermore,
they must work within the material constraints of their institutions.
Only so many tenure-track lines are available to begin with, and associate level hires are largely a research-intensive luxury. Whereas the
jWPA appointment may be *progress* from a department's perspective,
rhetoric and composition professionals yet understand the junior hire
as unethical (Horning) because an untenured WPA is placed in a risky
line as the means to a department's ends of getting the administrative
work done. This means/ends concern is quite compelling from our
disciplinary perspective even as it may not be the intent of the hiring
department.

    If we apply the "do no harm" standard here, we need to consider
whether the hiring department intends harm if it does not yet perceive
jWPA work as dangerous work, nor conceptually understand the dimensions of administrative work, not having earlier occasion to imagine or professionally define the work. If WPA work is new tenure-track
work, and the new hire must advance definitional claims—both disciplinary and administrative—before peer faculty *see* and understand
the work, can we expect hiring departments to meet our standard of

"doing no harm" and charge them with hiring and exploiting a junior person as the suspect *means* to a program's ends?

Surely, we should worry when any institution defines junior faculty's assets as "deep pools of dedication and energy," seldom found in "a senior faculty member" (Ranieri/Grutsch McKinney). The systemic abuse of junior hires in rhetoric and composition through their appointment as jWPAs should never be promoted, and most pointedly—this collection calls into question the naturalization of exploitive administrative workloads from within (our professional ideals) and without (patterns of institutional hiring). Not all hiring institutions may plead ethical and professional innocence, which we should afford others. Again, we should consider local conditions such as rhetoric and composition's disciplinary presence or absence as an indicator of an institution's awareness of our work. With this information, we may capably discern the department's intent to design a good position which will enable the new hire to secure tenure and to "do no harm" by exploiting them in a means/ends labor dynamic along the way. We also must remember that even our most experienced WPAs are wrongfully removed from WPA positions for political cause, rather than inexperience or incompetence. Finally, an unwieldy and overwhelming load in one institution's understanding may simply be standard work in the context of another (McGlaun).

A critical question and a most pressing need is how best to inform hiring institutions—to get the word out, or even intervene—so more and more job descriptions meet our disciplinary standards for "good work." So far, we have generated professional documents which define the scope of WPA work. However, we primarily advise jWPA applicants to define their work by informing hiring committees at the point of need—as part of their job interviews and subsequently in the context of negotiating an offer (Gebhardt). We might think further about the likelihood of a newly minted PhD effectively wielding rhetorical claims for a substantively different position than the one advertised in the MLA's *Job Information List* (Townsend). Not having heard of jWPAs successfully negotiating better workloads or job descriptions, such advice remains insufficient. If it is the case that a WPA establishes a credible ethos with experience and time in place (Ranieri/Grutsch McKenney), an applicant who needs a job and has no "time in place" is less likely to negotiate an alternate workload even as the top applicant in a pool of 200 others. When the WPA applicant asks a hiring institution with little understanding of rhetoric and composition as a discipline to embrace our WPA definitions of the "good WPA position," an applicant's petition may come off as a presumptuous and threatening challenge to the hiring institution's professional integrity.

Hiring institutions seldom hit the mark in their first efforts to define a good administrative line, and this is largely for the same reason that they will probably overwork their jWPAs and respond with alarm and distress when the new hire critiques their curriculum and instruction. Hiring institutions, more often than not, do not yet understand our discipline, nor WPA labor. They, too, learn about the work later on, surely as the jWPA attempts to move the program forward. In such predictable and unavoidable disciplinary encounters with WPA work, our hiring institutions and departments, as stakeholders, need to commit themselves to enabling the jWPA's work. They must respect our credentials and choose to learn and discover the perils and promises of a fully realized writing enterprise on the ground. We can and should ask this of our hiring institutions.

How then do we help hiring institutions craft good positions before they have enjoyed the company of a rhetoric and composition colleague, who might offer useful insight into such work? If newly minted PhDs are less capable of negotiating substantive changes in workload upon hiring, our professional organizations may yet reach out at another point of need—when academic advertising agencies such as the MLA define publication guidelines for job openings in higher education. Our WPA Council might work to ensure all inquiring institutions receive WPA workload and position statements, both descriptive and prescriptive, so any hiring institution receives a heuristic for assessing local needs, prioritizing them and building administrative lines with some professional guidance. We might further establish WPA consulting services for hiring institutions, contextualized by WPA principles for ethical hiring practices (Horning) as a constructive, enabling gesture, likewise promoted through the same advertising and hiring venues. Even further, we might then distribute professional standards perhaps within a mailing upon an agency's acceptance of an institution's advertisement. Imagine a trifold brochure in the health or medical tips informational mode, perhaps with a title like—"So, you want to hire a WPA?" Direct outreach (information distribution and consulting) at the institution's point of need is but one intervention strategy our professional organization could employ.

Another Turn of the Table: jWPAs on Location

As some graduate programs do conclude that jWPA appointments are necessary, useful and thus legitimate, we should proceed with heightened attention to the educational needs of this peculiar subclass of rhetoric and composition professionals by inviting jWPAs (gWPAs, NTTF serving as WPAs and jWPAs) to speak to the training issue. As Gebhardt imagines *strong* candidates capably succeeding in the *right* institutions, graduate programs must "durably train" (Bourdieu/ Passeron, qtd. in Dew) their students in the multimodal habits of WPA work before they accept appointments in the field. Given the politics of writing program administration, and the demands of WPA work, how might graduate education in rhetoric and composition be enriched?

Rhetorical skills are vital to administrative work. jWPAs must excel as practicing rhetors in multiple contexts—one's program, department, college and institution as well the external, civic contexts of community and state. Both dominant and marginal rhetorical principles and strategies enable us to establish strategic identities and advance claims on behalf of our programs, our discipline and our professional selves. We might thus extend our theoretical studies—move beyond the historical *appreciation* of rhetorical theory—to inquiry into the *production* of effective rhetorics across time and place, including ongoing opportunities to engage in rhetorical criticism.[3]

Both by discipline and by junior rank, jWPAs work as marginal rhetors in multiple institutional contexts, so critical, feminist and ethnic-minority theory offer us useful models and flexible strategies for "good work" in our administrative situations. Before securing our jWPA lines, we need practical rhetorical experience and training for advancing writing initiatives that require institutional critique and advocacy as integral to program administration.[4]

We should further review our regular practice of appointing graduate students as WPAs in training, as well as the ongoing proliferation of nontenure-track faculty WPA appointments. Both warrant local and disciplinary review to address concerns about their professional impact on all of us as stakeholders in the field. jWPAs within this collection offer insightful advice gleaned from their diverse administrative experiences. Graduate appointments by design should always advance WPA work as an intellectual/scholarly enterprise. Graduate

WPA assistantships are better delayed until students are advanced in their studies and accomplished in their teaching, and even further, WPA appointments may be most desirable as ABD or post-doctoral positions. Advanced students and new PhDs would thus enjoy WPA research appointments without teaching responsibilities as do many of their peers in literary studies. As a research appointment, the work may yet serve the local writing program while it enables the jWPA to conduct research and publish before going on the market.

Nontenure-track faculty WPA appointments remain as prevalent as jWPA lines, and they are arguably more problematic (Patton/Vogt). WPA policy should recommend that nontenure-track faculty administrative appointments be contractually constructed as transitional lines with negotiable boundaries. At a minimum, a delayed-tenure-clock contract (Townsend) is preferable to a static and inequitable category of nontenure-track faculty WPA work. Local initiatives to reconstitute positions may begin with a working agreement between rhetoric and composition professionals and their administrative supervisors to set long term goals to increase the number of professional appointments (tenure-track or full-time instructorships, etc.) offered at a specific site. Administrators may more easily commit to a working relationship— sustained dialogue and goal setting—with WPA appointment standards as the end goal. "Good work" might first be a good-faith agreement to explore venues for securing local resources collaboratively to enable such conversions.

Graduate programs with a commitment to educating their students for WPA work need to expand seminar offerings, so their students generate administrative research across their educational experience. A graduate concentration in writing program administration is preferable to a single seminar, as a concentration responsibly admits the depth and breadth of WPA work. Graduate seminars should guarantee deep practice in the production of administrative research and scholarship under the supervision of senior WPA mentors, and administrative mentors should be multiple and diverse. WPA seminars (already well known as areas of professional expertise in rhetoric and composition each worthy of a graduate faculty line, each with unique professional forums and venues for research and scholarly publication) which together may arguably constitute an intellectual baseline for good administration in most contexts would include the following:

- Writing assessment theory and practice, including methods of placement and exit assessment, research design and the review of published models of effective assessment on all levels—course, program and general education.
- Critical approaches to curriculum and program design and development, including the training and mentoring of teaching assistants and writing faculty at large.
- Critical approaches to teaching ESL, non-native and basic writing students, curriculum development and special needs assessment.
- Computer-mediated instruction, including pedagogical issues and practices in computers and writing, critical technological literacy and communication across the curriculum.
- Administrative research and publication, including a review of all WPA and NCTE statements of work standards, scholarship on tenure and promotion, and strategies for building tenure and promotion portfolios.[5]
- Issues in the politics and practice of writing program administration.

The scope of these proposed WPA seminars is expansive, indeed, but any of us who are now or have been WPAs recognize them as integral, even vital for sustaining a fully functional writing enterprise. Such courses are no longer a luxury if we commit to educating jWPAs. They clearly require us to hire more graduate faculty in vexed areas such writing assessment, the design and development of diverse programs—first-year, and WAC, for example—and critical issues of WPA politics and the rhetorical work of institutional critique and change. Many graduate programs rely upon the local WPA to both administer the program and train future WPAs, so the WPA's graduate seminars get restricted to the standard TA training seminar with perhaps a single WPA seminar that attempts to encompass the whole of WPA work. WPA education, in many contexts, remains constrained within the gWPA assistantship of practical work in the trenches. At the PhD level, we need multiple faculty with diverse administrative expertise to develop graduate seminars with the aim of securing their students' intellectual relationship with administration as a scholarly concentration.

When we move from the ever-popular gWPA assistant as our training ground to the graduate seminar as a forum for educating scholarly professionals, we firmly establish an intellectual framework for inculcating WPA work. This definitional move is necessary if we are to advance WPA work as scholarly production. The seminar structure calls students into an intellectual relationship with their subject matter and disciplines them into scholarly administrative practices. When we work on such parallel educational grounds with our colleagues in English and across the disciplines, we capably produce new professionals with the depth and breadth of intellectual training they need to succeed in the profession.

Furthermore, inventing a full, responsible WPA curriculum is only possible if we work to abandon our learned disciplinary impulse to get by, to make due, to forbear and content ourselves with administrative training in the trenches. We undermine our disciplinary health and make no progress as we perpetuate the myth of our own intellectual and material unworthiness for a fully realized graduate subspecialty or concentration in program administration.

The request for more WPA seminars is not a call for fewer theoretical or historical seminars, or for a narrowing or reduction of doctoral studies as we know it. Consider how effectively our expansive theoretical education enables both our deep contextual analysis and jWPAs' strategic action throughout this collection. Conversely, we seek to extend our theoretical education, to build upon it, by asking for an additional subset of WPA seminars, capably cohering as a subspecialty worthy of doctoral examinations in vexed areas of administrative work—writing assessment, curricular review and design, and administrative scholarship/research. In this vision, we experience breadth and depth, both vital to one's graduate education. If we constrain WPA graduate education to *training in the trenches,* to blue-collar labor (Dew) and/or outsourced administrative tasks and work (Helmbrecht) and do not advocate for more graduate seminars with their guaranteed intellectual production, we chase our own subdisciplinary administrative tails *ad infinitum.* We, indeed, do great harm to the jWPAs we produce and our own disciplinary selves, which still remain under professional construction in many hiring contexts beyond our PhD graduate programs.

In Closing, We Yet Imagine Openings

What should we presume about present jWPA interest in examining the proliferation of junior appointments, assessing our needs for enriched graduate education, and in calling for clear programmatic stands? Graduate programs can or cannot choose locally to commit to expanding our opportunities for administrative education and research and scholarly production at the graduate level. The jWPAs in this volume seek awareness, understanding, and a careful consideration of our experiences and learned strategies. We remain hopeful that clear and informed choices will follow. The critical wave of the 1990s taught many of us the value of decentering our authority and power, of shared control of our work, and the promise of multiple perspectives. When all stakeholders—graduate students in rhetoric and composition, their faculty, chairs, local administrators and program alumni—contribute to the discussion, our collaborative efforts may generate new energy and produce new knowledge. They can help us redress such complex and unwieldy issues as those integral to graduate education in writing program administration and the appointment of junior faculty as WPAs. In this spirit, we offer what we know and what we desire for such ends as will most benefit our next generation of jWPAs.

Notes

[1] See, "Reflexive Professional Development: Getting Disciplined in Writing Program Administration" by Theresa Enos in *The Writing Program Administrator's Resource: A Guide to Institutional Practice*. Ed. Stuart Brown and Theresa Enos. Mahwah, NJ: Lawrence Erlbaum, 2002. 59–70. Enos describes her program's integration of "reflexive practice and theory" in an effort to improve WPA training.

[2] Maybe a disciplinary consensus is neither desirable nor possible on the issue. Specific programs will choose to train students consciously for administrative work; others may responsibly defer, not having resources enough, nor safeguards to meet ethical criteria (Horning), nor the curricular offerings we propose. In either context, it is crucial for graduate faculty to deliberate carefully and make an informed decision, fully granting their programmatic liabilities for promoting jWPA hires.

[3] We might consider Susan Miller's proposal to reconceptualize our disciplinary work as "writing studies," as both our content and field name. Such a shift turns our attention to the "production of texts over their interpretation" (41). jWPAs would clearly benefit from a critical study of his-

torically-situated rhetorical production, of how specific rhetorics (political speeches, civic arguments) came into being. Each and every day, we are practicing rhetors advancing our disciplinary selves and advocating for our programs within specific institutional cultures. For Miller's engaging proposal, see "Writing Studies as a Mode of Inquiry" in *Rhetoric and Composition as Intellectual Work* Ed. Gary A. Olson. Carbondale, IL: Southern Illinois UP, 2002. 41–54.

⁴ See, Porter, James E., Patricia Sullivan, Stuart Blythe, Jeffrey T. Grabill, and Libby Miles. "Institutional Critique: A Rhetorical Methodology for Change." *College Composition and Communication* 51 (2000): 610–41. jWPAs need to know that institutional critique is integral to their administrative work.

⁵ See Gebhardt and Townsend chapters for a thick list of WPA research and field documents as but a snapshot of the scholarship now available for jWPA training. Our research is substantive enough to warrant a full seminar. Furthermore, we would be foolish to imagine that jWPAs have time on the job to absorb and implement all that our tenure and promotion research recommends. The information then arrives after the fact, too late to be useful. A jWPA's tenure argument is the most vital argument of her professional life, so administrative research seminars are more essential than ever. Integrating a research seminar is an ethical option we should endorse.

Works Cited

"The Portland Resolution: Guidelines for Writing Program Administrator Positions." *WPA: Writing Program Administration* 16.1/2 (Fall/Winter 1992). Rpt. Ward and Carpenter 352–56. Available http://wpacouncil. org/positions/portlandres.html.

Contributors

Roxanne Cullen is a professor of English at Ferris State University. She previously served as Associate Vice-President for Operations and Assessment and prior to that post served as administrative head of the Department of Languages and Literature. She has published articles on assessment and writing program administration in *The Writing Program Administrator as Theorist*.

Debra Frank Dew is an assistant professor of English and director of the writing program at the University of Colorado at Colorado Springs. In 2003, she received a CU system award for advancing diversity, and in 2004, the UCCS outstanding teacher award. Her work has appeared in *WPA: Writing Program Administration*. Her research interests include writing assessment, WPA training and disciplinary advocacy.

Suellynn Duffey is associate professor of English at the University of Missouri at St. Louis where she serves as writing program administrator, teaches graduate courses in composition, and is helping develop an undergraduate writing concentration. Her experience in writing programs at various institutions informs her jWPA scholarship. Her essays have appeared in *CCC*, *WPA: Writing Program Administration*, *Writing on the Edge*, *Rhetoric Review*, and in various edited collections.

Joseph S. Eng, Director, University Writing Program and Academic Skills Achievement Program, and Professor of English at California State University Monterey Bay, teaches writing and oversees related programs serving many first-generation college students. Formerly, he was Director of Composition and Associate Professor of English at Eastern Washington University in Cheney, Washington. He has taught undergraduate and graduate courses in writing, theories, pedagogy, and research methodologies for over two decades. Recent publications include articles and book chapters on grading and assessment, composition pedagogy, and writing program administration.

Rebecca Taylor Fremo is an associate professor of English at Gustavus Adolphus College, where she directs the writing center and teaches composition, secondary education pedagogy, and creative nonfiction courses. Her essays have appeared in *Journal of Basic Writing*, *Composition Studies*, and *Reader*.

Richard C. Gebhardt is professor of English and Director of the Rhetoric and Writing PhD Program at Bowling Green State University. His publications include *Academic Advancement in Composition Studies* (1997) and articles in *College Composition and Communication*, *College English*, *Rhetoric Review*, *JAC*, and *ADE Bulletin*; he edited *CCC* from 1987 to 1994. Rick received the 1978 Richard Braddock Award and the John Gerber 20th-Century Leadership Award presented by CCCC in 2000.

Brenda Helmbrecht is an assistant professor in Rhetoric and Composition at California Polytechnic State University (San Luis Obispo), where she serves as the director of the writing program. She teaches first-year writing, composition and rhetorical theory, advanced writing, and film.

Alice S. Horning is a professor of rhetoric and linguistics at Oakland University, where she directs the Rhetoric Program. She is the author of *Revision Revisited* (Hampton, 2002) and co-edited *Revision: History, Theory and Practice* (Parlor Press, 2006), and *The Literacy Connection* (Hampton, 1999). Her articles have appeared in *The Reading Matrix* and *College English*.

Connie Kendall is an assistant professor in the Center for Access and Transition at the University of Cincinnati, where she teaches courses in developmental reading and writing. Her essays appear in *Rhetorical Agendas: Political, Ethical, Spiritual* and *The Literacy Standard*. A chapter about the connections between literacy and rhetoric, cowritten with Morris Young, is forthcoming in the *SAGE Handbook of Rhetoric*.

Sandee K. McGlaun is Associate Professor of English and Director of the (brand new) Writing Center at Roanoke College, where she also teaches courses in first-year and advanced composition. Her essays have appeared in *Dialogue, The Writing Lab Newsletter,* and *Southern Discourse.*

Jackie Grutsch McKinney is an assistant professor and director of the Writing Center at Ball State University. She has recently published in *WPA: Writing Program Administration,* the *Journal of Teaching Writing,* and the *Writing Center Journal.*

Ruth Mirtz is an associate professor and director of the Crossroads Writing Project at Ferris State University, where she teaches composition, linguistics, and children's literature. Her work has appeared in *Classroom Spaces and Writing Instruction* (2004) and she has co-authored essays on writing program administration (*Writing Program Administrator as Theorist* and *WPA: Writing Program Administration*).

Martha D. Patton is assistant professor of English at the University of Missouri. Previously she served as the assistant director of the Campus Writing Program, also at the University of Missouri. She has published several book chapters as well as articles in journals such as *Language and Learning Across the Disciplines, The Writing Instructor,* and *WPA: Writing Program Administration.*

Paul Ranieri is an associate professor of English at Ball State University. He has published articles on learning, assessment, administrative styles, and liberal education, while serving as director of the Writing Program, department chairperson, and interim associate dean of the College of Sciences and Humanities.

Martha A. Townsend is Associate Professor and Director of Graduate Studies in English at the University of Missouri. Previously, she served for fifteen years as Director of MU's Campus Writing Program. Her most recent book chapter is "Understanding Ourselves, Our Work, and Our Working Conditions" in *The Promise and Perils of Writing Program Administration,* also published by Parlor Press.

Jo Ann Vogt has joined the staff of the Campus Writing Program at Indiana University in Bloomington, serving as Associate Director of CWP and Director of Writing Tutorial Services. Previously, she served as Assistant Director of the Campus Writing Program at the University of Missouri-Columbia.

Edward M. White, now a post-retirement visiting professor of English at the University of Arizona where he teaches a graduate seminar in writing program administration. He has published about 100 articles and book chapters, as well as thirteen books, on the teaching and assessing of writing and the administration of writing programs.

Index

academic inquiry, 144, 145, 147
academic slave labor, 140
activism, 118–119
adjunct faculty, 52, 139, 157, 163, 174, 207
administrative desire, 9, 110, 113, 115–117, 126, 131–132
administrative position, 6, 12, 22, 25–26, 29, 34, 59, 62, 73, 76, 173–174, 176, 178–179, 183, 184, 187, 236, 250, 252, 254255, 257–258, 261, 263, 272–276
administrative temperament, 110, 118
advocacy, 26, 128, 131, 287
African American: feminist theorists, 201–202; literary critics, 199
agency, 12, 70, 111, 120, 154, 221–222, 245, 283, 286
American Association for Higher Education, 143
American Association of University Professors, 19, 27–28, 32, 39, 40, 42, 48, 56, 86, 90
American Council on Education, 28, 37, 91
Amorose, Tom, 138
Anzaldua, Gloria, 199, 203–213
apprenticeship, 181, 213, 267
aptitude, 113
Aristotle, 42, 252, 256, 259, 268, 276–277; Aristotelian, 194

Asian-American WPA, 11, 153–154, 156, 159, 160, 162, 166, 168
assessment, 5, 6, 22–23, 27, 54–56, 68, 69, 85, 102, 104–105, 114, 117, 129, 164–166, 206, 208–209, 234, 265, 272, 283, 289–290
assistant professor, 15–17, 21, 29, 59, 64, 67, 72–73, 78, 92, 176, 185, 191, 199, 205, 219, 223, 226, 234, 240, 249, 258–259, 270
Association of Departments of English (ADE), 19, 26, 32, 36, 88, 92, 276
audience, 117, 122, 124, 195, 196, 200–201, 235, 243, 245, 257
Augustine, 256, 276
authority, viii, 5, 12, 45, 50, 58, 63, 64, 70, 74, 102, 122, 123, 125, 138, 153, 155, 159, 172, 175, 177–178, 183, 193, 194, 200–201, 207, 212–213, 215, 221, 227–228, 231, 242, 245, 291

Baldridge, Jason, 150, 152
Bell, David, 138
Beneficence, 43, 48, 55
Bible, 44, 46, 109
Bishop, Wendy, 71, 163–164, 169
Bitzer, Lloyd, 120, 194

Bledstein, Burton J., 138, 151
Bloom, Lynn, 28, 78, 84, 88
Bourdieu, Pierre, 110, 113
Bousquet, Marc, 143
Boyer, Ernest, 27–8, 36, 90,
    92, 144, 150–151, 271, 273,
    275–276
Brown, Stuart, 40, 56, 109,
    132–133, 177–178, 187–188,
    254, 291
Bruffee, Kenneth, 138
Bullock, Richard, 38, 89, 133, 170

call to serve, 5, 6, 9–10, 47,
    97–108
Campus Writing Program, 76–78,
    137, 148, 150
career suicide, 12, 250
Carnegie Foundation, 27, 36, 92,
    143, 151, 276
Carpenter, William J., 37–38, 40,
    57, 109, 127, 132, 217, 246,
    292
categorical imperative, 50, 55
cautionary tales, 73, 224, 250
CCCC Statement of Professional
    Guidance to Junior Faculty
    and Department Chairs, 24,
    26, 37
Chiang, Yuet-Sim D., 153, 160,
    167–169
Chiseri-Strater, Elizabeth, 254
Chronicle of Higher Education, 4,
    37, 52, 199, 217, 256, 278
Cicero, 256, 273, 277
collaboration, viii, 10, 65, 67, 125,
    137, 138, 144, 146–148, 150,
    159, 187, 265
collaborative, 51, 59, 66, 69, 89,
    125–7, 129, 130, 138, 141,
    142, 144–146, 148, 149, 150,
    182, 204, 257, 265, 272–273,
    291

competency exam, 253, 259
comprehensive writing program,
    74
constraints, 52, 70, 102, 120, 131,
    195–196, 198, 284
context, 12, 22, 23, 25, 28, 34, 50,
    98, 111, 122–123, 130, 151,
    159, 167–168, 195–198, 200,
    213, 219–220, 227, 236–237,
    239, 245, 250, 252, 256–258,
    262–263, 266, 268–269, 270,
    271–272, 274–275, 282–283,
    285, 291
Corder, Jim, 228
Council of Writing Program
    Administrators, 6, 7, 16, 22,
    25–26, 37, 40, 42, 44–45, 56,
    70, 81, 88, 93, 128, 151, 192,
    209, 255–256, 286
critical thinking, 123, 144, 202
critique: insitutional, 118–119,
    128, 131, 287, 289, 292
critique:, 88, 90, 128, 154, 159,
    166, 202
Crossley, Gay Lynn, 163–164, 169
Crowley, Sharon, 69, 71
culture, 24, 66–68, 79, 80, 117,
    125, 154, 16–22, 167, 169,
    192, 203, 207, 213–214, 216,
    251, 273

dangerous, 116
Decalogue, 44
de-centered, 126
delayed tenure clock, 288
desire, 111–113; activist, 119; for
    power, 103
discipline, 10, 31, 65, 80, 88, 89,
    115–116, 119, 121–124, 128,
    131, 143–144, 169, 202, 214,
    222, 228–229, 232, 241, 250,
    259, 279, 281–287, 290–291
distance education, 256, 265

Doctoral Consortium in Rhetoric
  and Composition, 255
double standard, 138–139,
  140–141, 143
duty theory, 8, 47–48, 55

Enders, Doug, 150, 152
Enos, Theresa, 56, 109, 132, 133,
  178, 187, 279, 291
ethic, 111, 114, 150; work, 111,
  114, 119
ethics, 141; standards, 65, 282
ethos, 12, 111, 122, 125, 195, 203,
  213, 220–221, 227–229, 231–
  232, 235, 237–238, 242–243,
  245, 252–253, 257, 259, 268,
  275, 285; professional ethos,
  12, 194, 220
Eurocentricity, 160
Evaluating the Intellectual Work
  of Writing Administration,
  18, 19, 27, 28, 31, 37, 93, 128,
  151, 209
exigence, 120, 173, 195, 196

Farrell, Edmund, 253
feminism, 88, 118, 154, 159–160,
  162, 163, 168, 192, 199, 201,
  202, 210, 217, 231, 287; feminized, 200
fidelity, 42, 55
Foss, Karen, 169, 202
Friedson, Eliot, 138, 151
frontloading, 112
full-time administrator, 63, 193
Fulwiler, Toby, 80, 149

Gates, Henry Louis, Jr., 199
general education, 3, 166, 253,
  255, 263, 265, 289
Gibson, Walker, 267, 274
Gilyard, Keith, 199
Glassick, Charles, 27, 28, 37, 93,
  143–144, 152

God, 98, 109
good work, 9, 56, 97, 99, 100–
  102, 104–105, 107, 108, 114,
  118, 281, 284, 285, 287
government G-scale, 142
graduate student WPAs, 4, 6, 7,
  10, 11, 16, 17, 47, 63, 99, 112,
  115, 119–120, 140, 155, 159,
  166, 173–177, 179–187, 193,
  253, 261, 264, 270, 272, 279,
  283, 287, 291
grant writer, 147
Gratitude, 43, 55, 103
Griffin, Cindy, 202
Groupie, 115, 118
Gunner, Jeanne, 28, 71, 125, 150,
  165, 232

habits of work, 113
habitus, 113, 115
Hansen, Kristine, 93, 133, 152
Harris, Muriel, 28
Harvard "Subject A," 232,
Hauser, Gerard, 257
Hawisher, Gail, 159
Heraclitus, 250
Hesse, Doug, 113, 117
hooks, bell, 160, 202
Huber, Mary, 27–28, 90
Hult, Christine, 89, 126, 129

identity, xi, 5–7, 10–11, 66, 74, 98,
  115–116, 138, 153–158, 160,
  162–164, 167–168, 172–178,
  192, 198, 202, 214, 240, 242,
  251, 274, 287
intellectual work, 8,-9, 18, 20, 31,
  73, 75–77, 87–88, 128, 130,
  131, 144–148, 150, 181, 209,
  282
Isocrates, 12, 251, 256, 273, 277

Jablonski, Jeffrey A., 150
Jackson, Rebecca, 254

Jaeger, Werner, 251
Janangelo, Joseph, 93, 133, 144
Jarausch, Konrad H., 138, 152
Jarratt, Susan, 160, 217
Jensen, Julie, 253
junior faculty writing program
    administrators, viii, ix, 4–12,
    20, 34, 42–46, 48, 50, 53,
    55–56, 75, 76, 86, 92, 97, 101,
    103–104, 106–108, 112–113,
    118, 120–124, 126, 128–132,
    138–141, 144–146, 149–150,
    175, 191–192, 196–198, 201,
    206–209, 215–2116, 220,
    221–222, 224–225, 227–228,
    230–231, 236, 239, 240, 242,
    244–246, 249, 256, 268,
    273, 280–283, 285–287, 289,
    290–292
Justice, 43, 55, 119
jWPA desire, 6, 7, 9, 10, 47, 119

kairos, 257, 269, 272
Kant, Immanuel, 50, 55
Kimball, Bruce, 251
Kinneavy, James, 251, 253, 259,
    277

labor, 114
labor force, 50
learning communities, 256; living-
    learning program, 270
LeFevre, Karen Burke, 220
liberal education, 250–251, 253,
    259, 275
location, 7, 11, 75, 107, 110,
    116, 153, 156, 159, 160, 163,
    166–169, 192, 194, 199, 216,
    220–222, 227–228, 231,
    236–237, 239, 240, 242–243,
    245–246, 283
Logan, Shirley, 198
logic, 100, 122, 144

logos, 235, 238, 251–252, 256–
    257, 267, 272, 274

macrolevel teaching, 99
Maeroff, Gene I., 37, 152
Making Faculty Work Visible, 19,
    27, 32, 35–37, 93, 144, 152
Malencyzk, Rita, 227
marginalization, 160, 162, 200
Marrou, Henri, 251
Marshall, Margaret, 19
Marxism, 143
material, 9, 60, 62, 111, 113–114,
    118, 120–122, 125–126, 128,
    130–132, 140, 142–143, 173,
    216, 280, 284, 290
McLeod, Susan H., 28, 84, 89,
    149
mentoring, 10, 23–24, 36, 51, 59,
    73, 74, 81, 84, 131, 177, 182,
    214, 225, 273, 282, 289
Micciche, Laura R., 47, 57, 159,
    163, 170
millennial generation, 256; stu-
    dents, 272
Mishnah, 46
MLA Job Information List, 3, 61,
    67, 205, 253, 279
Modern Language Association,
    3, 18–19, 26–27, 32–33, 35,
    37–38, 40, 56, 61, 67, 73,
    87–38, 93, 101, 144, 150, 152,
    162, 176, 185, 205, 249, 253,
    277, 279, 285–286
Moxley, Joseph, 16
Mullin, Joan, 129, 150
multimodal, 112, 120, 130, 132,
    287
Myers, Nancy, 254

National WAC Network, 82
National Writing Project, 154
noble, 6, 10, 103, 110, 114, 115,
    117–118, 179

non-malfeasance, 43, 48, 55
non-tenure-track, 10, 73, 137–143,
    146, 147, 149, 234, 287
novice, 68, 126, 207, 213, 269

Ohman, Richard, 70
Okihiro, Gary, 168
Olson, Gary, 16
"other," 154
overproduction, 118, 120, 124,
    131

Passeron, Jean,Claude, 110, 113,
    132
pathos, 235, 238
Peeples, Tim, 229
Perception, 35, 45, 62, 65, 75, 113,
    150, 227, 237, 240, 270–271
Perry, David, 229
phronesis, 256–257, 268, 272–
    273, 275; practical wisdom,
    256, 269, 272
Piercy, Marge, 97–98
policing agency, 51
Portland Resolution, 25–26, 29,
    38, 43–44, 47, 56, 59, 60–62,
    70–71, 88, 217, 255, 277, 292
postmodern, 162, 164–166
power, 4, 5, 18, 40, 45–46, 50,
    70, 71, 77, 97–98, 102–103,
    105, 125, 138, 161, 177–178,
    194–195, 200, 201–202, 208,
    220, 226, 231, 238, 240, 242,
    257–258, 268, 269, 272, 274,
    291; desire for, 103; powerless-
    ness, 9, 104, 108, 197
Prendergast, Catherine, 153, 167,
    170
production, 130; administrative,
    125, 127–128, 130, 132; multi-
    modal, 112; rhetorical, 127–8,
    292; scholarly, 114–115, 126,
    290–291

production:, 129
professionalism, vii, 4–8, 11–12,
    16–20, 22, 25–26, 29–31, 33,
    34, 36, 40, 45, 47, 52, 60, 62–
    70, 73–74, 81–82, 85–90, 107,
    110–112, 115–119, 123–129,
    131, 137–150, 153, 156–157,
    159, 160, 162, 167–168, 174,
    176, 179, 181–182, 184–186,
    192, 194, 206, 212, 216,
    220–221, 224, 226, 239, 245,
    251, 255, 274–275, 279–290,
    292; professional standards,
    138, 286
publication, 3, 7, 22–24, 32,
    42–43, 48, 89, 91, 102, 107,
    128–131, 143, 148, 176, 178,
    212, 239, 249, 255–256, 261,
    273, 283, 288

queer theory, 168
Quintilian, 256, 277

rabbinic law, 46
race, 11, 158, 160, 162, 164,
    167–168
regular faculty, 77, 91, 147
Reid, Neil, 150, 152
Reparation, 42, 55
Report of the Commission on
    Writing and Literature, 26,
    38, 93
Reynolds, Nedra, 220
rhetor, 147, 194–195, 197, 199,
    201–202, 268
rhetoric, 147, 160, 194–195, 197,
    199, 201–202, 268; rhetorical
    work, 119, 122–124, 126, 131,
    289
rhetorical network, 120
rhetorical situation, 12, 59, 120,
    194–198, 201, 211, 216, 250,
    257–258

Rice, Eugene, 143
Roen, Duane, 28, 89, 171
Ronald, Kate, 220
Rose, Shirley K, 145
Roskelly, Hephzibah, 254
Royster, Jacqueline Jones, 18, 198, 217
Ruszkiewicz, John, 253

sacrifice, 34, 99, 103, 107, 114, 117, 149, 250
Schell, Eileen, 127, 159–60
scholarly work, 68, 77, 84, 88, 90, 113, 129, 150, 212, 271
scholarship in composition, 19, 26, 32, 38, 88, 92
scholarship of teaching, 8, 27, 90, 150, 273, 275
Schuster, Charles, 16, 71, 110, 116, 217, 273
Schwalm, David, 26, 38, 220, 226, 232, 246
self-improvement, 43, 48, 55, 56
self-sacrifice, 110, 114, 119
service, 9, 18–19, 22, 24, 26, 30, 32–33, 35–36, 44, 46, 75, 78, 87–88, 90, 98, 100, 105, 107, 110, 112–15, 117, 119–21, 166, 175, 185, 193, 197, 200, 212, 220, 230, 239, 241, 243, 244, 271–272, 280; and sacrifice, 113
signifyin(g), 199
Slevin, James, 88
small college, 11, 12, 192, 194–198, 202, 205–207, 209, 216, 226, 244
Smitherman, Geneva, 199
Soven, Margot, 149, 152
Starhawk, 231, 238
stereotyping, 11, 168
strategic plan, 262, 263
syllabus: common, 207; core, 208

technology-enhanced classrooms, 256, 269
Ten Commandments, 44
tenure, vii, 3–6, 8,-9, 11, 15–26, 28, 29–34, 37, 40, 42–45, 50, 52–53, 58, 60–69, 73–80, 83, 84, 86–89, 91, 111, 116, 118, 120, 127–128, 130, 137–142, 144–146, 178–179, 185, 192–193, 205–207, 209, 211, 213, 215, 219, 224–225, 227–228, 239, 244, 250, 255, 259, 260–261, 263, 270–271, 275–276, 280, 282, 284–285, 288–289, 292
tenure and promotion, 11, 18–21, 25–26, 28–34, 45, 61, 69, 73–80, 83, 86–88, 91, 116, 127, 239, 263, 289, 292
tenure clock, 76; delayed, 288
tenured faculty, 28, 37, 209
tenure-first principle, 17, 18, 22, 23
tenure-track faculty, 91, 139–142
testing, 89, 256
the great leveler, 66
theory, 7, 11, 42, 50, 85, 99, 108, 118–19, 123–124, 129, 160, 164, 166, 168, 185–186, 199, 201–202, 207, 209, 212–213, 217, 224, 229, 232, 235, 251, 254, 271, 287, 289, 291; hope, 119
Thomas Hobbes, 50
Thoreau, Henry David, 252
Townsend, Martha, 9, 47, 149, 151

upper-level writing courses, 225–226, 233, 236

values, 10, 18, 26, 41, 47, 55, 77, 80, 112, 114, 117, 127, 138, 150, 197, 198, 211, 252

victim narrative, 63, 70, 113, 117,
    121, 130, 154, 203, 219, 222,
    250
victim narratives, 6–7, 60, 115
Villanueva, Victor, 159

Walvoord, Barbara, 82, 85
Ward, Irene, 37–38, 40, 57, 109,
    127, 132, 217, 246, 292
Weiser, Irwin, 38, 145, 152, 248
White, Edward, xi, 5, 45, 47, 78,
    84, 268
witnessing, 202–3, 212
Worsham, Lynn, 199
WPA-centric, 125
WPA-L listserv, 45, 105, 153, 159,
    164, 168
writing across the curriculum
    WPAs, 79
writing across the curriculum:,
    3, 22, 46, 73–75, 77, 79–82,
    84–86, 129, 137, 144, 146,

149, 174, 191, 193, 196–197,
    203–206, 208–215, 223, 233,
    238, 240, 243, 289
writing center, 3, 16, 19, 22, 36,
    74, 137, 191, 193, 196–197,
    204–205, 210, 213–215, 219,
    220, 223, 224, 230, 232, 233,
    234, 239, 240, 241, 242–244,
    246, 247, 254, 261–262, 266,
    270–271, 276
writing concentration, 224–226,
    228, 233, 237
writing in the disciplines, 74, 151,
    210
writing intensive, 78–80, 84, 197–
    198, 203–204, 207, 210–212,
    215, 233, 238, 277
Wyoming Resolution, 69

Young, Art, 149, 151

Zinsser, William, 210

Printed in the United States
116843LV00001B/285/A